Resource Management Excellence

The Art of Excelling
in Resource and Assets Management

Resource Management Excellence

The Art of Excelling in Resource and Assets Management

Book 5 in the five-part series
The Five Pillars of Organizational Excellence

H. James Harrington, Ph.D.

Foreword by
Yoshio Kondo

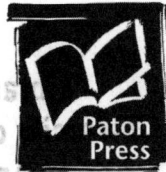

Paton Press LLC
Chico, California

Most Paton Press books are available at quantity discounts when purchased in bulk. For more information, contact:

Paton Press LLC
P.O. Box 44
Chico, CA 95927-0044
Telephone: (530) 342-5480
Fax: (530) 342-5471
E-mail: *books@patonpress.com*
Web: *www.patonpress.com*

Printed in the United States of America

10 09 08 07   5 4 3 2 1

ISBN-13: 978-1-932828-12-2
ISBN-10: 1-932828-12-5

Library of Congress Cataloging-in-Publication Data
Harrington, H. J. (H. James)
    Resource management excellence: The art of excelling in resource and assets management / H. James Harrington; foreword by Yoshio Kondo.
        p. cm. — (The five pillars of organizational excellence; 5)
    Includes index.
ISBN 1-932828-12-5
1. Capital. 2. Human capital—Management. I. Title.
HD39.H37 2006
658ædc22
                          2006034372

Notice of Liability
The information in this book is distributed on an "as is" basis, without warranty. Although every precaution has been taken in the preparation of the book, neither the author nor Paton Press LLC shall have any liability to any person or entity with respect to any loss or damage caused or alleged to be caused directly or indirectly by the information contained in this book.

Staff
Publisher: Scott M. Paton
Editor: Karen Bleske
Book design: David Hurst
Cover design: Caylen Balmain

CONTENTS

ABOUT THE AUTHOR

H. James Harrington

In the book *Tech Trending* (Capstone, 2001) by Amy Zuckerman, H. James Harrington was referred to as "the quintessential tech trender." The *New York Times* referred to him as having a ". . . knack for synthesis and an open mind about packaging his knowledge and experience in new ways—characteristics that may matter more as prerequisites for new-economy success than technical wizardry . . . "

H. James Harrington, Ph.D.
CEO, Harrington Institute Inc.

Present Responsibilities

Harrington now serves as the chief executive officer for the Harrington Institute. He also serves as the chairman of the board for a number of businesses and as the U.S. chairman of Technologies for Project Management at the University of Quebec.

Harrington is recognized as one of the world leaders in applying performance improvement methodologies to business processes.

Previous Experience

In February 2002, Harrington retired as the COO of Systemcorp ALG, a leading supplier of knowledge management and project management software solutions. Prior to this, he served as a principal and one of the leaders in the Process Innovation Group at Ernst & Young. He was with IBM for more than thirty years as a senior engineer and project manager.

Harrington is past chairman of the prestigious International Academy for Quality and past president of the American Society for Quality. He is also an active member of the Global Knowledge Economics Council.

Credentials

The Harrington/Ishikawa Medal, presented yearly by the Asia Pacific Quality Organization, was named after Harrington to recognize his many contributions to the region. In 1997, the Quebec Society for Quality named its quality award "The Harrington/Neron Medal," honoring Harrington for his many contributions to Canada's quality movement. In 2000, the Sri Lanka national quality award was named after him.

Harrington's contributions to performance improvement around the world have brought him many honors and awards, including the Edwards Medal, the Lancaster Medal, ASQ's Distinguished Service Medal, China's Magnolia Award, and many others. He was appointed the honorary advisor to the China Quality Control Association, and he was elected to the Singapore Productivity Hall of Fame in 1990. He has been named lifetime honorary president of the Asia Pacific Quality Organization and honorary director of the Chilean Association of Quality Control.

Harrington has been elected a Fellow of the British Quality Control Organization and the American Society for Quality. He was also elected an honorary member of the quality societies in Taiwan, Argentina, Brazil, Colombia, and Singapore. He is listed in *Who's Who Worldwide* and *Men of Distinction Worldwide*. He has presented hundreds of papers on performance improvement and organizational management structure at local, state, national, and international levels.

Harrington is a prolific author, having published hundreds of technical reports and magazine articles. He has authored twenty-eight books and ten software packages.

OTHER BOOKS BY H. JAMES HARRINGTON

- *The Improvement Process* (McGraw-Hill, 1987, a best-selling business book that year)
- *Poor-Quality Cost* (Marcel-Dekker, 1987)
- *Excellence—The IBM Way* (ASQ Quality Press, 1988)
- *The Quality-Profit Connection* (ASQ Quality Press, 1988)
- *Business Process Improvement* (McGraw-Hill, 1991, the first book about process redesign)
- *The Mouse Story* (Ernst & Young, 1991)
- *Of Tails and Teams* (ASQ Quality Press, 1994)
- *Total Improvement Management* (McGraw-Hill, 1995)
- *High Performance Benchmarking* (McGraw-Hill, 1996)
- *The Complete Benchmarking Implementation Guide* (McGraw-Hill, 1996)
- *ISO 9000 and Beyond* (McGraw-Hill, 1996)
- *The Business Process Improvement Workbook* (McGraw-Hill, 1997)
- *The Creativity Toolkit—Provoking Creativity in Individuals and Organizations* (McGraw-Hill, 1998)
- *Statistical Analysis Simplified—The Easy-to-Understand Guide to SPC and Data Analysis* (McGraw-Hill, 1998)
- *Area Activity Analysis—Aligning Work Activities and Measurements to Enhance Business Performance* (McGraw-Hill, 1998)
- *Reliability Simplified—Going Beyond Quality to Keep Customers for Life* (McGraw-Hill, 1999)
- *ISO 14000 Implementation—Upgrading Your EMS Effectively* (McGraw-Hill, 1999)
- *Performance Improvement Methods—Fighting the War on Waste* (with Kenneth C. Lomax, McGraw-Hill, 1999)
- *Simulation Modeling Methods—An Interactive Guide to Results-Based Decision Making* (McGraw-Hill, 2000)
- *Project Change Management—Applying Change Management to Improvement Projects* (with Daryl R. Conner and Nicholas L. Horney, McGraw-Hill, 2000)
- *E-Business Project Manager* (ASQ Quality Press, 2002)
- *Process Management Excellence: The Art of Excelling in Process Management* (Paton Press, 2006)
- *Project Management Excellence: The Art of Excelling in Project Management* (Paton Press, 2006)
- *Change Management Excellence: The Art of Excelling in Change Management* (Paton Press, 2006)
- *Knowledge Management Excellence: The Art of Excelling in Knowledge Management* (Paton Press, 2006)
- *Making Teams Hum* (Paton Press, 2007)

DEDICATION

I dedicate this book to my wife, Marguerite, who has made my life worth living. Without her help and encouragement I could never have accomplished as much as I have. She is my best friend and my only lover.

I also dedicate this book to my son, Jim, of whom I am very proud.

ACKNOWLEDGMENTS

I want to acknowledge Candy Rogers, who converted and edited endless hours of dictation into the finished product. I couldn't have done it without her help. I want to thank my friends at the American Society for Quality and the International Academy for Quality for their many contributions to the concepts expressed in this book.

I also want to thank Abdul Rahman Awl for his work in preparing the financial chapter in this book and for his friendship throughout the years.

I'd like to recognize the contributions made by the team from Harrington Institute Inc. I particularly want to recognize Thomas McNellis for all the research he did in developing the DMAIC scorecard presented in Appendix D.

But most of all, I want to recognize the contributions made by my wife, Marguerite. She's always there when I need her.

FOREWORD

It goes without saying that quality, cost, and productivity are important management indicators for companies. It's essential from a business management perspective to keep improving and sustaining not only quality but also production volume, delivery performance, productivity, and cost. Given productivity's status as a representative of quantity, I'd like to outline the somewhat different nature of quality relative to cost and productivity.

For example, quality pundits use the term "total quality management" more widely than "total productivity management," and we never use the term "total cost management." Why? Quality culture is a well-known concept, but we don't use the terms "cost culture" or "productivity culture." One theory for this bias is that quality has more to do with human nature than cost and productivity.

There are a few reasons to support this. For one thing, humankind's interaction with quality is far longer than its relationships with cost and productivity. Human beings are said to be animals that can use tools. The quality of the tools they use has been important to them ever since they evolved a few million years ago.

For eons, our ancestors led self-contained and self-sufficient lives. Then they started to trade with their neighbors, at first simply by bartering. As transportation methods developed, the distance of trade increased gradually but remarkably. Humans started to seek out and use precious materials such as gold, silver, and gemstones. These eventually spurred the development of money; when that happened, the concept of cost was born. As a concept, productivity began only a few centuries ago with the development of mass production.

Manufacturers are keenly concerned about quality, cost, and productivity. In contrast, customers are concerned about quality, price, and after-sales service. Even though their relative emphasis may be different, both manufacturers and customers have a common concern for quality and service. This concern is also shared between employees up- and downstream of a process within a company. If the quality of competitive products or services is the same, customers are primarily concerned about the price of the goods or services. Usually they're not interested in how productivity affects the competitiveness of a product or service. Instead, customers are more interested in after-sales service.

Employees are more likely to accept an appeal for quality improvement from upper managers than appeals for cost reduction and increased productivity. This is due to quality's appeal to human nature, something that both managers and employees can share.

One of the most frequent responses to a quality improvement effort is, "We understand its importance, but when quality is improved, cost goes up. It mustn't be taken too far." Does this contradictory relationship always exist? The answer is no. It's often possible to convert a win-lose relationship into a win-win one by seeking out creative solutions. This process then becomes the productivity breakthrough itself. In fact, W. Edwards Deming said a half century ago that "productivity goes up as quality goes up: This fact is well-known but only to a select few." Then not only does the superficial optimization in a win-lose relationship become inevitable but also the transformation into a creative, win-win relationship.

All of us know that motivation, both positive and negative, is a vital prerequisite for the success of our work. In his theory of motivation, Frederick Herzberg emphasizes that situations that provide for both dissatisfaction and satisfaction are indispensable.

In our current affluent society and in the future as employees' incomes and educational levels continue to rise, it's increasingly important to provide opportunities for satisfaction. Quality is fundamentally linked with human nature and an important human satisfier. It's thought that quality's importance as a source of satisfaction, and hence, motivation, will increase in the future.

—Yoshio Kondo
Past president, International Academy for Quality
Honorary member, American Society for Quality

PREFACE

"You are part of the change parade. Do you want to be a bandleader or sweep up the horse droppings after the parade has passed? It's up to you."

—HJH

This series was written for a small group of organizations. It's not for traditionalists, the weak of heart, or for organizations that believe winning a national quality award is their ultimate objective. This series was written for organizations that aren't content with being anything less than the best they can be. It's for organizations that want to stand out from the crowd and that hunger to obtain optimum results in the five Ps:

- *Pride*. Employees are proud of their work and their organization.
- *Performance*. The entire organization operates at high levels of efficiency and effectiveness.
- *Profit*. The organization is profitable, able to pay its employees good salaries, and pay higher-than-average dividends to its investors.
- *Prestige*. The organization is considered an admirable place to work in and is known for its highly desired products and services.
- *Pleasure*. Employees enjoy coming to work because they're doing something worthwhile in a friendly, supportive environment.

Good is no longer good enough. Doing the right thing "right" isn't good enough. Having the highest quality and being the most productive doesn't suffice today. To survive in today's competitive environment, you must excel (see figure P.1). To excel, an organization needs to focus on all parts of itself, optimizing the use and effectiveness of all of its resources. To excel you need to provide "knock their socks off" products and services, and be so innovative and creative that customers say, "I didn't know they could do that!"

> *"To compete and win, we must redouble our efforts, not only in the quality of our goods and services, but in the quality of our thinking, in the quality of our response to our customers, in the quality of our decision making, in the quality of everything we do."*
> —E. S. Woolard
> Former chairman and CEO, Dupont

After years of working with all types of organizations and using many different approaches to improve performance, I've come to realize that five key elements must be managed for an organization to excel. I call them the "five pillars of organizational excellence." All five must be managed creatively and simultaneously. Top management's job is to keep all these elements moving ahead simultaneously. To concentrate on one or two alone is a surefire

Figure P.1   **Organizational Excellence**

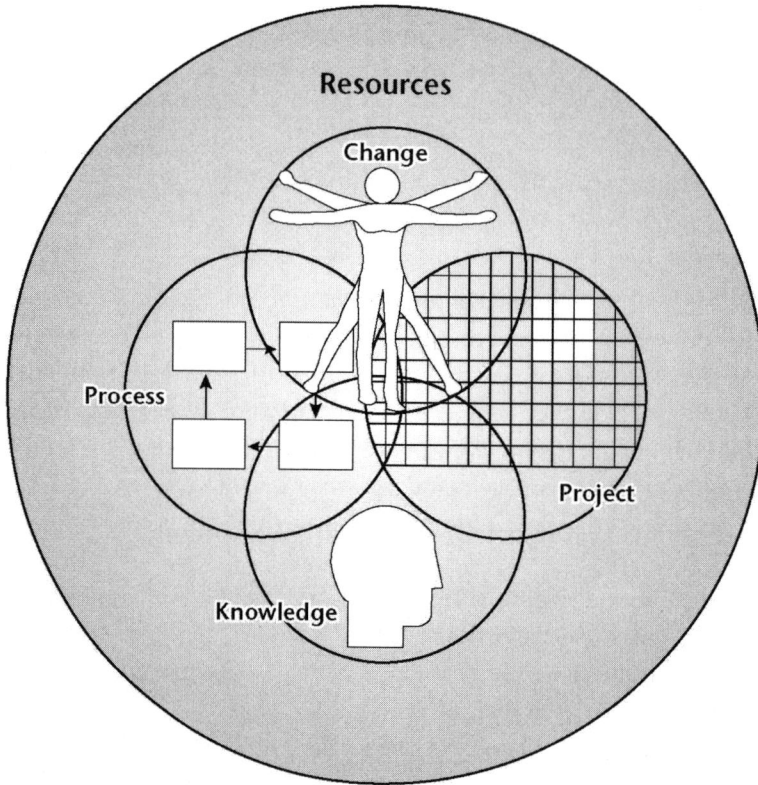

formula for failure. Priorities might shift, causing an individual pillar to move from "very important" to simply "important," but it should never shift lower than that.

The processes discussed in this series are designed to permanently change an organization by skillfully managing its five key pillars. None of these management pillars is new by itself, but by combining and managing them together, a holistic approach to improving an organization's performance is possible. (See figure P.2.)

The five pillars of organizational excellence are:

■ *Process management excellence.* We must manage our processes and continuously improve them because they're the way we do business.

■ *Project management excellence.* We must manage our projects because they're the way we obtain major improvements in our processes.

■ *Change management excellence.* We must manage the organization so that it can cope with the chaos it will be subjected to by the magnitude and quantity of necessary changes.

■ *Knowledge management excellence.* We must manage the organization's knowledge, its most valuable asset. (Knowledge gives an organization its competitive advantage, as technology can easily be reverse-engineered and transferred to any place in the world almost overnight.)

■ *Resource management excellence.* We must manage our resources and assets because they're what drive our business results.

By effectively managing these five key pillars and leveraging their interdependencies and reactions, an organization can bring about a marvelous self-transformation. It will emerge from its restricting cocoon and float on the winds of success and self-fulfillment.

"These companies [excellent organizations] implement their results through effectiveness in developing and deploying management capital's intellectual, technical, human information and other resources in integrating a company's hard and soft assets."
—Armand V. Feigenbaum and Donald Feigenbaum
Authors of *The Power of Management Capital*

Organizational excellence is designed to permanently change an organization by focusing on the five pillars of excellence. Learning to manage the pillars together is the key to success in the endless pursuit of improved performance. To help you in this endeavor,

Figure P.2 The Five Pillars of Organizational Excellence

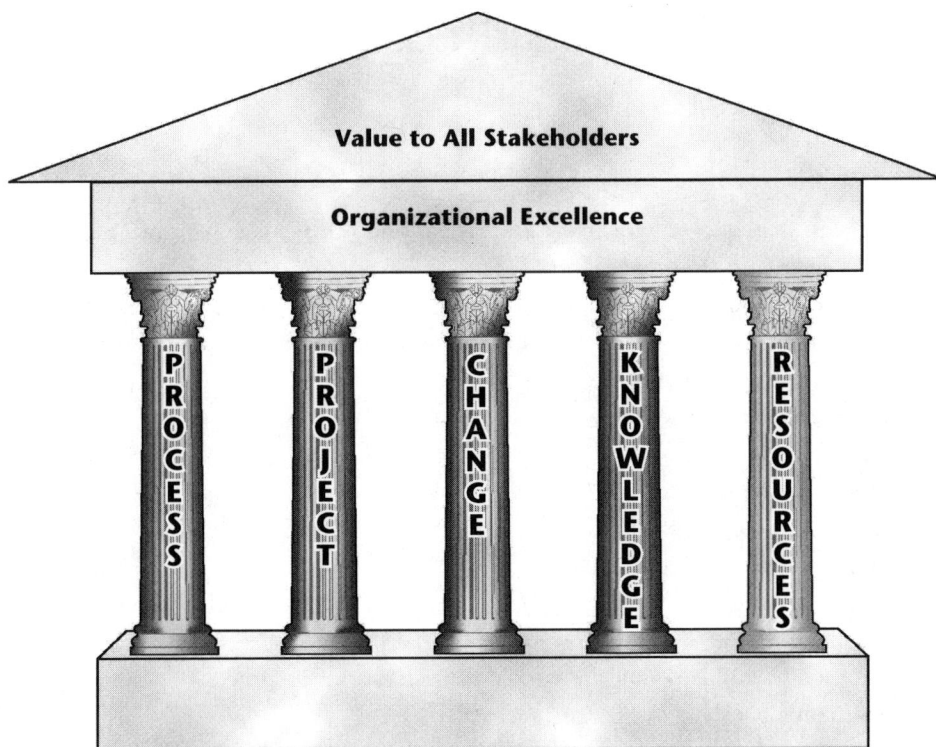

Value to All Stakeholders

Organizational Excellence

PROCESS   PROJECT   CHANGE   KNOWLEDGE   RESOURCES

each volume in this five-book series addresses one of the pillars. The series consists of the following books:

- *Process Management Excellence: The Art of Excelling in Process Management*
- *Project Management Excellence: The Art of Excelling in Project Management*
- *Change Management Excellence: The Art of Excelling in Change Management*
- *Knowledge Management Excellence: The Art of Excelling in Knowledge Management*
- *Resource Management Excellence: The Art of Excelling in Resource and Assets Management*

None of the five pillars can individually support organizational excellence. All of them must be present and equally strong to support the weight of success for all of its stakeholders. The challenge that excellent organizations face today is how to nurture an innovative learning culture while maintaining the procedures and structure needed to ensure optimum performance as well as customer and investor satisfaction. The Five Pillars of Organizational Excellence series was designed to help solve this dilemma.

Because it's important to understand how the five pillars interact with and support each other, a short discussion about each of them follows.

PILLAR I—PROCESS MANAGEMENT EXCELLENCE

"Your processes manage the organization, not your managers."
—HJH

The process management concept certainly isn't new to management professionals; it's the basis of most improvement methodologies.

A *process* is a series of interconnected activities that takes input, adds value to it, and produces output. It's how organizations do their day-to-day routines. Your organization's processes define how it operates.

To manage a process, the following must be defined and agreed upon:

- An output requirement statement between process owners and customers
- An input requirement statement between process owners and suppliers
- A process that can transform suppliers' input into output that meets customers' performance and quality requirements
- Feedback measurement systems between process and customers, and between process and suppliers
- The method by which people are trained to understand the process
- A measurement system within the process

You should address these six key factors when designing a process. However, the problem facing most organizations is that many of their support processes were never designed in the first place. They were created in response to a need without understanding what a process is.

> "If you [management] create an expectation of continuous product or service improvement, but fail to deliver on that expectation, you will see a build-up of fear and negative forecasting."
> —Stephen R. Covey, Ph.D. Author, *The Seven Habits of Highly Effective People*

The Two Approaches to Process Management

There are two basic approaches to managing processes:

■ The micro-level approach, which is directed at managing processes within a natural work team or an individual department

■ The macro-level approach, which is directed at managing processes that flow across departments and/or functions within the organization

Most of the work that quality professionals do involves continuously improving processes. Some of the tools they use include design of experiments, process capability studies, root cause analysis, document control, quality circles, suggestions, Six Sigma, Shewhart's cycles, ISO 9001, and just-in-time manufacturing and supplier qualification.

In excellent organizations, management requires each natural work team (or department) to continuously improve the processes it uses.

Refining the process is an ongoing activity. If the refinement process is working as it should, the total process's efficiency and effectiveness should be improving at a rate of 10 to 15 percent a year. In most cases the project team focuses on the major problems that reflect across departments and reap such a harvest within three to twelve months. At that time the project team can be disbanded and the process-refinement activities turned over to the natural work teams involved in the process. Area activity analysis methodology, which was discussed in book one of this series, is the most effective approach to process refinement.

Figure P.3 What Different Types of People Have to Say About a Half-Full Glass

■ The optimist: It's half full.
■ The pessimist: It's half empty.
■ The process manager: We have twice the number of glasses as we need.

By focusing on its processes and working with its suppliers, IBM reported that, "Between 1997 and 2001, the hardware reliability of our high-end servers improved by more than 200 percent while computing power increased by a factor of four."

PILLAR II—PROJECT MANAGEMENT EXCELLENCE

"How can you compete when more than 70 percent of your improvement efforts are unsuccessful?"

—HJH

According to the 2002 Chaos Report compiled by the Standish Group International:
- Only 26 percent of all projects are successful.
- Forty percent of all information technology (IT) projects fail or are canceled.

A *project* is a temporary endeavor undertaken to create a unique product or service.

Projects in most organizations are mission-critical activities, and delivering quality products on time is nonnegotiable. Even with IT projects, things have changed. Benchmark organizations are completing 90 percent of their projects within 10 percent of budget and schedule. Information systems organizations that establish standards for project management, including a project office, cut their major project cost overruns, delays, and cancellations by 50 percent (Gartner Group, August 2000).

Process redesign and process reengineering are two of the most important projects that organizations undertake. These types of projects have a failure rate estimated to be as high as 60 percent. The two main causes for these high-cost failures are: poor project management and poor change management. For example, IBM launched eleven reengineering projects, the focus of which varied from the way it manages internal information systems to the way it develops products and serves customers. "We have reduced IT spending by 31 percent for a total savings of more than $2 billion," the company reports. "Since 1993, cycle time for large systems development has been slashed from fifty-six months to sixteen months. For low-end systems, it's seven months—down from two years."

The Professional Project Manager

People liken project management to quality management. Everyone thinks he or she knows what quality is, so organizations assume that anyone can manage quality. This same thought pattern applies to project management, but just as a quality manager is a special type of professional, so is a project manager. Project managers require skill, training, and effective leadership specifically related to project management.

The Project Management Body of Knowledge (PMBOK) defines sixty-nine different tools that a project manager must master. Few project managers have mastered all of these tools. In today's complex world, most organizations have numerous projects going on at the same time. Many of them are interlinked and interdependent. Their requirements and schedules are continuously changing, which causes a chain reaction throughout the organization. For this reason, organizations can't afford to manage each project in isolation. They must instead manage their project portfolios, making the appropriate trade-offs of personnel and priorities.

Project Management Excellence: The Art of Excelling in Project Management, book two in this series, focuses on how to use project management tools to effectively manage an organization's projects and integrate them into the total operations. This requires the effective integration of projects, resources, and knowledge to obtain business intelligence.

PILLAR III—CHANGE MANAGEMENT EXCELLENCE

People like to think of themselves as change masters, but, in truth, they're change bigots. Everyone in the management team supports change. They want to see others change, but when it comes to the managers themselves changing, they're reluctant to move away from past experiences that have proven successful for them. If an organization is going to change, top management must be the first to do so.

Change is inevitable, and you must embrace it if you're going to be successful in the challenging world in which we live. *Change Management Excellence: The Art of Excelling in Change Management*, book three in this series, discusses a change management system that's made up of three distinct elements:

- Defining what will be changed
- Defining how to change
- Making the change happen

> **"Research confirms that as much as 60 percent of change initiatives and other projects fail as a direct result of a fundamental inability to manage their social implications."**
> **—Gartner Group**

Most of the books written to date about change management have been theoretical in nature. They talk about black holes, cascading sponsorships, and burning platforms, but these are only the last phase of the change process. Most organizations don't understand or follow a comprehensive change management system. An effective change management system requires the organization to step back and define what will be changed. It's not about reducing stock levels, increasing customer satisfaction, or training people; it's about the fundamentals. Which of the key business drivers must be changed, and how do they need to be changed?

An organization must develop crisp vision statements that define how key business drivers will be changed through time. This requires the organization to have an excellent understanding of what its business drivers are and how they're operating. Then the organization must define exactly how it wants to change these key business drivers through a set period of time. Once the organization has defined what it wants to change, it can then define how to change. During this stage, the organization looks at the more than 1,100 different improvement tools that are available today, determines which tools will bring about the required changes to these key business drivers, and schedules the implementation of these tools and methodologies. This schedule makes up a key part of the organization's strategic business plan.

The last phase in the change management process is making the change happen. This is the area in which behavioral scientists have developed a number of excellent approaches to break down resistance and build up resiliency throughout the organization. It's this phase that most change management books have concentrated on, but it's the last phase in the total change management system. Book three of this series focuses on all three phases, discussing in detail how to define what will be changed, defining how to change it, and how to make the change happen.

PILLAR IV—KNOWLEDGE MANAGEMENT EXCELLENCE

"When a person dies, a library is lost."
—HJH

Today, more than ever before, knowledge is the key to organizational success. To fulfill this need, the Internet and other information technologies have provided all of us with more information than we can ever consume. Instead of having one or two sources of information, the Internet provides hundreds, if not thousands, of inputs, all of which must be researched to find that key nugget of information. People are overwhelmed with so much information that they don't have time to absorb it.

To make matters worse, most of an organization's knowledge is still undocumented; it rests in the minds and experiences of its employees. This knowledge disappears from the organization's knowledge base whenever an individual leaves an assignment. *Knowledge Management Excellence: The Art of Excelling in Knowledge Management*, book four in this series, defines how to establish a knowledge management system (KMS) that will be designed to sort out unneeded and/or false information and capture the "soft" knowledge needed to run an organization.

Because an almost endless amount of information clouds up computers, desks, and minds, a KMS must be designed around the organization's key capabilities and competencies.

What Is Knowledge?

Knowledge is a mixture of experiences, practices, traditions, values, contextual information, expert insight, and sound intuition that provides an environment and framework for evaluating and incorporating new experiences and information.

There are two types of knowledge: explicit and tacit.

Explicit knowledge is defined as knowledge that's stored in a semistructured medium, such as in documents, e-mail, voice mail, or video media. I call this hard or tangible knowledge. It's conveyed from one person to another in a systematic way.

Tacit knowledge is defined as knowledge that's formed around intangible factors embedded in an individual's experience. It's personal, content-specific knowledge that resides in an individual. It's knowledge that an individual gains from experience or skills that he or she develops. It often takes the form of beliefs, values, principles, and morals. It guides the individual's actions. I call this soft knowledge. It's embedded in the individual's ideas, insights, values, and judgment. It's only accessible through direct corroboration and communication with the individual who has the knowledge.

Knowledge management is defined as a proactive, systematic process by which value is generated from intellectual or knowledge-based assets and disseminated to the stakeholders. *Knowledge Management Excellence* discusses the six phases required to implement an effective KMS. These are:

■ Phase I—Requirements definition (seven activities)
■ Phase II—Infrastructure evaluation (sixteen activities)
■ Phase III—Knowledge management system design and development (twelve activities)
■ Phase IV—Pilot (fifteen activities)
■ Phase V—Deployment (ten activities)
■ Phase VI—Continuous improvement (one activity)

> "Knowledge takes us from chance to choice."
> —HJH

The true measure of success for knowledge management is the number of people who have access to and implement ideas from the knowledge networks. These networks bring state-of-the-art ideas and best practices into the workplace. This allows the organization to develop areas of critical mass to implement standards that work, and it also provides access to all employees—allowing them to make comments to improve those standards. Even the newest employee can look at the materials and make recommendations based upon personal insight, creativity, and experience.

A big challenge related to implementing a KMS is transforming knowledge held by individuals, including process and behavioral knowledge, into a consistent technological format that can be easily shared with the organization's stakeholders. However, the biggest challenge is changing the organization's culture from a knowledge-hoarding culture to a knowledge-sharing one.

PILLAR V—RESOURCE MANAGEMENT EXCELLENCE

Nothing can be accomplished without resources. Resources are at the heart of everything you do. If you have too few, you fail. If there are too many, there's waste, which hinders the organization's competitive ability. Too many organizations limit their thinking about resources to people and money. These two are important, but they're only a small part of the resources that an organization must manage.

"The essence of competitiveness is liberated when we make people believe that what they think and do is important—and then get out of their way while they do it."

—Jack Welch
Former CEO of GE

When resource management is discussed, it's in the broadest sense—all the resources and assets that are available to the organization. This includes stockholders, management, employees, money, suppliers, inventory, boards of directors, alliance partnerships, real estate, knowledge, customers, patents, investors, goodwill, and brick and mortar. When all of these are considered, it quickly becomes apparent that effective resource management is one of the most critical, complex activities within any organization. This book will discuss resource management excellence in detail.

THE SKY IS NOT THE LIMIT

"You are limited only by what you can envision."
—HJH

People used to say, "The sky's the limit" when they were thinking of the limits of possibility. Today there's no limit—if you can dream it or imagine it, then you can do it, or there's someone out there who can do it for you.

You must start thinking differently. The word "impossible" should be stricken from your vocabulary. Thinking outside of the box isn't good enough; you must tear down the walls of the box and build a culture without walls.

The work force is becoming more mobile. Organizations are cutting back by outsourcing all but their core capabilities and competencies. Business offices are shrinking as increasingly large numbers of people are working from their homes. No organization can afford to do that one-of-a-kind job with its own people, not when consultants can do it faster, better, and with reduced risk.

WHY DO YOU NEED ORGANIZATIONAL EXCELLENCE?

Times have changed, and our thinking about the way we manage our improvement activities must change with them. Only the very best organizations will attract customers in today's competitive environment. Producing excellent products isn't enough today; we must excel in all parts of our organization. Piecemeal approaches such as total quality management (TQM), Six Sigma, and customer relationship management must give way to a holistic view of the organization and its improvement efforts. An organization should wow its customers, not just satisfy them. Customers should rate the total organization as outstanding, not just very good.

Customers remember an organization's name for two reasons and for two reasons only:

- If it produces a poor product or service
- When it produces an exceptional product or service that makes them say, "Wow! That was a great experience."

If you simply meet your customers' requirements, you don't build customer loyalty. They can be attracted away from you if your competition undercuts you by a few cents. Your organization must radiate excellence in everything it does.

For the last fifty years, the quality professional, management professional, and consultant have tried—largely unsuccessfully—to impose improvement systems on business, government, and academia. Consider the following attempts:

- Quality control—failed
- Total quality control—failed
- Zero defects—failed
- Total quality management—failed
- Process reengineering—failed
- Six Sigma—failing
- ISO 9001:2000—added little real value

"We must simply learn to love change as much as we have hated it in the past."
—Tom Peters
Author, *Thriving on Chaos*

The question is, "Why, after great spurts of success, do these sound improvement systems fall into oblivion?" They're much like an old toy that gets put back in the dark corner of the closet when a new toy is found under the Christmas tree.

These exercises in futility stem from applying improvement initiatives to an organization as if they were bandages. What's really needed is fundamental organizational change. Treating symptoms usually doesn't affect a cure; it just prolongs the agony.

These approaches failed because the initiatives were applied as separate activities instead of with the intention of making a total organizational transformation. It's similar to giving a person who has pneumonia an aspirin for his or her headache, thinking it will cure the disease.

From decade to decade, business focus continually changes:

- 1970s—people
- 1980s—teams
- 1990s—processes
- 2000s—knowledge and adaptability

In keeping these changes in focus, the approaches to performance improvement have also changed:

- ISO 9001 and ISO 14001—process-driven, lacking in business focus
- Total quality management—process-driven, with statistical analysis and teams that are customer-focused
- National quality awards—quality-driven, plus results
- Six Sigma—problem/solution-driven, with a customer focus
- Total improvement management (TIM)—performance-driven/total organization-driven sales, marketing development, personnel, and production. It included organizational change.
- Organizational excellence—performance-driven, including processes, projects, organizational change, information technology, resources, and knowledge management

"Only 5 percent of the organizations in the West truly excel. Their secret is not what they do, but how they do it."

—HJH

The following list gives a point score to these approaches' effectiveness in improving organizational performance.

- Casual—no recognized system (0 points)
- ISO 9001 and ISO 14001—minimum requirements (200 points)
- Six Sigma—problem-focused (400 points)
- TQM—"womb to tomb" quality and teams (500 points)
- National quality awards—result-based (600 points)
- TIM—combined quality, reliability, performance, and results (800 points)
- Organizational excellence—five pillars (1,000 points)

"You can win the National Quality Award with 600 points out of a maximum of 1,000 points. That's 60 percent of the way to the goal."
—HJH

You might ask, "Where are we today?" A survey conducted by Harris Interactive Europe for Dow Corning provides the status for 2003. It included sixty-nine executives from a wide range of industries in the Americas, Europe, and Asia. This survey revealed that TQM was the most important business innovation for these organizations during the last four years. Although Six Sigma has received a lot of press during the past thirteen years, it didn't rate in the top three most important business innovations. The top three, in descending order, are:

- TQM
- Process engineering
- Supply chain management

> "We want to operate far more efficiently. We want to operate at a new level of excellence."
> —Robert J. Herbold
> Former COO, Microsoft

The American Society for Quality recently sponsored a survey of 600 executives from manufacturing, service, government, health care, and education. It reported that 99 percent of the executives surveyed believe that quality contributed to the bottom line. Also, it indicated that 92 percent of the executives believe that an organizationwide effort to use quality techniques provides a positive return. Figure P.4 gives a breakdown of the most frequently used quality techniques.

The survey indicates that a wide gap exists between the executives' awareness of quality improvement processes and their implementation. Again, the survey reveals that TQM is used 300 percent more than Six Sigma. The quality profession suffers by continuously changing the name of its activities despite little change in content.

Figure P.4 Quality Technique Familiarity Versus Use

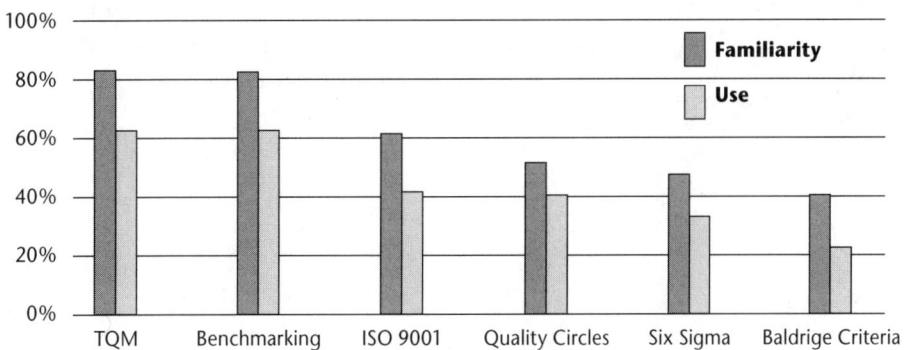

ORGANIZATIONAL EXCELLENCE SUMMARY

> "Being good is good. Being the best is great!"
> —HJH

When you look at the five pillars that must be managed to achieve excellence, you'll see common threads that run through all of them:

- Communication
- Teamwork
- Empowerment
- Respect for one another
- Honesty
- Leadership
- Quality
- Fairness
- Technology

> **"The sizeable gap between usage and awareness leads me to believe that businesses and organizations either don't use quality method-ologies to improve their operations, or they just don't realize that the processes they have in place are attrib-utable directly to the quality discipline."**
> **—Ken Case**
> **Former president, American Society for Quality**

All of these key factors are built into the word "manage-ment." They turn an employee into an individual who owns his or her job, thereby bring-ing satisfaction and dignity to the individual for a job well done.

In today's worldwide marketplace, customers don't have to settle for second best. Over-night mail brings the best to everyone's doorstep. The Internet allows people to shop inter-nationally, making it easy for them to get the best quality, reliability, and price, no matter who offers it. Customers are concerned about the products they buy, but they're equally or more concerned about dealing with organizations that care, are quick to respond, and that will listen and react to their unique needs. This means that, to succeed in the twenty-first century, organizations must excel in all parts of their busi-nesses. Your organization must excel at what it does, but its stakeholders must also recognize your efforts as excellent. This will win over today's savvy customers.

> **"We expect a lot—highly motivated people consciously choosing to do whatever is in their power to ensure every customer is satisfied . . . and more. Every day. Without this concentrated effort, attempting a flawless service is really quite futile."**
> **—Fred Smith**
> **Founder, Federal Express**

CHAPTER I

INTRODUCTION TO RESOURCE MANAGEMENT EXCELLENCE

"Even the best ideas need resources to transform them into results."
—HJH

Merriam-Webster's Collegiate Dictionary defines "asset" as "anything owned that has exchange value." It defines "resource" as "something that lies ready for use or that can be drawn upon for aid or to take care of a need." For the purposes of this book, assets are included as part of resources.

The following discussion covers resource and assets management in its broadest sense, which is all resources and assets that are available to an organization. Resource/assets management includes:

- Alliance partnerships
- Boards of directors
- Bricks and mortar
- Customers
- Employees
- Equipment
- Floor space
- Goodwill
- Inventory
- Investors
- Knowledge
- Management
- Money
- Patents
- Real estate
- Stockholders
- Suppliers
- Work in process

"We think that in today's economy the intangible assets of a corporation are more valuable than land, buildings, and cash. A company like Infosys is in the knowledge business, so we recognize people as our most strategic asset."
—**Nandan Nilekani**
CEO, Infosys

When all these resources are considered, it's easy to see that effective resource management is among the most critical and complex activities within any organization. It's extremely important that an organization manage not just its financial and physical resources, but also its human, intellectual, informational, organizational, and technical resources to ensure proper planning, execution, and delivery of products and services that will wow customers.

More than 1,100 different tools and methodologies are available to manage resources. Among the most widely used are:

- Accountability matrices
- Activity-based budgeting
- Activity-based costing
- Activity-based management
- Alliance partnerships
- Application evaluation
- Automation
- Business to business (B2B)
- Business to consumer (B2C)
- Balanced scorecards
- Corporate governance
- Creativity training
- Customer relationship management (CRM)
- Customer surveys
- Design of experiments
- Employee opinion surveys
- Error-proofing
- Executive dashboards
- External audits
- Five Ss (i.e., sort, set in order, shine, standardize, and sustain)
- Inventory control
- Just-in-time
- *Kaizen*
- Lean
- Lean Six Sigma
- Opinion surveys
- Organizational restructuring
- Outsourcing
- Performance appraisal systems
- Performance evaluation systems
- *Poka-yoke*

- Policy deployment
- Poor-quality cost
- Process redesign
- Process reengineering
- Project management
- Pull concept
- Self-managed employees
- Single-minute exchange of die
- Strategic planning
- Suggestion systems
- *Takt* time
- Total preventive maintenance
- Total Six Sigma
- Visual workplace
- Waste elimination

For a complete list of tools and methodologies, see *Performance Improvement Methods—Fighting the War on Waste* by Kenneth C. Lomax and H. James Harrington (McGraw-Hill, 1999).

Enough information exists about these resources to write a book about each one, and in fact numerous books are available that do just that. This book provides an overview of resource management along with key recommendations about the best ways to go about it. Chapters 2 and 3 begin the discussion by focusing on human resource management because that's the one skill that separates truly excellent organizations from merely good ones. Along with executive and staff resources, this book also examines the following critical resources:

- Corporate governance
- Products and services
- Alliance partnerships
- Customers
- Technological resources
- Financial resources
- Suppliers
- Property
- Inventory
- Investors

As you think about your resources, remember that *you* are your most important one. Examine how you use this important resource, and be sure you're making the most effective use of yourself. Former GE CEO Jack Welch's Six Rules for Self-Examination are helpful in this context. They are:

1. Face reality as it is, not as it was or as you wish it were.
2. Be candid with everyone.
3. Don't manage; lead.
4. Change before you have to.
5. If you don't have a competitive advantage, don't compete.
6. Control your own destiny, or someone else will.

> **"Americans believe more than anything else in the last four letters of their title: Amer-I-Can."**
> **—Anonymous**

In *The Power of Management Capital* (McGraw-Hill, 2003), Armand V. Feigenbaum and Donald S. Feigenbaum point out that pace-setting organizations recognize twelve key channels of management capital. They are:

1. New product and service development, which includes supporting product leadership through rapid economical development
2. Effective market leadership and top-line growth, including customer-relationship management
3. Business expansion and globalization to increase value by leveraging resources and capabilities across international boundaries
4. Total quality management for product, process, and service excellence to ensure complete customer satisfaction, profitability, and top-line growth
5. Tracking of performance and improvement via key operating measurements
6. Development of partnerships and alliances for competitive leadership through effective production liaisons and strategic business relationships
7. Improvement of operational effectiveness to ensure operating cost leadership, performance excellence, and integrated management of processes
8. Effective supplier management to reduce costs and delivery time
9. Establishment of effective human resources to encourage the integration of individual knowledge, skills, attitudes, commitment, and effectiveness
10. Integrated business information management to improve the availability and integrity of information required to manage the business
11. Effective financial operations to support and ensure growth, profitability, and complete customer satisfaction
12. Asset management for effective acquisition, use, and disposition of necessary assets and infrastructure

Note that all twelve of these channels affect the way resources are managed in an organization.

CHAPTER II

EXECUTIVE RESOURCES

"An organization is a mirror image of its executives."
—HJH

THE LEADERS

Considering the complexity of resource management, you might ask, "Where do you start?" There is no right answer to this question. I like to start with investors' selecting the right management team, as this is critical to every organization. There is no substitute for experienced, qualified, proven executives. The executive team is the first thing that professional investors look at when evaluating organizations. They make a decision to invest based upon considerations such as:

- What is the executive team's track record?
- Have its members led other successful organizations?
- Are they visionaries?
- Do they attract other successful managers to their team?

"Quality is made in the boardroom. When I want to know what a company stands for, I look first to the actions of senior managers."
—W. Edwards Deming

A good executive with a fair product will have a successful business. Just look at the amazing turnaround Lou Gerstner led IBM through in the 1990s. A poor executive with a good product has a high probability of leading the organization into bankruptcy.

Do you need different executives based upon the maturity of the organization? As an organization progresses, it needs very different leadership styles. A young start-up company requires the executive team to have a detailed understanding of its products and services. Its members usually are the organization's best salespeople. They need to have entrepreneurial personalities. Often they design the offering themselves. This type of leader develops a very creative and unstructured environment. Everyone shares the vision, and interactions between the employees and the executive team are ongoing.

Bill Gates in the early days of Microsoft is a typical example of excellent executive leadership of a young organization. But by 1994, Gates realized that there was an operational crisis in Microsoft. Microsoft was maturing; its laid-back, creative atmosphere was at odds with the needs of the organization. The executive team and the culture of Microsoft needed

"They (excellent organizations) emphasize the quality
of management, which rec-
ognizes and is measured in
terms of the leadership and
networking capability for
focusing a company's total
resources on sustaining business growth."
—Armand V. Feigenbaum and
         Donald Feigenbaum
    Authors of *Principal
Management Capital Channels*

to change drastically. As a result, Gates turned the organization over to Robert J. Herbold, who served as Microsoft's
COO for the next seven years. Herbold had spent most
of his career at Procter & Gamble, an organization with a
very mature culture. You might ask, "How well do soap and
software mix?" Well, they mix very well. Under Herbold's
guidance, Microsoft's operating expenses decreased from 51
percent of revenue to 40 percent. Revenue quadrupled and
its profitability went up seven times. Herbold states, "In the
case of driving for excellence in these functional areas, you
have to draw attention to the crisis to really make people take notice and say, 'Yes, we want
to do it differently here.' It should be clear what the goal is: We want to operate far more
efficiently. We want to operate at a new level of excellence."

Examples of creative and effective management styles are also found in public sector
organizations, including international development organizations. Omar Kabbaj, the president of the African Development Bank, achieved a major turnaround at the bank at the
end of the 1990s. He took over when the bank was in deep
financial and management troubles that threatened its existence. The bank had lost its Moody's AAA rating because bad
loans had been mounting, the credit standing of many of its
borrowing members had plummeted, and internal squabbles
between management and the board had reached a crisis level. These events also hit hard the most important asset that
the bank had enjoyed since inception—trust between the
African shareholders (governments) and their nonregional partners, mostly the developed
countries. Within a very short period, the new president achieved wonders. His dynamic,
no-nonsense approach resulted in a complete turnaround. He restored the bank's financial and management credibility. He demonstrated to the shareholders that the partnership between the borrowing members and the donor community was worth keeping. He
selected new managers who believed in change—and he achieved all this without affecting
the African character of the bank. His combination of technical and political skills, coupled
with courage and a strong determination to succeed, saved the bank from destruction and
laid a new foundation for growth.

"The business of leaders, of
heroes, is tricky. Leadership
is not something that is
done to people, like fixing
your teeth. Leadership is
unlocking people's potential
to become better."
             —Bill Bradley
      Retired U.S. Senator

Beginning in 1995, Jim Wolfensohn, the dynamic president of the World Bank, "re-
created" the world's biggest development financing institution and brought focus and direction into its operations. In a remarkable act of determination, he succeeded in convincing
everyone that the bank's real business was reducing poverty in the developing countries,
where the majority of the people lived on less than a dollar a day. The World Bank bureaucracy up to that time was moving in all directions, almost trying to be the answer to the

world's every problem. Wolfensohn understood that the World Bank's enormous financial and labor resources could make a difference in fighting poverty only if the bank became more focused on the real problem. He transformed the bank's operational strategy dramatically by sending most of the staff out of the comfortable Washington headquarters and into the field where the problems were. His efforts in the last seven years have not only reinforced the reputation of the World Bank as a leader of the development industry, but they have actually changed the way other development institutions conceive and administer international development strategies. Rarely have the poor in the world's developing countries found such a strong voice of support as they have in Jim Wolfensohn's.

> "If you know *how* to do it, you will always have work. If you know *why* to do it, you'll be the manager."
>
> —HJH

Yes, the executive personality and management style must be different for young organizations and mature organizations. Figure 2.1 demonstrates the differences between the two kinds of organizations.

One of the major problems that young organizations and family-owned organizations face is how and when to transform from an entrepreneurial-type environment to a mature business environment.

Figure 2.1 Young Organizations/Mature Organizations

Young Organizations	Mature Organizations
Creative	Planning
Likeable	Respected
Knowledgeable leader	Understands the product/business
Unstructured	Process-focused
Technology-driven	Customer-driven
Networker	Manager
Reactionary	Structured
Highly motivating	Sets the example
Optimistic	Realistic
Sales-oriented	Organizational-oriented
Inspirational	Demanding
Optimistic	Realist
Visionary	Strategic
Results-oriented	Process-oriented
Product-driven	Performance-driven

The organization's management team is the key resource that has the biggest impact upon an organization's performance. Why are its members so crucial? Just look at what the management team is responsible for:

- Articulating a vision
- Identifying business opportunities
- Building business strategies
- Selecting and training employees
- Setting priorities
- Preparing job descriptions
- Setting performance standards
- Selecting the leaders
- Allocating resources
- Providing the measurement-and-reward system
- Making job assignments
- Developing the processes
- Establishing the organizational structure
- Building strategic alliances

Considering the importance of management's responsibilities, it's obvious that the management team must execute these responsibilities in a superior manner if any organization is going to excel. Unfortunately, the management team is one of the biggest problems that organizations face today. Donald Stratton, manager of quality at AT&T Network Systems, reported the following findings in an April 2002 *Quality Digest* article:

- 82 percent of the problems analyzed were classified as common cause. These are process problems owned by management.
- 18 percent of the problems analyzed were special cause. These are problems that were caused by people, machinery, or tools. Only a small share of these problems can be solved by employee teams.
- Of the 82 percent management controlled:
  - ☐ 60 percent of the corrections could be implemented by first- and second-level management.
  - ☐ 20 percent could be implemented by middle management.
  - ☐ 20 percent could be implemented only by top management.

AT&T is not an unusual case. In fact, its management team performs far better than most organizations' management teams. All organizations invest significant amounts of their total resources into the management team. For the most part this produces unsatisfactory results.

My studies indicate that the average executive makes between fifty and eighty behavioral errors—such as showing up late for a meeting or not returning calls in a timely manner—per week, largely because these behavioral errors aren't measured nor are standards set for them. Once agreed-to standards of performance are in place, behavioral errors drop significantly.

The other part of managerial responsibility is decision making and here, the average executive performs much better. An analysis of the executive's decisions one year after the executive made the decisions indicated that:

- 5 percent of the decisions were bad decisions.
- 15 percent of the decisions were excellent decisions, and based upon the additional knowledge that was available one year later, no change would have been made to the decision.
- 85 percent of the decisions were good decisions but could have been better.

For organizations to excel, a minimum of 50 percent of the executive decisions should be perfect decisions when viewed one year later. This requires some drastic changes in the way decisions are made and in the information that is available when the decisions are made. It doesn't mean that decisions should be put off; they can't be. No decision is often worse than a bad decision. What it means is that members of the executive team must be better prepared and understand how confident they can be in the data they are provided. They have to have a much better understanding of the impact their past decisions have had on the organization's performance.

Management's Role

A typical organization has three distinct levels of management. They are:

- Top management
- Middle management
- First-line/supervisor management

Each of these levels of management has unique and different responsibilities.

- Top management's role is to:
    - ☐ Create and communicate the business vision
    - ☐ Develop and communicate the business objectives
    - ☐ Approve functional missions
    - ☐ Review business progress

> "Among the effective executives I've known and worked with, there are extroverts and aloof, retiring men, some even morbidly shy. Some are eccentric; others are painfully correct conformists. Some are fat, and some are thin. Some are worriers, and some are relaxed. Some drink quite heavily, and others are total abstainers. Some are men of great charm and warmth: Some have no more personality than a frozen mackerel."
> —Peter Drucker
> Author and consultant

> "I doubt that anybody outside Toyota could perceive how much time, effort, discussion, and sensitivity we have regarding the human side of our business."
> —Gary Convis
> President, Toyota Motor Manufacturing, Kentucky

- ☐ Obtain funding
- ☐ Interact with customers
- ☐ Interact with investors
- ☐ Set the role model for the rest of the organization
- ☐ Interact with the board of directors
- ☐ Ensure compliance with plans and processes
- ☐ Set priorities
- ☐ Develop succession plans

- ■ Middle management's role is to:
  - ☐ Establish functional priorities
  - ☐ Develop cross-functional interfaces and processes
  - ☐ Select and train first-line managers
  - ☐ Align plans with priorities
  - ☐ Communicate business directions
  - ☐ Review team progress
  - ☐ Ensure compliance to procedures
  - ☐ Develop succession plans
  - ☐ Solve problems that the first-line manager can't handle
  - ☐ Set work objectives

- ■ The first-line manager's role is to:
  - ☐ Select the employees and align them with suitable assignments
  - ☐ Train the employees
  - ☐ Negotiate team objectives
  - ☐ Create improvement strategies
  - ☐ Ensure department's objectives are met
  - ☐ Evaluate employees' weaknesses and assist them in improvement
  - ☐ Align employees' strengths with job assignments
  - ☐ Set work schedules and standards
  - ☐ Solve problems that are common cause

> **"The best leader is the one who has sense enough to pick good men to do what he wants done, and the self-restraint to keep from meddling with them while they do it."**
> **—Theodore Roosevelt**

We are finding that to accomplish these tasks, today's knowledge worker wants more involvement in defining his or her work and more participation in managing the way the work is done. To accomplish this, management must create an environment in which:

- Management must share power and responsibility.
- Management must provide employees with much more information than in the past.
- Management at all levels must practice participative management/employee involvement.
- Management must trust its employees to earn the trust of its employees.
- Management must feel comfortable with decentralized decision making.
- Management must not perform hindsight appraisals.
- Management must accept failure as being part of the learning cycle and recognize risk-taking as a dominant trait of people who get ahead.
- Management must make time available to train the employees in how to make decisions, learn new jobs, and perform business analyses.
- Management must have the courage to reject poor solutions but also take the time to explain why the suggestions are being rejected.

The fact is that management's role has changed drastically in the past twenty years and will change even more in the future. (See figure 2.2.)

The following are the eleven key activities performed by executive teams:
- Hire really good people.
- Focus on the products and services.
- Have excellent market research.
- Focus on speed and decisiveness.
- Stay close to the support processes such as procurement and information systems.
- Cut bureaucracy.
- Set high standards for products and people.
- Excite people about change.

> "Being a responsible manager in the Toyota entity means you have a great responsibility to take care of the people who are donating their lives to the company."
> —**Gary Convis**
> **President, Toyota Motor Manufacturing Kentucky**

Figure 2.2 The Way Management Is Changing

Activity	Yesterday	Today	Tomorrow
Management style	Dictating	Coaching	Assisting
Providing direction	Orders	Consensus	Define results
Goal setting	Management's goals	Common goals	Employee's goals
Evaluation	Criticism	Appraisal	Two-way evaluations
Decision making	Management decisions	Team decisions	Individual decisions
Compensation	Pay for years worked	Pay for performance	Pay for knowledge
Way to correct problems	Focus on the individual	Focus on the activity	Focus on the process

- Focus innovation and creativity on the parts of the organization that develop great products that excite your customers and those that have a lot of interaction with customers.
- Know and talk to the customers (make sales calls).
- Insist on open and honest communications.

Management styles have evolved through five unique stages. They are:

- *Individualistic management stage.* This is a nineteenth-century management style, which was very dictatorial and was responsible for creating most of the large family wealth that existed at the turn of the twentieth century. Families such as Ford, Rockefeller, Mullin, Sloan, Vanderbilt, and Watson are all characterized by individuals who built and managed great organizations.

> **"Effective leadership is the common denominator in all performance. If I had a buck, I'd spend ninety-nine cents on picking great leaders."**
> **—Dennis Donovan**
> **Executive VP, Human Resources, Home Depot**

- *Professional management stage.* The professional manager's goal was to produce the maximum output with a minimum of expenditure.

- *Scientific management stage.* This movement was led by Frederick Winslow Taylor and was based upon four principles:
  - ☐ Scientific design of the job
  - ☐ Scientific selection of workers to match the job requirements
  - ☐ Scientific training of the workers to perform the jobs as designed
  - ☐ Spirit of cooperation about the work to be done

- *Human relations management stage.* As workers became more educated, human relations management became an effective management style. It's based upon the belief that if management treats employees with respect and dignity, the employees' performance will be maximized. This is a very simple idea for a simple situation.

- *Participative management stage.* As laborers gave way to knowledge workers, their managers' style had to change, and they began to practice participative management. This has allowed for a much larger span of control and for a virtual work environment. Participative management involves the employees and empowers them to be responsible and accountable for their jobs.

> **"The art of leadership is being ready and able to subordinate one's self-interest often to the greater good of the unit or the organization."**
> **—Fred Smith**
> **CEO, Federal Express**

Frank Cary, past chairman of the board for IBM, stated: "Wholesale imitation of the Japanese won't travel well, but we can and should emulate their success in making people productive and bring out the best that's in them." The challenge to management in a participative management environment is to learn how to manage groups effectively so that eventually the group itself can identify and make business decisions related to its activities. At that level, responsibility and activities are maximized.

James Harbour, automobile industry consultant, stated, "The Japanese don't manufacture a car with any better technology than we do, but they are stomping us into the ground because of absolutely superior management."

> **"We became overorganized, overstaffed, short-term, and myopic."**
> —**Donald Beall**
> **Chairman/CEO,**
> **Rockwell Corp.**

PARTICIPATIVE MANAGEMENT

The theory of participative management states that "people who are involved in the decisions that have an impact on them have a tendency to implement these decisions much more effectively and efficiently." No doubt about it—today you must involve the employees and staff more in the decisions that affect them. But management must be ready to handle the large number of suggestions it will get when it asks the employees, "What is wrong and what should be done about it?" This pressure on the first-line manager is passed on up the organization, and if the total system is not prepared, it will come apart. Never ask an employee for a suggestion or an opinion unless you are ready to use it or explain why you can't.

Why Managers Don't Like Participative Management

Joseph M. Juran predicts that the first-line manager's role will change drastically in the next few years.

In a survey conducted by Harvard Business School of first-line managers:

- 72 percent viewed employee involvement as being good for the organization.
- 60 percent thought it was good for the employees.
- 31 percent thought it was good for themselves.

The U.S. national performance excellence award—the Malcolm Baldrige National Quality Award—highlights the importance of employee participation and empowerment by stating that it:

- Gives employees the authority and responsibility to make decisions and to take actions
- Enables employees to satisfy customers on first contact, to improve processes, to increase productivity, and to better the organization's business results

> **"If I may be permitted another look into my fallible crystal ball, I suggest that self-managing employee teams will become the dominant successor to the Taylor system."**
> —**Joseph M. Juran**

- Results in decisions' being made closest to the "front line," where work-related knowledge and understanding reside

Management Roadblocks

Why have organizations been so slow to implement a participative management system? When a company's leaders decide to implement participative management, they anticipate that the employees and the unions will be roadblocks. The truth is that the employees take to it like ducks take to water, but the first-line and middle managers are the ones who don't want to get their feet wet. Lockheed in Sunnyvale, California, was one of the first companies in the United States to put quality circles into operation, but the program collapsed when its main mover, Wayne S. Rieker, left to become a consultant in 1976. Why weren't the quality circles continued? Because first-line and middle managers were not convinced that the results were worth the expenditure, and they saw little benefit to themselves in continuing the program.

First-line and middle managers resist participative management because they're not familiar with it, and they feel uncomfortable facing the uncertainty. They have, through the years, developed management styles that are uniquely theirs. Their styles are the ones that work for them. They are natural and not put on. They perceive that to change at this point in their careers is a high-risk activity. They admit that participative management is good for the employee and good for the company, but they don't view it as being beneficial to themselves. In fact, they see it as a threat, taking away some of their authority.

Too often, the executive team dictates participative management processes to first-line management, who are told that if they can't adjust they'll have to find work elsewhere. However, participative management processes are very carefully sold to employees. The first-line managers are ordered to give the employees more say about their work environment without any change in the way top and middle management interact with the first-line managers. As a result, they implement the program half-heartedly. This attitude is quickly recognized by employees, who begin to wonder if they are not being "used" by management.

A high level of concern is shared by most first-line and middle managers, regardless of their ages, leadership styles, or backgrounds. Their concerns usually can be divided into the following categories:

- Loss of job security
- Loss of authority
- Increased workload
- Loss of responsibility and measurements
- Erosion of one-on-one relationship between the manager and employee
- Loss of power
- Doubt about upper management commitment
- Fear of failure

Upper management must deal with the fear and concern about the loss of power, prestige, and control very seriously. Through the years, middle and first-line managers developed and refined the techniques required to survive and prosper in a hierarchical organization. It's unrealistic to expect them to discard this successful experience to try some new fad without devoting a great deal of time to help them develop a new set of management skills.

Before participative management is introduced, a plan must be carefully developed and implemented to train and prepare the total management team to change its management style. Then management should practice participative management within its own ranks before it is used at the employee level.

It's important to note that that management can involve employees to different degrees:

- *Dictator.* Manager makes the decision; employees participate by carrying it out.
- *Leader.* Manager listens to the employees and then makes the decision.
- *Politician.* One person/one vote.
- *Optimist.* Manager gets consensus.
- *Theoretical.* Manager gets full agreement.

Remember that as the manager you are always held responsible. You must reject bad decisions but always explain why you rejected them.

> "Remember that participative management does not mean democratic management."
> —HJH

What Makes It Work?

If participative management is to work effectively:

- Managers must be willing to share some powers and responsibilities.
- Managers must trust employees.
- Management must make training in problem solving and prevention paramount.
- Work must be viewed as a cooperative effort between management and employees. Workers must accept majority decisions, and management must have the courage to reject suggested solutions that are not beneficial to the company.
- Management must be willing to accept a system that decentralizes decision making. People like to be able to point at a single individual who made the decision. With participative management, this is impossible. Upper management must resist the tendency to hold the department manager responsible for any decision that is made by the group. Business needs to get out of the finger-pointing mode of operation and on to something that is more productive.

- Management must believe that everyone has good ideas and that combining individual ideas will produce the best possible solution.
- Management must be willing to implement employees' suggestions when feasible.
- Management must provide an environment conducive to developing employee loyalty.
- Management must recognize the group's accomplishments.
- Organized labor must become an active partner in developing a participative system.
- Managers must accept participative management as a long-term effort and not expect immediate results. Westinghouse estimated it would take two years for any significant results and ten years before the full benefits of participative management would be realized.

Benefits to the Business

If participative management is effectively implemented, the following benefits will be realized by the company:

- Quality and productivity, both inside and outside the company, will greatly improve.
- The business will develop and improve.
- Communication, both upward and downward, will improve.
- Employee morale will improve as a stronger management-employee relationship develops.
- Problems will be solved that would otherwise never get high enough priority to get attention.
- The employees will help things run smoothly as the goals of the informal leader of the department and those of the formal leader and of the company become aligned.

The *IndustryWeek* 2001 Census of Manufacturers reported that in organizations that empowered more than 75 percent of their employees, the employees' median productivity was 20 percent to 60 percent higher than that of their competition that didn't empower their employees.

Benefits to the Employees

As much as the company stands to gain from participative management, employees have even more to gain:

- All employees find opportunities to grow.
- The employees get the feeling they are part of the action and are making things happen.
- Employees gain increased job satisfaction as monotony is eliminated and job stature improved.
- Individuals are given new training and provided with opportunities to demonstrate their abilities, and new doors for recognition and promotion are opened.
- Job security is enhanced because the profitability of the company is improved.
- Employee intellectual stature is heightened.

To Make Participation Work

To be successful, participative management must start at the top with the executive team giving up some of its power and decision-making responsibilities to middle management. (See figure 2.3.) With this additional work, middle management, which is already overworked, will then be glad to give some of its responsibilities to the first-line managers. In turn, the first-line managers will be grateful to be empowered to make more important decisions. But now the first-line managers have more than they can do, so they pass on to their employees the right to make more decisions related to their assignments. When the participative/empowerment management process is implemented correctly, the people who have less work to do are the members of the executive team, who have been working sixty hours per week to get their jobs done. Now the executives, who are usually workaholics, have the time to go out to the work areas and talk to their employees in their own environments. The executives should also use this extra time to meet their customers so that they can better understand their needs and expectations.

I strongly disagree with Deming's quote below. MBWA works very effectively in organizations such as Hewlett-Packard, IBM, and many others. James L. Donald, CEO of Pathmark Stores, a $4.8 billion retail supermarket chain, agrees. He stated, "CEOs have to spend time where the action is, or they are not going to get the true picture." Donald stays in touch with his employees and managers by spending 40 percent of his time in Pathmark Stores, visiting all shifts.

"MBWA (Management By Walking Around) is hardly ever effective."
—W. Edwards Deming

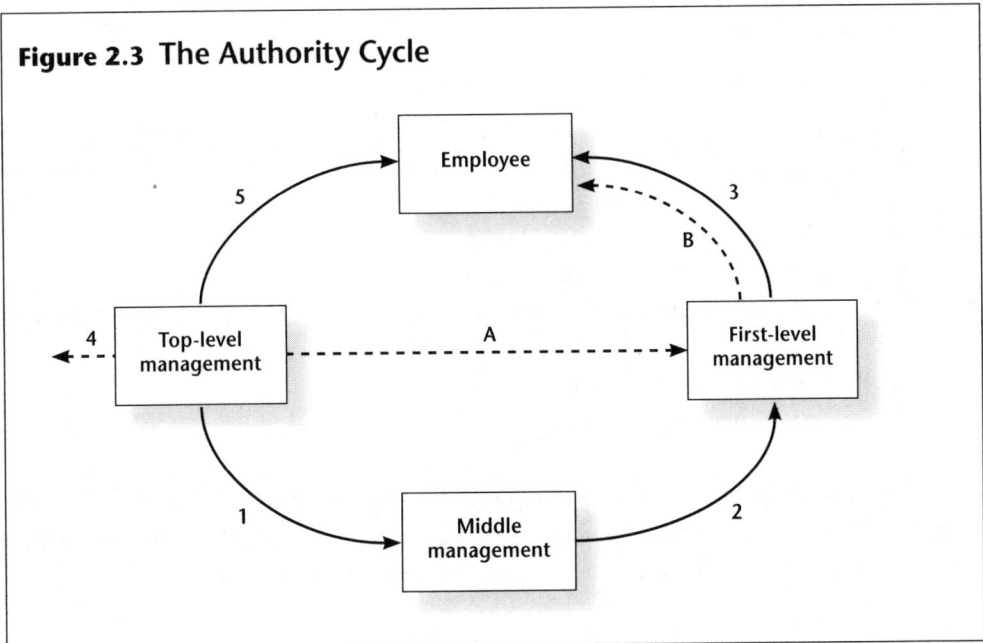

Figure 2.3 The Authority Cycle

"Pacesetting companies lead, manage, and systematically structure quality as a fundamental strategy for continuous quality alignment with hands-on senior management leadership."
—Armand V. Feigenbaum

Middle management's fear and concern about loss of power, prestige, and control must be dealt with seriously for participative management to be successful. Its fears are not all unfounded. If you look at the layoffs that have occurred in the past ten years, you can see a disturbing trend. Middle managers account for about 5 percent of the work force and they have accounted for 22 percent of the people laid off. Keeping this in mind, you can understand middle managers' concern about giving up any of their responsibilities without upper management's giving them additional responsibilities.

"Never be bigger than your frontline selling associates."
—Sam Walton
Founder, Wal-Mart

CHANGING MANAGEMENT STYLES

Management's style is changing, and the survival of the manager lies in his or her ability to keep pace with this changing environment and to be a role model for the employee. (See figure 2.4.)

When employees start to participate in planning their work, they soon become empowered and take on more responsibilities. That will lead to their acting as if they were owners of the organization. They will begin to look for ways to cut costs, improve productivity, and increase customer satisfaction. Basically you would like each employee to think of himself or herself as being self-employed. With this mindset, employees will be concerned about building their own businesses, developing fine reputations, and ensuring that the people who pay for their work are satisfied.

"The whole employee involvement process springs from asking all your employees the simple question, 'What do you think?' "
—Donald Peterson
Former chairman,
Ford Motor Co.

Ken Jennings and John Stahl-Wert in their book *The Serving Leader* (Barrett-Koehler, 2004) make five important points:

- Build the confidence and self-esteem of others.
- Keep raising the bar of expectations of those you lead.
- Teach those you lead the knowledge, skills, and strategies they need to succeed and work hard to remove obstacles that prevent progress in these areas.
- Build on the strengths of those you lead.
- Provide a compelling vision that people will want to run to achieve.

To start your personal transformation, look back over the past thirty days and list the things you have done to follow these five points. Then do the same thing thirty days from now. The ideas are not new, but sometimes people forget what they already know.

Figure 2.4 Old Management Style Versus New

Old Management Style	New Management Style
Gives orders	Gets agreement on objectives
Holds back data	Openly exchanges information
Expects employees to work long hours	Requires results
Emphasizes individual performance	Emphasizes team performance
Gains approval decisions from above	Makes decisions after discussions with the affected employees
Primary job is to get the assignment completed	Primary job is to enable the employee to complete the assignment
Takes credit for employees' work	Gives credit to the employees
Tells how to do it	Explains why it needs to be done
Works within the organization's structure	Changes the organization's structure to meet the activities' needs
Chief reward is self-promotion	Chief reward is growing employee capabilities
Thinks of himself or herself as boss	Thinks of himself or herself as a manager of human development
Follows the chain of command	Works with anyone necessary to get the task completed
Thinks of himself or herself as a manager of a discipline	Thinks of himself or herself as a manager of processes
Sets schedules	Emphasizes urgency of the job—approves schedules set by employees
Dodges unpleasant tasks	Takes immediate action on unpleasant tasks
Delegates unimportant, uninteresting jobs	Makes job assignments based upon individual capabilities and skills
Gives the best worker more assignments	Keeps a balance of work expectations between both good and bad performers
Pay is based upon time on job	Pay is based upon knowledge and contribution
Stays aloof from the employees	Employees and management share outside activities
Thinks minorities and women have to be treated specially	Treats everybody specially
Worries about employees who could replace him or her	Develops a backup for himself or herself
Manages all employees the same way	Adjusts management style to meet the employee's personality and task assignment
Checks to be sure employee never fails	Allows employees to learn from failure, as long as the impact is not too detrimental to the organization

The Impact of Pushing/Pulling

If the bandleader with his big baton goes marching down the street in one direction and the band takes off in another, he's doing no one any good. His big stick is useless. Any organization is only as effective as the number of people who follow its leader. You can liken leadership to pulling a piece of string with your finger. (See figure 2.5.) No matter where your finger goes, the string will follow right along behind; it will bend and curl and go in the same direction that your finger does. On the other hand, if you try to push the string, it wads up and goes nowhere. This is exactly what happens when managers try to lead by force rather than by inspiration. If you lead by setting an example and inspiring individuals to follow, your employees will be behind you all the way.

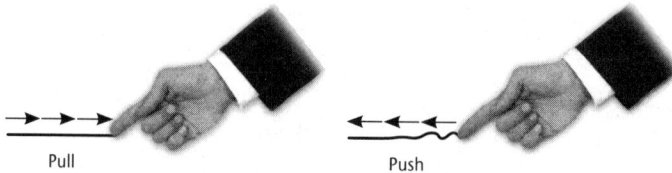

Figure 2.5 Impact of Pushing/Pulling

Pull   Push

VARIABLES IN MANAGEMENT STYLE

An effective management style must have many facets. Today, managers are expected to adjust their management style to meet the personality traits of the employee. In the future, managers will have to adjust their management style to the individual's personality and to his or her job assignments. People's working personalities can be divided into four categories:

- *Planners.* People who excel in taking an idea and laying out a systematic approach to its implementation. Planners tend to be introverts.
- *Networkers.* People who establish excellent communication systems between groups. They are excellent negotiators and politicians. Networkers tend to be extroverts.

- *Doers.* People who take a plan and carry it out. They like to be assigned a problem and get it corrected. They make things happen.
- *Leaders.* People who through their charisma, appearance, or example, attract others to them. People follow them because it's unpopular to do otherwise.

Each of these personality traits imposes very different needs on management. These needs can be classified into two types:

- *Social needs.* The needs that are satisfied by management contact, public recognition, and demonstrated interest in the individual and his or her career and personal life.
- *Technical needs.* The skills required to perform a given task.

Two factors drive the degree to and frequency with which both needs have to be fulfilled. They are:

- How well the individual is performing the assigned task
- The type of personality that composes the individual's makeup

Figure 2.6 shows how management styles must change versus the employee's performance level. It's easy to see that, based upon how the individual is performing, management styles must be changed to meet the employee's needs.

- Employees who do not meet requirements need a coach. They need someone who will tell them what to do, show them the correct way when they can't accomplish a task, and minimize their chances of making an error. They need someone who will help them feel good about themselves, even when they aren't doing well.

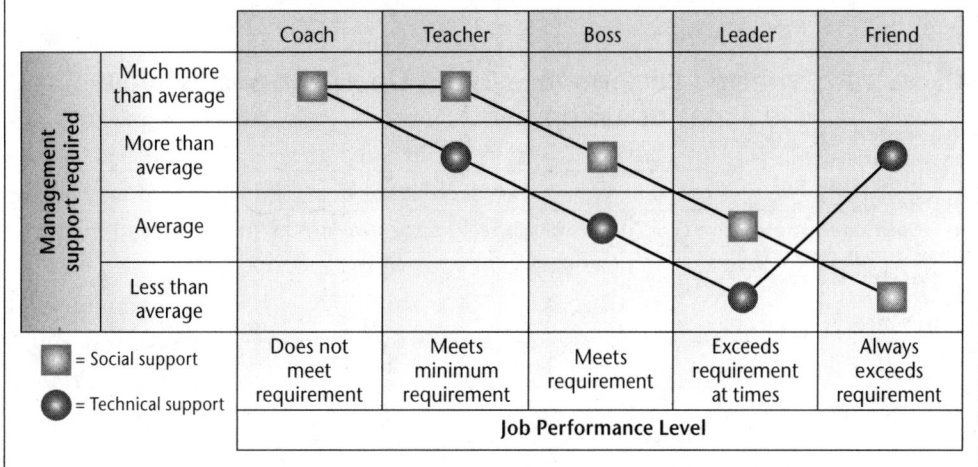

Figure 2.6   Management Support Required Versus Job Performance Level

21

■ Employees who meet minimum requirements need a teacher. They need someone who can help them understand the concepts. They need someone who will measure their performance and show them when they make an error. They need someone who recognizes their success and helps them to succeed.

■ Employees who meet requirements need a boss. They need someone who gives them assignments and follows through to be sure they are accomplished. They need someone who helps them develop and improve the quality of their output and their productivity.

■ Employees who exceed requirements at times need a leader. They need someone who knows what needs to be done and who has empowered the employees to take on responsibility and accountability for their jobs. The leader works with the employee to ensure that barriers to completing the job are eliminated and focuses his or her effort on coordinating the employee's interfaces and providing feedback. The leader sets the example for the employee—for his or her technical and personal style at work.

■ Employees who always exceed requirements need a friend. At this level of performance, management can delegate the responsibilities for the assignment to the employees and hold them accountable for its outcome. Management should develop an open, two-way personal relationship with the employees, sharing experiences and family concerns. Technical interest and understanding are developed by providing a ready ear to discuss project operations and exchange ideas, but the technical decisions are made by the employees. The employees are empowered to make decisions and take actions on all tasks assigned to them without management direction.

It's easy to see that a management style must vary from coaching all the way to friendship, based upon varying degrees of performance. But performance is as much the responsibility of the manager as it is of the employee. (See figure 2.7.) If a person has a networking personality and is assigned to do networking (coordinating between areas), his or her

Figure 2.7 Expected Performance Based Upon Personality Traits and Types of Assignments

		Type of Assignment				
		Planner	Networker	Doer	Leader	
Personality Traits	Planner	Outstanding	Very poor	Good	Poor	Performance Level
	Networker	Very poor	Outstanding	Poor	Good	
	Doer	Good	Poor	Outstanding	Very poor	
	Leader	Very poor	Good	Poor	Outstanding	

chances of meeting requirements are extremely high. But if a networker is assigned to a planning activity, it will be hard for him or her to meet requirements. Unfortunately, in today's and tomorrow's complex environment, employees will be moving back and forth through many types of job assignments. As a result, management style for an individual employee will have to vary based upon the task that the individual is performing. Management can't hold an employee responsible for poor performance if management misassigns the individual.

COMMUNICATION MANAGEMENT

Successful communications management ensures timely and appropriate generation, collection, dissemination, storage, and ultimate disposition of your organization's information. Communication is the lifeblood of any organization team, and it's particularly important for global organization teams. It can be difficult to keep all organization members abreast of organization status and key activities in any organization. In the case of global organizations, differences in culture, language, and time make it even more difficult. However, use of a formal communications process and some simple techniques can keep communications flowing and organization teams synchronized.

A communications plan, regular communications, and use of e-mail and other collaborative tools are essential components of communications management for global organizations, and they are critical for the successful management of the organization. A formal written plan is good practice and should be divided into internal and external communications. The plan should be put in place when the organization is created and updated periodically. It should be made available to the organization team and placed in the organization file or central repository.

The internal communications plan addresses communications within the organization team. The plan specifies the types of communications, frequency, responsible parties, method of distribution, and procedure for archival. In the case of meetings, the plan should specify the types of meetings (in person, videoconference, teleconference), where meetings will be held, how often they will be held, party responsible for minutes, and how meeting minutes will be distributed and posted. Other types of communications include updates on team member status and planning documents (for example, development plans and quality plans).

The external communications plan deals with communications outside the organization and includes communications such as management's status reports to stakeholders, press, consultants, and the general public. The plan should include the same basic information as the internal plan but should be more specific, since the sensitivity and impact of external communications are greater. Review and approval procedures should be included in the plan. Executing the communications plan is an important aspect of global organization management, but there are some fundamental practices that you should also keep in mind.

Frequent communications are important to keep team members synchronized. Regularly scheduled meetings keep the lines of communications open and are essential to keep team members current. A written agenda and meeting objectives distributed in advance keep meetings focused and allow participants to be prepared. Distributing updates about team member status before the meeting is also good practice, and templates can be used to ensure consistency in approach and content. Up-front preparation not only saves time but also allows you to obtain more detail and better organized presentations than oral updates normally provide. Timely written meeting minutes are mandatory and head off misunderstandings. Minutes are particularly important when organization team members don't share a common language.

Written presentation materials should be used for face-to-face meetings when participants don't share a common language. Use of new technologies can improve communications for the global team. Electronic mail and electronic repositories have been well accepted and allow effective asynchronous communications within and outside the organization. Extending these capabilities using new collaborative tools can increase the effectiveness of global communications by allowing multiple authors of a document, automated review-and-approval workflows, and Web-enabled application sharing and viewing to improve the effectiveness of teleconferences. Videoconferences can also be a useful addition to your communications mix. They are a cost- and time-effective alternative to travel. They can be more effective than teleconferences by improving the focus and extending the attention of meeting participants. In summary, communications is the most important part of any successful organization. Establishing a formal plan and conducting regular meetings can help your global organization team avoid many problems and misunderstandings.

Five-Way Communication

One of the most important parts of human resource improvement is to improve the transparency and the effectiveness of the organization's communication process. Most organizations are talking about improving the effectiveness of a two-way communication system (up and down) and have started to make real progress in that area. But that is wholly inadequate. Organizations that are going to excel must establish a five-way communication system. (See figure 2.8.)

This five-way or star communication system is a key part of a participative team environment that is based upon a strong supplier-customer relationship. In this information-rich environment, it's absolutely essential that organizations establish a five-way communication system in which management can no longer ration information to employees, and

Figure 2.8 **Five-Way Communication**

1. Up
2. Down
3. Sideways
4. Customer
5. Supplier

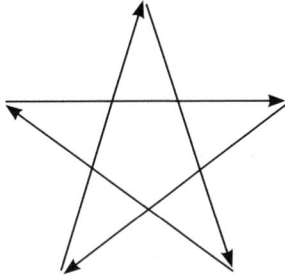

all employees have an obligation to communicate their knowledge to the organization. Today's technology and personal interactions can easily take care of the communication problem if they are both used correctly. Computer networking, voice mail, centralized database, telecommunications, video conferencing, town hall meetings, and bowling leagues are just some of the means that are included in today's communication system. The effectiveness of the system is limited only by the unwillingness of management and the employees to use this system. As a result, how effective the individual user is in five-way communication must become part of the individual performance evaluation.

Toyota puts communication with its employees high on this priority list. One of the ways that Toyota keeps the communication channels open is by the use of a hotline, which any employee can call to ask a question or to register a complaint. The caller does not have to give his or her name. Management takes each call very seriously and responds to it. This is just another way to keep the five-way communication system working.

Today and in the future, technology is and will continue to be an even more important key enabler in the five-way communication process. Without it you would be back to two-way communication.

All in all, the United States isn't doing too badly when it comes to keeping employees informed and satisfied (see figure 2.9). The following is the result of a survey that asked employees how satisfied they were with the organizations they work for. Here is the percentage of responses that indicated that they were very satisfied.

"Communicate up, down, around, and throughout the organization. Be visible. Be open to suggestions and keep moving forward."
—**Rosemary Gregory NASA**

"Employees regard IBM's intranet as their most trusted source of company information—surpassing external media, co-workers, and their immediate managers."
—**IBM Report "We Rewired the Enterprises"**

Figure 2.9 **Satisfaction Survey**

	Canada	United States	European Union	Japan
Employees	39%	43%	28%	17%
Executives	22%	21%	5%	9%

COMMITMENT

The U.S. Marine Corps prescribes eleven principles of effective leadership in its *Guidebook for Marines*. The following is an adaptation of these leadership principles that can serve as a useful starting point for establishing the basis of commitment to leadership and for demonstrating personal commitment. They have served the U.S. Marines well for years and they will also serve you well.

- *Take responsibility.* If you wish to lead, you must be willing to assume responsibility for your actions and those of the people who depend on you. Use your authority with judgment, tact, and initiative. Let your organization be the one to lead the charge and provide the energy to the organization.

- *Know yourself.* Be honest when you evaluate yourself. Constantly seek feedback and self-improvement. If you believe that you're truly the best in your department, admit that to yourself. Then set out to be the best in your organization.

- *Set an example for others to follow.* Your people look to you for a standard of correct behavior. The manner in which you conduct yourself is more influential than any instructions you may give or any discipline you may impose. Be a role model.

- *Develop your people.* Tell your people what your expectations are and give them some clear time frames for results. Then, get out of the way and let them do the job. If you are confident of your own abilities, then you will also believe in the competence of those around you. Answer requests for advice, but leave the details to them.

- *Be available.* Be sure that employees clearly understand their tasks. Tell them why you think that certain issues are important and offer to be available for advice, coaching, and support. Stay aware of their progress and the problems they are encountering, but don't take any initiative away from them.

- *Look after the welfare of your employees.* Know their problems and make sure they receive all the appropriate help and benefits that they need, but don't pry. Respect their need for privacy.

- *Keep everyone well informed.* When in doubt, overcommunicate. Your job is to prevent rumors from occurring through a free flow of timely information. Take action to stop rumors when they exist; rumors cause only undue disappointment and unwarranted anger. Make sure that people know that they can always look to you for the truth. Then, when there is something you can't tell them, they will understand.

- *Set goals that are achievable.* Setting unrealistic goals creates frustration and hurts morale. Instead, set reasonable but slightly more challenging objectives. Your goals should require you to continuously improve. People get neither a sense of accomplishment nor failure when they succeed or meet an easy goal.

- *Make sound and timely decisions.* If you think that you have made a bad decision, have the courage to change it before it is too late.

- *Know your job.* Stay abreast of current events in your field. Talk with people who have recently attended seminars or those who have shown expertise in areas that you are unfamiliar with. Don't look back to the way things were done in "the good old days."
- *Build teamwork.* Whenever possible, assign projects to your entire staff. Ensure that employees understand the contributions that each one makes to the entire effort. Insist that everyone pull his or her share of the load. When something goes well, celebrate it. Managers in excellent organizations show commitment to their assignment and their employees' every day in the way they perform their day-to-day tasks.

URGENCY AND PERSISTENCE

Today's work environment is very fast moving, and management must create a sense of urgency in every employee's mind. People who make things happen radiate energy and a sense of urgency. A good manager is a person who doesn't put off until tomorrow anything that someone can be made to do today. The world is full of good intentions. Many well-meaning, brilliant people turn out to be unsuccessful because they have made a habit of putting things off until tomorrow. These are the people who don't start working on a project until it's almost due and then something interrupts them so that they miss the schedule. Success comes to the manager who makes things happen on schedule without sacrificing quality or cost. The quality of that last-minute job is usually compromised. Good managers know how to communicate a sense of urgency without being obnoxious and overbearing. They do it by showing interest, by reviewing plans, by checking progress, by being there to help break down the roadblocks that get in the way of their employees. There is no substitute for management interest. The things that management is interested in get done. The other things may or may not get done.

> "We can't stand here doing nothing; people will think we're workmen."
> —**Spike Milligan**
> **British comedian**

> "Two salesmen went to the Congo. One reported back that there was no business there because the natives don't wear shoes. The other salesman reported that there were great opportunities in the Congo because the natives don't wear shoes."
>
> —HJH

Today, requirements to reduce cycle time and speed up everything you do is driven by a sense of urgency. Reengineering or redesign is popular because it reduces cycle time. Restructuring is designed to make organizations more agile and responsive. Software that gets things done faster with fewer resources sells fast. Reduced cycle time is a significant competitive advantage. Product life cycles that used to be three to five years are now three to five months. Getting a new product to the market two months late can transform it from a winner to a loser. Organizations that don't have a sense of urgency find themselves without customers. Managers must convince each employee to squeeze as much productivity as possible out of each minute. Each employee must be an accelerator to the process. There's a lot of room for improvement. Tor Dahl, chairman of the World Confederation of Productivity Science, reported that the average U.S. worker spends his or her time as follows:

- 23 percent waiting for approvals, materials, or support
- 20 percent doing unnecessary things
- 18 percent doing things that he or she should not be doing
- 16 percent doing things over
- 15 percent doing things that should be done by someone else

> **"It's not so much the size of the ROI that matters (anymore), but the speed of return."**
> **—Leo Apotheker**
> **President, Global Field Operations, SAP-AG**

Everyone must believe that it is urgent to increase the operating velocity throughout the organization. Everyone must accelerate the way the organization functions.

All employees must have a strong sense of urgency. They can't be held back with endless preparation directed at having everything perfect before they make a move. It's understood that high quality is crucial, but it must come quickly. Your people all need to be accelerators. They need to learn fast, fail fast, fix it quickly, and move on. This drives the organization quantum leaps forward.

Just think about how eager you were when you were hired to help drive the organization in new directions, to prove yourself, to make your mark. What happened to that sense of urgency and the eager drive to make things happen? Isn't it time that you set aside the things that are bogging you down to regain that drive to make things happen fast?

The combination of urgency and persistence make a winning formula for management and employees alike. As important as a sense of urgency is, it takes persistence to get the job done.

The way excellent organizations are managed has changed greatly during the past thirty years and will need to change even more in the next ten years. Figure 2.2 depicts this trend.

Persistence and perseverance in taking risks and failing often is the forge that makes the metal that success is built on. Look at this example. This list shows the age at which this man enjoyed successes and suffered failures as he moved through a life that made him one of the greatest people in U.S. history.

- Failed in business: 22
- Ran for legislature—defeated: 23
- Failed in business again: 24
- Elected to legislature: 25

- Sweetheart died: 26
- Nervous breakdown: 27
- Defeated for speaker: 29
- Defeated for elector: 31
- Defeated for Congress: 34
- Elected to Congress: 37
- Defeated for Congress: 39
- Defeated for Senate: 46
- Defeated for vice president: 47
- Defeated for Senate: 49
- Elected president of the United States: 51

> **"Nothing in the world can take the place of persistence. Talent will not: Nothing is more common than unsuccessful people with talent. Genius will not: Unrewarded genius is almost a proverb. Education will not: The world is full of educated derelicts. Persistence and determination alone are omnipotent. The slogan 'press on' has solved and always will solve the problems of the human race."**
> **—Calvin Coolidge**
> **Former U.S. president**

Who was this man who wouldn't give up? You've probably guessed it—Abraham Lincoln.

Persuading people to accept a new point of view is often difficult at best. It takes patience and endurance. Benjamin Franklin, the great U.S. statesman, is a good example of a person who could get people and nations to accept new ways of thinking. He used five rules to guide his bargaining approach:

- Be clear in your own mind about exactly what you're after.
- Do your homework, so that you are fully prepared to discuss every aspect and respond to every question and comment.
- Be persistent. Don't expect to "win" the first time. Your first job is just to start the other person thinking.
- Make friends with the person with whom you are bargaining. Put your bargain in terms of his or her needs, advantages, and benefits.
- Keep your sense of humor.

SETTING PRIORITIES

All members of an organization must set priorities for their work—to do what is important, which may not be what they like to do. They must define what gets results and what wastes their time. Everyone has spent too much time doing unimportant things that have poor payback to himself or herself and the organization. People set aside the things that need to be done because someone stopped by to see them. They answer phone calls that are not in line with today's priorities. They put the business at risk because they don't want to cut a conversation short. They react to the problem at hand, putting off the problems that are really important. As a result, they miss schedules, lose customers, and work far more hours than they should.

You should identify and cultivate the things that work well for you. You should drop or cut back significantly the ones that don't. Each day make a list of what needs to be done and spend most of your time doing it. Record the number of hours you worked on the items in the priority list versus the hours spent doing other things. Then work on improving this ratio.

> **"A typical pattern will show that 80 percent of output results from 20 percent of inputs; that 80 percent of the consequences flow from 20 percent of causes; or that 80 percent of results come from 20 percent of effort. A few things are important; most are not."**
> **—Richard Koch**
> **Author, *The 80/20 Principle***

SUCCESSION PLANNING

In April 2003, *Chief Executive* magazine rated IBM and Johnson & Johnson in a dead heat as number one and General Electric as a close number three in having the best leaders. In her article on the subject, Leah Nathans Spiro wrote, "Whatever their strategy, CEOs are convinced that grooming top leaders is absolutely key to their company's ability to compete."

IBM, Johnson & Johnson, and General Electric all put leadership development and succession planning as a high priority on all of the executives' lists. Sam Palmisano, CEO of IBM, spends 30 percent of his personal time in leadership development. Palmisano stated, "I talked to CEOs all over the world, and I cannot name anyone who doesn't think this is core and essential."

Talking about leadership training is not just talking about classroom or distance-learning training. Sure, they are good idea generators, but in themselves, they don't work. Education, not put to use, is wasted effort. Just because you have an MBA degree does not mean that you'll be a good leader. It's like having all the parts that are required to assemble a car engine, but having the parts is just the starting point. It cannot produce the thrust needed until the parts are put together in the right order with the proper clearances. But even then, it serves no purpose until it's installed in a car. Education is the parts. The manager's mind assembles the education and ideas (parts) and then puts them together. But the real skill is installing leadership within the organization. The proof lies in how the managers apply their learning and their skills to bring people together so that they function effectively within the organization.

> **"In this era of nervous boards, directors are interested in home-grown talent vs. outside messiahs."**
> **—Jeffrey Sonnenfeld**
> **Associate dean, Yale School of Management**

This means that the real training field for leadership is not in the classroom but in the office and the factories. Johnson & Johnson decentralized the organization structure of its more than 200 different operating units, headed by individual presidents or directors, and provided an excellent opportunity for career growth for its managers. Managers who do well in small units are moved up to larger units and finally up to one of the seventeen group operating chairmanships. This provides the executive team with an excellent opportunity to view many high-potential leaders and to help them develop.

Succession planning is a key building block in every excellent organization. All managers need to think about who will sit in their chairs when they get the chance to move up or retire. That means that for every management assignment throughout the organization, at least two potential replacement candidates should be identified and developed. Managers who think that no one can replace them are digging a hole for themselves, for if that is true, they are never going to be considered for promotion to a more responsible assignment.

If your goal is to refine and retain great people, there is no better way than to give them challenging assignments, keep them learning new skills, and keep moving them to more responsible assignments. Many organizations identify their high-potential leaders and put them on a fast track with an executive mentor assigned to help them develop. PepsiCo CEO Steven Reinemund each year takes forty of his high-potential middle managers on a five-day retreat in Virginia, where they discuss the twenty-seven attributes of leadership. All of the forty attendees leave the retreat with goals that they have agreed to work on.

At General Mills all employees are encouraged to do voluntary work with local nonprofit organizations such as the American Society for Quality. This gives all employees the chance to develop their leadership skills in an environment that is nonthreatening. General Mills Institute even works with the employees who want to be involved in the program by helping them to find nonprofit organizations to work with. A startling 70 percent of General Mills employees are involved in this program.

In December each year, General Electric's board meets, without any members of the management team, to agree on who would be a successor to the CEO if the CEO were to leave for personal or business reasons. This doesn't mean that the CEO is about to be replaced, but it does ensure the shareholders that plans are in place to handle the situation if it occurred.

> **"We believe very strongly that 'leadership development' not only drives our business but drives the culture that supports our business. It demonstrates the outcome we care the most about."**
> **—Steven W. Sanger**
> **CEO, General Mills**

The U.S. Army requires that each officer have multiple subordinates ready to step in and take command in case it's needed. This is a good rule for all organizations, as the fate of the organization can't be dependent upon one individual. If a key manager at any level is pulled out, the organization can't be left unable to function. Succession planning goes far beyond just reacting to emergencies. It must include planning to groom individuals at all levels to step into their new roles when the opportunity occurs.

EXECUTIVE RESOURCES SUMMARY

"The bandleader is out in front strutting,
but it's the drummer who sets the beat."
—HJH

"The meek might inherit the earth . . . but the strong will always retain the mineral rights."
—John M. Capozzi
Why Climb the Corporate Ladder When You Can Take the Elevator?

Your organization should not feel like a jail. Your employees should not think they are being punished because they come to work. Unless you are actually in jail, leaders cannot force people to follow them. People follow leaders because they respect and trust them. Real leaders make their employees feel that they are part of the organization and that what they do is a vital part of making the organization a success.

"The problem is—we have too many managers and too few leaders."
—HJH

CHAPTER III

STAFF RESOURCES

HUMAN CAPITAL

"There is such a thing as investment in human capital as well as investment in material capital," noted Arthur Cecil Pigou in his groundbreaking *A Study in Public Finance* (Macmillan, 1928). During the early 1960s, Gary Becker, the 1992 Nobel Prize winner, was credited with the best-known application of the idea in his book, *Human Capital* (Blackwell Publishing, 1964). "It is fully in keeping with the capital concept to say that expenditures on education, training, medical care, etc., are investments in capital," said Becker. "However, these investments produce human capital—not physical or financial capital—because you cannot separate a person from his or her knowledge, skills, health, or values the way it is possible to move financial and physical assets while the owner stays put."

A study conducted by Deloitte & Touche found that the organizations that invested the highest percentage of their budget in human capital practices far outperformed the average organization:

- 66 percent higher market-to-book ratio
- 300 percent higher five-year return to shareholders

Another study performed by PricewaterhouseCoopers found that organizations with a documented human resources strategy have:

- 35 percent higher revenue per employee
- 12 percent lower absenteeism

The 100 U.S. organizations that are rated the "Best Companies to Work For" have outperformed the major stock indexes for years.

An organization gets the best from its employees when you:

- Train them
- Trust them
- Challenge them

"Our most valuable national resource is clearly our human resources. If we squander that valuable resource, we will have paid a terrible price, and it will show up and be reflected in the position of our country in the twenty-first century. We simply cannot afford to do that."

—Neal Lane
Assistant to the president for Science and Technology; Director, Office of Science & Technology Policy

"Half the challenge is finding talent; the other half is maximizing the performance of the people we do have. CEOs also must ensure that the people they already employ have the right skills, knowledge, and behaviors."
—**Joe W. Forehand
CEO, Accenture**

- Encourage them
- Understand them
- Reward them

If your managers are your most valuable assets, your staff runs a very close second. Employee management includes activities such as training, appraising, inspiring, encouraging, and rewarding. Organizations must manage their staffs to help them grow to be more productive, to share their ideas, to encourage them to be more creative and to take reasonable risks. Developing an environment that will allow all employees to excel is a key part of organizational excellence. Organizations that are effective at recruiting and retaining people have an appeal that money cannot buy.

Figure 3.1 presents two lists of personal characteristics—one for desirable and one for undesirable characteristics. Evaluate each statement on each list to rate the characteristics of your organization's employees, using the following scale.

"The essence of competitiveness is liberated when we make people believe that what they think and do is important—and then get out of their way while they do it."
—**Jack Welch
Former CEO, General Electric**

4—Strongly agree

3—Agree

2—Neither agree nor disagree

1—Disagree

0—Strongly disagree

Add up the two columns. In the ideal organization the sum of the desirable characteristics list would be eighty and the undesirable would be zero. In an excellent organization, the ratio of desirable to undesirable characteristics is higher than six to one.

Example:

Desirable characteristics $= \frac{60}{10} = 6$ to 1

Undesirable characteristics $= 10$

A world-class organization has a ratio of at least four to one. Organizations with a ratio of less than three to one have a significant opportunity to improve the effective use of their human resources. For these organizations, carrying out the following activities can improve this ratio.

- Focus on building trust and loyalty in the organization through open and honest communication.
- Expand the use of teams, both at the departmental and cross-functional levels.
- Provide continuous training in customer relationships to all individuals who interact with the customer in any way.

Figure 3.1 Desirable and Undesirable Characteristics

Desirable traits	Rating	Undesirable traits	Rating
Employees are loyal.		Employees are distrustful.	
Employees are happy.		Employees are haphazard.	
Employees are helpful.		Employees are unhappy.	
Employees are hardworking.		Employees are self-serving.	
Employees are creative.		Employees are lazy.	
Employees are organizationally focused.		Employees need directing.	
Employees are punctual with assignments.		Employees are self-focused.	
Employees are forgiving of management mistakes.		Employees are not dependable.	
Employees are team-focused.		Employees miss schedules.	
Employees will go the extra mile.		Employees are unforgiving of management's mistakes.	
Employees give 110 percent of their effort.		Employees put themselves ahead of the team.	
Employees are trustworthy.		Employees do enough to get by.	
Employees are self-starting.		Employees give 90 percent or less of themselves.	
Employees are honest.		Employees are untrustworthy.	
Employees are motivated.		Employees' output should be better.	
Employees trust management.		Employees are sometimes dishonest.	
Employees trust each other.		Employees need motivation.	
Employees' output is excellent.		Employees don't trust management.	
Employees are dependable.		Employees are not loyal.	
Employees have realistic expectations.		Employees have unrealistic expectations.	
Total		**Total**	

- Train the employees and have them participate in problem solving related to their assignments.
- Align employees' thinking about their jobs with the organizational strategy by installing an area activity analysis process in each natural work team.
- Install a suggestion system and do everything possible to accept as many suggestions as possible. Aim to have 80-percent minimum acceptance rate for suggestions.
- Increase general and job-related training for all employees.
- Emphasize team performance and quality when assessing nonmanagement employees.
- Emphasize face-to-face visits with customers to get their feedback about the products and services provided. Use this information to drive your corrective action process.

- Focus on simplifying processes.
- Make heavy use of process value analysis.
- Focus your quality strategy on building it in and inspecting it in.
- Implement fast action solution teams (FAST).

Some things that you should not do:

- Emphasize quality when assessing your senior managers.
- Encourage widespread participation in quality meetings.
- Use world-class benchmarking to set operating standards.
- Rely on surveys to obtain feedback from your customers.
- Emphasize empowerment as a means of improving performance.
- Remove quality control inspections.
- Lay off employees as a result of improvement activities.

> **"If we did all the things we are capable of doing, we would literally astonish."**
> **—Thomas Edison**

"World-class companies are making tremendous improvements in all areas of human resources," says Chris Bogan, president and CEO of Best Practices LLC. "These companies are investing billions of dollars to develop systems that will increase employee retention and overall work force morale." A study conducted by Best Practices found:

- One organization that set its training budget at 3.3 percent of its payroll allowed it to reduce prices up to 22 percent.
- Another organization that required 85 percent of its employees to participate in continuous training was able to turn out products at a rate that was four times that of its competitors, giving it a very significant advantage. (Source: *Quality Digest*, September 2003.)

> **"[At General Electric] we know the answer—the antidote because we saw it at work, at least in pockets, during the eighties. It's self-confidence. Give people the chance to make a contribution to winning, let them gain the self-confidence that comes from knowing their role in it, and before long, they abandon the paraphernalia of status and bureaucracy. They simply don't need it anymore. Self-confidence is the fuel of productivity and creativity, decisiveness and speed."**
> **—Jack Welch**
> **Former CEO, GE**

Gallup polled 309,000 employees from 11,000 business units to show a direct link between financial results and employee engagement. In those organizations with highly engaged business units, employee retention rates are 1.4 times higher, profitability is 1.3 times higher, productivity is 1.5 higher, and customer outcomes are 1.6 times better than average.

When William McKight, former CEO of 3M, was asked what type of organization he would like, he stated: "An organization that would continually self-mutate from within, impelling forward by employees exercising individual initiative."

HUMAN CAPITAL INVESTMENT

With human capital being such a critical part of the organization's resources, its outcome needs to be managed like any other resource. To accomplish this, you must look at the process that develops this resource. This is a six-phase process:

- *Phase I*—Developing the job description
- *Phase II*—Defining the performance standard
- *Phase III*—Selecting the individual
- *Phase IV*—Training the individual
- *Phase V*—Feedback to the individual
- *Phase VI*—Growing the individual

Phase I—Developing the Job Description

The purpose of the job description is to define what the organization expects from the individual. A *job description* is defined as "a list of activities, duties, tasks, and responsibilities that an individual is required to perform within a specific job classification or process area." The job description also defines the education and experience requirements that the person should have to be considered for the job. The job description is written in a way that describes how the individual should be capable of performing after being trained.

Phase II—Defining the Performance Standards

Standards allow people to understand what is expected of them and lets them know when they are competent in performing their assigned tasks. Too often, in too many jobs, the standard of acceptable performance is not defined. As a result, the person performing the task is put at an unfair disadvantage as management can't say clearly what is expected. A performance standard is a measurable, observable criterion by which a person can determine if a specific assignment has been performed expending no more than the planned-for resources (processing time) and at the required quality level. Standards should be set at a level that represents the expectations for an individual who is performing at the meets-requirements level in an assignment. The meets-requirements level is what is expected of all individuals performing the assignment who have completed the required training related to the job. People who are meeting the standard are meeting requirements and are considered competent. They are not exceeding requirements.

Job descriptions define what is to be done; standards define what resources are required to do the assignment and the required quality of the output. Standards are also used to define the training requirements for people assigned to a new activity. They are needed to evaluate the effectiveness of the training, and they are key inputs into the individual's performance plan and periodic performance evaluation. They also provide a way to encourage and develop competency without requiring formal training. A good feedback system is often more effective in helping a person to develop competency than formal training. You can learn only so much in the classroom. The ultimate experience is performing the act itself. You can sit in a classroom and look at movies of people skydiving, the teacher can explain the principles of how a parachute opens and how to roll when you hit the ground, but you never experience the thrill of skydiving until you stand in the open door of a plane at 10,000 feet and jump out into the wild blue yonder.

Phase III—Selecting the Individual

The most important and difficult phase in the human capital cycle is selecting the right person to do the assignment. It's the process of matching assignment requirements (job description and standards) to the individual candidate to minimize the possibility that the individual won't be able to master the assignment and to minimize the cost of training and the time it takes to develop the person to the point where he or she is fully competent. This is a costly and time-consuming activity. This process includes both hiring new employees and considering current employees for transfer, reassignment, or promotion. It's the most important part of the whole human capital cycle, for if you start with defective materials, the end product will not meet requirements or it will cost the organization an excessive amount to develop an individual who just gets by. Too often, organizations promote people to their maximum level of incompetence.

The recruiting process is key to attracting high-potential human capital to the organization. Management realizes that it's costly to obtain desirable, qualified high-potential candidates, but it often doesn't understand the complexity of the process. This process must be very effective because the cost of turnover in money and lost productivity has a major impact upon all organizations; a 1 percent increase in turnover can cost the organization 8 percent of its profits. Recruiting is not a process in which management should look for ways to cut costs; it should invest heavily to be sure that the new employee is going to fit into the organization's culture, be able to excel in the initial assignment, and have the ability to grow and accept additional responsibilities within the organization.

Every organization wants the brightest, most talented people to come work for it, but only a very few become the organization of choice for these talented, scarce individuals.

The University of Melbourne in 2002 conducted a survey to define what influenced new hires' decision to accept a job offer. The results were:

- On-site facilities—56.5 percent
- Career opportunities—55.5 percent
- Work environment—51.7 percent
- Job security—46.4 percent
- Location—31.8 percent
- Pay/remuneration—28.4 percent

- Prestige—23.2 percent
- Hours—23.2 percent
- Family-friendly policies—9.5 percent

Selecting the correct internal person for a new assignment or promotion presents its own problems. Internal selection reduces the risk of errors because the employee has already developed a track record within the organization. But because the person can do one job well doesn't mean that he or she will be able to perform a different assignment effectively. Organizations typically make the error of promoting outstanding salespeople, engineers, or accountants to management positions, thinking that because they know how to do the work, they will be able to lead other people who are doing the work. Doing a task and leading people require very different talents, and there is no direct correlation between these two very different assignments.

When you are considering internal people for new job assignments and promotions, look at their career plans. Ask yourself, "Is this new assignment in line with the individual's career objectives?" Review the self-study programs the person has been taking to prepare for the new career assignment. Don't make the mistake of putting people who are doing outstanding jobs into positions where they will fail or just squeak by.

When one organization realized it had too many managers, it started a management technical vitality program. In this program, 25 percent of the managers were rotated out of management for a one-year technical assignment. After the one year, they were offered another management assignment. More than 20 percent of the people involved in this program refused to go back into management because they got more satisfaction out of doing work in their professional disciplines than they did managing people.

Phase IV—Training the Individual

The organizational environment is one of lifetime learning. Organizations must continuously reinvest in training their people and not just the ones who are rotating into new assignments. Every employee must be constantly trained just to keep pace with the changing environment. Professional employees who stay in their present assignments should receive a minimum of forty hours per year of training, and nonprofessional employees (in other words, factory workers, clerks, maintenance, etc.) should get a minimum of thirty hours per year of training. Management should get sixty hours per year of training. New employees and people who are reassigned or promoted will require more training.

Training is defined as "the process by which individuals acquire the ability to do something job-related that they were unable to do before. It can be formal or informal, structured or unstructured, self-directed or facilitated."

At each budget cycle the organization should prepare and fund a formal training plan for each employee. This training plan should become part of the individual's performance plan, along with the expected improvements in the individual's performance that occur as a direct result of the training.

Study after study indicates that there is a very positive correlation between investment in training and both profits and revenue. Harrington Institute estimates that U.S. organizations spent more than $100 billion in training in 2003. Ray Abu Zayyad, past president of IBM's General Product Division, stated: "Every year IBM employees spend the equivalent of 4 million student days in class. That is like having a student body of 40,000."

Despite all this, much of the training effort is wasted. Harrington Institute estimates that as much as 35 percent of the training budget is wasted because the employee never uses the approaches that were taught. If you don't use a newly learned technique during the first thirty days after the training, there is only a 60 percent chance that you will ever use it. If you don't use it during the first ninety days after the training, the probability of using it drops to less than 25 percent. That's the very reason to strongly recommend just-in-time training, in which the lessons learned are put to use immediately after they are presented in class.

Training must be treated like any other investment. There should be good return on your investment. The first rule in training is to direct your training at correcting skills deficiencies. That means you must define the gap between your employees' present state of skills and what is required to perform at the standards level. Filling this gap is the first priority of the training program. The next priority is to improve the employees' skills so they can excel in their job assignments. The last priority is to prepare the employees for future growth within the organization. No organization can afford to spend any of its training budget on things that don't have a direct impact upon an individual's ability to do his or her present or future assignments unless it is a legal requirement.

Here are some guidelines that will help you prepare your training plans:

- Define the skills gap between your employees' present skills and the desired future-state skills they need to have.
- Define what benefits the organization will receive from closing this gap.
- Develop training programs that are directed at closing the gap and that are economically justifiable.
- Define how you will measure the results of the training and its impact upon closing the gap.
- Establish a way to measure the effectiveness of the training.
- Measure the organization's improvement in performance that comes from the training.

You should calculate a return on investment (ROI) from your training process each year. You can accomplish this by subtracting the cost of the training from the increased organizational performance that results from the training (impact) and dividing it by the cost of the training.

ROI = (impact – training cost) divided by training cost

Phase V—Feedback

As with any process, the human capital cycle relies on good feedback of information from its stakeholders to improve. It's a five-way communication system that includes up, down, sideways, customers, and suppliers, relentlessly providing information to the individual. It's the way people refine and improve their performance. Without it they can slip backward rather than continuously improving. Although the performance plan and performance evaluation conducted periodically between employee and manager provide a major feedback source, the day-to-day communication between the employee and the manager is the most effective way for a manager to help the employee grow and develop.

But even this is not adequate—employees must obtain feedback from their customers, suppliers, and associates to fully develop and grow. This closed-loop feedback system is an essential part of the human capital development cycle.

Phase VI—Growing the Individual

Helping the individual to grow within the organization is crucial to maximizing the organization's retention rate. Turnover is a drain on the organization's finances and capabilities. The state of Iowa estimates that it cost the state $113,300 to replace an employee earning $64,500 per year. The Jack Phillips Center for Research, a division of Franklin Covey, in 1999 developed estimates of the typical costs of turnover by job function or role. (See figure 3.2.)

Figure 3.2 Typical Costs of Turnover

Job type or category	Turnover cost percent of annual salary
Entry level—hourly, nonskilled	0–50 percent
Service/production workers—hourly	40–70 percent
Skilled hourly (e.g., machinist)	75–100 percent
Clerical/administrative (scheduler)	50–80 percent
Professional (sales, nurse, accountant)	75–125 percent
Technical (e.g., computer technician)	100–150 percent
Engineers (e.g., chemical engineer)	200–300 percent
Specialists (e.g., computer software designer)	200–400 percent
Supervisors/team leaders	100–150 percent
Middle managers	125–200 percent

Source: The Jack Phillips Center for Research, a division of Franklin Covey. Copyright 1999. All rights reserved.

The question remains, "Why does an employee leave the organization?" Two major classifications of turnover must be considered: mandatory and voluntary.

Three major conditions cause the mandatory turnover rate:

■ Increased productivity that reduces the need for the present number of employees
■ Decrease in sales
■ Poor performance, usually caused by selecting the wrong employee for the assignment

Although the mandatory turnover rate hurts the organization, the voluntary turnover rate really cuts at the heart of the organization. Management has a tendency to believe that people voluntarily leave the organization to get a better-paying job or for increased job security; this is often the excuse employees give. The real reason most employees leave is seldom communicated to management. The top reasons employees leave an organization are:

■ Lack of appreciation
■ Lack of involvement
■ Lack of respect
■ Low use of skills
■ Lack of fulfillment of promises made during the hiring process (overpromised and underdelivered)
■ Lack of development opportunities

It's absolutely critical to do a better job of retention because in the next fifty years, growth in the U.S. labor force will be much slower than in the past fifty years. From 1950 to 2000 the U.S. labor force grew by more than 100 percent; it grew from 62 million in 1950 to 141 million in 2000. The U.S. Government Accountability Office projects that the labor force growth rate will drop to 0.6 percent per year in the next fifty years. This will have a very significant impact upon the United States' ability to increase revenue growth at the rate it has in the last fifty years unless there are huge gains in productivity.

According to a 2000 report by the Coca-Cola Retailing Research Council, the average annual cost of turnover per supermarket is about $190,000. The cost of turnover in the supermarket industry as a whole per year is about $5.8 billion; this is more than its total net profit in 1999 of $4.1 billion.

How do you stop this turnover? By the time someone has reached the point of considering leaving your organization, you have invested thousands of dollars in recruiting and training that person. Too often management stops investing in employees after they are trained, but this is absolutely the wrong thing to do. Companies that are really interested in their employees develop career paths within the organization for each person to keep him or her challenged and interested. It doesn't mean that you have to keep promoting people because, in today's environment, upward movement is often limited. To keep good employees today requires imagination and creativity. Many things other than promotion will keep your employees happy and challenged, not the least of which is just basic good management principles. Nothing does more to offset employees' wandering feet than a manager who sincerely cares about them and listens to their ideas. It's time to empower your employees—get them involved in designing their assignments. Tell the employee *what* you want done, not how to do it. Encourage them to take risks and when they fail, and they will fail sometimes, help them to recover and encourage them to try again.

> "Real progress is made by the risk takers, not the caretakers."
> —HJH

WORLD-CLASS STAFF OR BETTER

If your ratio puts your organization in the world-class category or better, you will find the following helpful to improve the use of your human resources.

> "Organizations begin to understand the foolishness of trying to simply institute someone else's improvements without the knowledge of their underlying aim, processes, and internal system."
> —Frank Voehl, COO
> Harrington Software

- Provide customer-related training when new employees are first hired.
- Emphasize quality and teamwork when assessing all levels of management.
- Encourage widespread participation in quality meetings among nonmanagement employees.
- Empower employees at all levels with particular emphasis on empowering employees who interact directly with the customer.
- Provide creative training to all employees.
- Use world-class benchmarking information in defining processes and establishing work standards.
- Involve the entire work force in the strategic planning process.
- Emphasize quality, reliability, and responsiveness as key to your reputation.
- Apply increased focus on developing innovative support processes.
- Emphasize performance and adaptability in your base products/services and in your support activities.

Some things that can get world-class organizations into trouble are:

> "Passion is found in leadership that recognizes the pursuit of excellence is the most powerful emotional motivator in any organization."
> —Armand V. Feigenbaum

- Increasing participation in department-level improvement teams
- Increasing hours of training in general-knowledge subjects

- Making education and championing a primary role of the quality assurance function
- Having an executive team that does not personally practice participative management with the employees who report directly to them
- Trying to manage all employees using the same management style
- Not performing regular employee opinion surveys with effective corrective action
- Frequent reorganizations
- Not giving organized labor a key role in improvement activities
- Carrying out too many changes/improvements at the same time

> **"Inspired people create inspired teams. Inspired teams create inspired communities. Inspired communities will create an inspired world."**
> **—Lance Secretan**
> **Author, *Inspirational Leadership***

It doesn't make any difference where you are in the world; these truths are self-evident. When you look at the 100 best companies in the United Kingdom, they all share the same characteristics. It doesn't matter whether they are in the service or manufacturing sector; the key elements contributing to their success are the same. They focus on three core issues:

- Champions of change
- Employees
- Customers

The UK's best companies empower their staff, unlocking the potential of their people. This creates a culture in which the staff is empowered to focus on the customer.

Building Trust and Loyalty

The management team talks quality, teamwork, and dedication, but it cuts jobs and pushes more throughput. As a result, today's employees have less trust in and loyalty to the company. Most employees look at their jobs as a temporary assignment before they move on to the next one. Employees used to think about making a career with the company; today they consider it a job or a temporary holding-point while they look for something better. Most employees want to trust management and be loyal to the organization, but they have been given little reason to do so.

Here are some suggestions on how to build trust and loyalty within your organization:

- *Treat employees as adults.* Too often managers ask employees to come to work and to "check out" their minds on the way in. They ask people to follow procedures blindly. That doesn't even work with teenagers.
- *Trust them.* Organizations prepare their processes to ensure that the 0.5 percent of their people who are dishonest will not be able to have a negative impact on the organization and as a result, they punish and limit the 99.5 percent of employees who truly are trying to do a good job.

■ *Share information.* Too many managers believe that information is power. They believe employees don't have the ability to handle confidential information in an appropriate way. As a result, they continuously limit the flow of information to the employees.

■ *Appreciate their viewpoints.* When I worked at Ernst & Young, I had a secretary who had to be smarter than I am. She was a single mother with two children she was putting through college on a salary of $25,000 a year. I know I couldn't have done that. Certainly a person who can manage her life as effectively as that can provide good input into the way we should manage our business.

> "Many employees are afraid to ask questions or take a position, even when they do not understand what the job is or what is right or wrong. People will continue to do things the wrong way, or to not do them at all. The economic loss from fear is appalling. It is necessary for better quality and productivity that people feel secure."
> —**W. Edwards Deming**

■ *Be genuinely interested in them.* People trust people who are interested in them, and understand their problems and their desires. Too many managers give lip service to their employees without a sincere interest in their future and in their families. "How's the family?" is easy to say and too hard to mean.

■ *Be concerned about them in their careers.* Your employees spend approximately 50 percent of their waking hours at work. Their jobs and careers are important to them. The management team has a responsibility to help them grow and develop along the lines that they are interested in. You need to promote from within.

Management has to build credibility within the organization. You cannot buy trust and loyalty. Management has to earn it. Credibility builds trust. Trust builds loyalty. Loyalty breeds success for the individual and for the organization.

> "I do think there has been an increased emphasis on trying to build trust inside organizations in order to get quality up and costs down and get more innovation."
> —**Stephen R. Covey, Ph.D.**
> Author, *The Seven Habits of Highly Effective People*

Think of a manager-employee relationship as a marriage. If you don't trust and respect each other, it won't work. Too many managers think that they get respect and trust as a result of their position. The truth is that you must earn employee trust and respect and then work very hard to keep the employees' trust and respect. One little slip and a year of work building trust and respect can go down the drain.

What are some typical mistakes that management makes that detract from its credibility?

■ *Hides bad news.* The management team thinks that the employees can't cope with the negative side of the business. As a result, they have a tendency to hide negative trends and major problems from the rest of the organization.

■ *Tells half-truths and outright lies.* Too frequently management doesn't provide the employee the total story. In other cases, when the employee asks a specific question, management thinks that it's not able to answer that question or not empowered to answer the question. As a result, management will give a false answer. A typical example is as follows:

☐ Employee question: "Are we going to shut down this location?"

☐ Management's answer: "No, not that I know of" or "I don't know the answer to that question."

■ *Not living up to values and visions.* Too often organizations establish vision statements that are worded something like, "We will be the biggest and best." But in reality, this vision is completely out of the question and the employees know that. In other cases organizations establish sets of value statements that are theoretically and ethically correct, but in reality management doesn't live up to them.

■ *Not taking action on poor performers.* One of the major complaints Harrington Institute gets when we interview employees is that management doesn't step up and fire performers who aren't carrying their weight. Certainly this is the most negative and most undesirable part of a manager's job assignment. As a result, they often look for excuses for putting off the undesirable activities, thus allowing poor performers to slip by. Meanwhile, the other members of the department are quick to recognize poor performance and come to believe that management doesn't care about the level of performance. They believe that if management cared about the level of performance, it would take action and get rid of the poor performers.

■ *Decision dodging.* "I'll look into that. I don't know if I can make that decision. I need more information. I'll get back to that later." These are all bad answers to an employee's suggestions or questions. Management must step up and make decisions. Being decisive is a key part of management's job.

The legendary football coach, Bear Bryant, had three key rules to develop team loyalty and spirit. They were:

■ "If anything goes bad, then I did it.
■ If anything goes semigood, then we did it.
■ If everything goes really good, then you did it."

One of management's top priorities in the improvement process is to build a competent, close-working team that performs both efficiently and effectively without stifling the creativity of the individual. This requires that all members on the team trust and understand each other. Management must trust its employees and share the power that information about the organization provides to everyone. In the past, management spoon-fed employees with only enough data to do their jobs, holding back most of the key operational information. This builds a false sense of power for management and fosters a feeling of distrust in the employees. Providing everyone with as much data as possible is always best because it short-circuits the rumor mill that acts something like this:

- Unknown (first person)—John tells Mary: "I think there could be a layoff," or "I don't know if there will be a layoff or not."
- Rumor (second person)—Mary tells Ruth: "We could have as many as 1,000 employees laid off."
- Fact (third person)—Ruth tells Harry: "There will be 1,000 employees laid off next month."
- Results (fourth person)—Harry tells John: "They are going to lay off 1,000 people next month. I have started looking for a new job. How about you?" John says, "I am going to get out of here before the market gets flooded with people from this company."

As the Old Testament states, "People perish from lack of knowledge." To earn trust and understanding from its employees, management must provide them with a secure environment. Management must realize that any improvement process will cause the employees to ask themselves the following questions:

- What's in it for me if I make the organization more productive?
- Will productivity improvements cost me my job or reduce my standard of living?
- Am I willing to change jobs or relocate to stay with the organization?
- What will my future be with the organization?

To provide a secure environment, management must help the employee answer these "silent questions." Management's positive actions, not words, can best accomplish this.

Tell Them Why

Everyone wants to have self-respect and to be respected by others. This is a universal need, and it's a need management must fulfill more today than ever before. For without self-respect, it's impossible to build trust and loyalty. Showing that you respect a person is a sincere form of flattery. Think of how you handle people. The higher the level a person is, the more you respect him or her, and the more time you take to explain why you are doing something. When you don't think a person is important, you have the tendency to tell him or her what to do. You tell your children to take out the garbage or to do the dishes. The more you respect an individual, the more time you take to explain why he or she should do something. Management often falls into the trap of telling its employees what to do without explaining why it's worth their time and effort to do it. It's always preferable to tell employees why they need to do something than how to do it.

> "In all the research on behavior, effective human relations has always boiled down to the same thing: The more convinced people are that you care about them, the more demanding you can be."
> —**Ed Gubman**
> **President, Gubman Consulting**

Bosses tell an employee how to do something. Modern managers tell the employee why it needs to be done, taking the managers out of the boss role and putting them in the role of a modern leader and associate. No longer are you ordering employees to do something.

You are helping them to understand the results that must be accomplished, the impact the activity has on the organization, and imparting a sense of urgency. Telling an employee how to do a job may get it done, but explaining why the job needs to be done gets it done with enthusiasm. People who understand the *why* develop their own approach for accomplishing the task, make fewer errors, and complete the assignment faster because they have a sense of ownership. They will also feel free to change their approach as the situation changes. If employees don't understand why they are doing the task, they charge ahead, carrying out management's direction until they are stopped.

Do It With a Smile

A smile goes a mile, while a frown drives you down. A smile unlocks the door of acceptance. It denotes friendship, caring, and a willingness to listen to both sides of the story. Managers who have smiles on their faces, twinkles in their eyes, and sincerity in their voices breed an environment of friendship and cooperation into the entire workplace—the energy level of the total department surges. People like to work for managers who are friendly, likable, and have positive attitudes. Too often, under the pressures of the job, managers forget that everyone looks to them to set the attitude of the organization. Other managers think that they won't be taken seriously if they don't appear to be a little aloof, firm, and stern. They rely on the harsh personality to give them stature and respect. But that's not true. Sure, you can get short-term results by threatening people, but you build long-term team relationships and performance by creating an enjoyable work environment.

"They said, 'Cheer up, things could get worse.' So I cheered up and, sure enough, things got worse."
—Unknown author

People just perform better when they are happy and satisfied with their jobs, and when they are not threatened by their jobs and their managers. What are the key management characteristics that make a work environment enjoyable?

- Shows sincere interest in the employee
- Is easy to talk with
- Treats everyone as equally important
- Is comfortable to be around
- Has friendly and pleasant personality
- Is not above doing any job
- Realizes that other people are busy, too
- Does not bring personal problems to work
- Has a consistent personality that can be depended upon
- Remembers commitments
- Shares success and shoulders blame

President Dwight D. Eisenhower typified this type of person. There was never any doubt that he was in command and meant what he said, but he always had a smile for everyone. Although a smile or a frown can make management convincing, it's meaning what you say and following through to be sure it's accomplished that really counts.

Listening

Managers must be good listeners. God gave people two ears and only one mouth. I believe he was trying to tell us to listen twice as much as we talk. Employees cannot tell you what their problems are or what they are thinking when you

"Few behaviors underscore the value you place on another person as much as the ability to listen."
—Kenneth Blanchard, Ph.D.
The One Minute Manager

are talking. Make effective use of silence to encourage your employees to talk. Take the time to develop good listening habits. Some useful guidelines are:

■ Gather as many ideas as possible before making a decision.
■ Look directly at the person who is talking to you.
■ Use words of encouragement such as: "Yes, I understand, tell me more."
■ Put your phone on hold when someone comes in to talk to you.
■ Ask probing questions and don't jump to conclusions.
■ Take time to chat with co-workers.
■ Ration the time you talk.
■ Understand what is behind their words.
■ Listen with your eyes and ears.

"The same letters spell *listen* and *silent*.
You cannot learn when you are talking."
—HJH

Education, Training, and Learning

As Peter Senge notes, the root for the word "educate" is *educare*, which in Latin means "to draw out of," not to fill up. Throwing information or techniques at people is not building knowledge or capacity; creating conditions for facilitating honest, fear-free discussion and insight sets the stage for people—from executives to operators—to make a personal connection with what it means to work on systematic improvement.

Just as you bring your car in every 5,000 miles for an oil change and just as you have good preventive maintenance programs for your manufacturing equipment, you must invest in keeping your employees current with the latest developments in their fields of work. Estimates are that a four-year bachelor of science degree is obsolete within four years after the diploma is issued. Obsolete employees cost the organization large amounts of

"The skill sets your people can bring to the organization are much more likely to be a differentiator than they were in the past."
—Susan Meisinger
CEO, Society for Human Resource Management

money if they aren't providing the best possible outputs. They work hard, but the results they accomplish are just mediocre.

An essential part of an excellent organization's activity is continuous education—training and learning programs for all employees. At a minimum, each employee should receive forty hours of update training each year. For knowledge workers the minimum training should be sixty hours or eighty hours, depending on the speed at which the particular knowledge area is changing. For their managers the minimum training should be sixty hours on technical subjects and forty hours on managerial subjects. Organizations can't afford to have obsolete employees on staff, and they also can't afford to let old employees go and hire new ones because that is even more expensive. Most organizations are unwilling to invest the time required to keep their people up to date. It's impossible to change without providing the required training. Management always has a good excuse about why it's the wrong time to train its people. When things are busy, it doesn't have the time to send them to training classes and when things are slow, it doesn't have the money.

> **"The average (training) is between forty to sixty hours a year (per employee)."**
> **—Gary Convis**
> **President, Toyota Motor Manufacturing, Kentucky**

A study of Chrysler dealers found that the difference between an experienced salesperson and a new one in the first three years was $140,000 in profit.

Today's trend has moved from classroom training to distance learning and online training. Distance learning is growing at a rate of almost 200 percent per year, while classroom training is growing at less than 2 percent. Distance learning has a number of advantages. They are:

- The students take the class at a time that is convenient for them.
- The subject matter is always the same and presented in the same way.
- It does not require a minimum size class.
- The students can progress at their own rates.
- The students can have an ongoing interaction with the teacher.

> **"You have this wonderful development opportunity as an individual. As a company, you get to develop people."**
> **—William C. Weldon**
> **CEO, Johnson & Johnson**

IBM spends more than $1.1 billion a year on training and leadership development.

It's not enough to set aside the money and time for training. Of course, that's an important start, but the executive team needs to understand what's being taught and how it's being delivered. Jim Donald, CEO of Pathmark Stores, urges other CEOs and executives to ". . . get involved. Actually go through the courses yourself. Lead by example. You've got to get down there and make sure the training program is the right training program." Nothing is worse than to train your employees in problem-solving tools and performance improvement tools and then to have the executive team not understand these tools when the employees use them and present the results.

When people talk about training, they tend to think about instructor-led classroom training. The best training occurs when the formal training is followed up with a mentoring program on the job. Other forms of training are also important and include computer-based training, Internet training (distance learning), self-study, and linear and interactive videos.

No Layoffs

"Layoffs are horribly expensive and destructive to shareholder values."
—Frank Poppoff
Former CEO, Dow Chemical

Excellent organizations have a commitment to their employees. Management understands that the fastest way to stop the free flow of good ideas is to reduce the head count as a result of an improvement initiative. Everyone understands that improvement initiatives, such as Six Sigma, suggestion systems, total quality management (TQM), and reengineering, result in greater productivity—fewer people can produce the same output. So how can you expect your employees to give freely of their ideas to increase your productivity and minimize waste if it means that their jobs or their friends' jobs will be eliminated? If you start a continuous improvement process and then have a layoff, what you end up with is a continuous sabotage process.

Management wants the employees to implement programs that will reduce the labor that is required to provide a quality output. As you can understand, the employees' objective of having a job and management's objective of producing more with less conflict with each other. It's agreed that the job-for-a-lifetime concept that organizations such as IBM and Sony used to practice died in the 1990s. Neither the organization nor the employees expect lifetime commitment any longer, but to make the continuous improvement process work, there must be some compromise. Management must look at the employees as an investment, not a cost—an investment it wants to protect.

It costs from 50 percent to 150 percent of an employee's annual salary to replace that employee. You would normally think of that total replacement cost as being the cost to find, interview, train, plus the cost of the learning cycle. These are important costs, but the biggest cost is the loss of momentum within the processes in which the old employee was involved and the loss of soft knowledge. Dow Chemical estimates that it costs the company between $30,000 and $100,000 to replace a technical or managerial person.

Layoffs are not only costly for the organization from a financial standpoint, but they also have a negative impact on the hiring cycle. Many of the very best people lose trust in the organization and look elsewhere for work.

Federal Express calls its no-layoff philosophy its "guaranteed fair treatment procedure." It is an important concept that supports and makes its improvement processes so successful.

It may be necessary to lay off people when business turns down, and your employees will accept that as a fact of life. What they can't accept is to be put out of work because they shared ideas that reduced the effort required to produce the output. It's effective to have management release a no-layoff policy that reads something like this:

"No employee will be laid off because of improvements made as a result of the improvement process. People whose jobs are eliminated will be retrained for an equivalent or more responsible job. This doesn't mean that it won't be necessary to lay off employees because of a business turn-down. In any case, we will look at all other economically feasible alternatives before people are laid off."

Some of the alternatives to layoffs are:

- Increase customer demands for output.
- Remove the "dead wood" from the process.
- Eliminate or reduce overtime.
- Stop hiring new employees.
- Offer skills training.
- Offer train-the-trainer programs.
- Increase marketing and sales efforts.
- Allow employees to take voluntary leaves of absence.
- Start job rotation programs.
- Offer incentive retirement programs.
- Shorten workweeks.
- Send people to external schools to fill in desired skills.
- Volunteer people to support local civic programs.
- Relocate employees to another office or plant that needs workers.
- Offer job sharing.

When Bill Clinton was governor of Arkansas, he signed a bill in 1991 that ensured that no state employee would lose employment because of an effective quality management program.

STAFF OPINION SURVEYS

To focus on improving employee satisfaction, PNC Financial Services' top management developed what it called its "employee satisfaction improvement process (ESIP)." It used an employee satisfaction survey to gauge the status of and to measure the improvement in employee satisfaction. (This is not a new approach; IBM started conducting employee opinion surveys every eighteen months in the 1950s.)

Using an employee opinion survey correctly is a very important part of an overall program aimed at employee and management satisfaction and retention. To start an improvement process, one of the first things an organization should do is to complete a management-employee opinion survey. The survey's purpose is to set the baseline for measurement and to help identify areas for improvement. It also serves as a communication link between top-level managers and their employees and first-line management. The opinion survey provides another means to help management develop sensitivity and awareness. Through awareness of the team's overall attitudes, management can anticipate problems before they occur and take action to prevent them from developing.

You should approach the opinion survey carefully, keeping in mind that it will be repeated a number of times to measure trends. The survey questions cover at least eleven areas. They are:

- Overall satisfaction with the company
- The job itself
- Salary
- Advancement opportunities
- Management
- Counseling and evaluation
- Career development
- Productivity and quality
- Work environment
- Handling of concerns
- Company benefits

> **"The bottom line was, when employee satisfaction is high, so is customer satisfaction— and satisfied customers tend to do more business with you and recommend you to other customers."**
> **—James E. Rohr**
> **CEO, PNC Financial Services**

In addition, a section for write-in comments enables the employee to provide more detailed information and address concerns not covered. Possible questions might be:

- Everything considered, how would you rate your overall satisfaction with the company?
  - ☐ Completely dissatisfied
  - ☐ Very dissatisfied
  - ☐ Dissatisfied
  - ☐ Neither satisfied nor dissatisfied
  - ☐ Satisfied
  - ☐ Very satisfied
  - ☐ Completely satisfied

- How do you rate your job?
  - ☐ Very poor
  - ☐ Poor
  - ☐ Average
  - ☐ Good
  - ☐ Very good

■ How would you respond to the statement: "My job makes good use of my skills and ability"?
- ☐ Strongly disagree
- ☐ Disagree
- ☐ Neither agree nor disagree
- ☐ Agree
- ☐ Strongly agree

■ How would you rate your salary considering your duties and responsibilities?
- ☐ Very poor
- ☐ Poor
- ☐ Average
- ☐ Good
- ☐ Very good

■ How do you rate the job being done by your immediate manager?
- ☐ Very poor
- ☐ Poor
- ☐ Average
- ☐ Good
- ☐ Very good

■ How much trust and confidence do you have in your immediate manager?
- ☐ Very little or none
- ☐ A little
- ☐ Some
- ☐ Quite a bit
- ☐ A great deal

■ What seems to be management's biggest concern?
- ☐ Costs
- ☐ Schedules
- ☐ Quality
- ☐ Personnel

■ What seems to be management's least concern?
- ☐ Costs
- ☐ Schedules
- ☐ Quality
- ☐ Personnel

It's imperative to maintain confidentiality and anonymity if survey results are to be meaningful. You must exercise care when the survey form is being filled out, during the data-analysis cycle, and when results are reported to the management team. You should take special care in providing feedback to small units.

To help define problem areas, each manager should be provided a report showing how his or her people responded. This report should compare the survey results of the natural work team to those of the total function and of the organization as a whole.

> **"You have to put your employees at the center, making your employees first, even ahead of the customer."**
> **—Jeff Taylor**
> **Founder and CEO,**
> **Monster.com**

Each manager should conduct a feedback session in which the results of the survey are presented to the employees. These sessions are important because:

- The employees will be curious about the results in general and how the department compares to the rest of the company in particular.
- It provides management an opportunity to discuss employee concerns.
- It provides an excellent way to receive ideas and suggestions.
- It shows that management is serious about the results.
- It allows the team to develop corrective action.

The natural work team should develop action plans to improve the areas in which the team's average is statistically lower than the total function's or organization's average. The executive team should develop action plans to improve areas in which the total organization's average is lower than world class. That is anything that is average or below. World-class organizations' total averages run between 4.4 and 4.8 out of a maximum of 5.0.

"The effort has dramatically increased employee satisfaction," says James E. Rohr, chairman and CEO of PNC. "There is a strong relationship between employee and customer satisfaction and our company's performance."

Does this work only in the United States? No, it works around the world. Harrington Institute used the employee and management opinion survey as part of the change process at an organization in Zimbabwe, in 2002 and got the same kind of positive results.

STAFF PERFORMANCE PLANS

W. Edwards Deming classified "evaluation of performance, merit rating, or annual review" as part of the deadly disease that was crippling corporate management. Deming was a great quality professional. He did a lot to bring the importance of statistical quality control and problem solving to the attention of management around the world. The statement above is part of his well-known "14 Points for Management." Most of his fourteen points are right on target, but these recommendations prove that even great men are not right all the time. The only people who do not want to be measured are the poor performers. The good performers want to be measured to show how well they are doing and if you don't measure them, they will develop ways to measure themselves, and these measurements may not be in line with what management wants to get accomplished.

In my personal discussions with Deming, I realized that the reason he was against performance plans and management by objective was that he had seen so many of these poorly developed and misused. He agreed that all employees should know what is expected of them and have some way to determine how well they are performing. I agree with Deming that no performance plan is better than a poor plan that is misused.

The keys to an effective individual performance process are:

- The right things are measured.
- Both the employee and the manager agree on the performance standards.
- It includes an ongoing measurement and feedback system that provides information to the employees and management.

"The only people who don't want to be measured are the poor performers. The good performers want to be measured so that management will know how well they are doing."

—HJH

Any business plan should involve everyone, from the boardroom to the boiler room. With this as a basic starting point, it's easy to see that the individual's performance plan should be based upon how the person's performance is going to support the organization's business plan. Concepts of this nature have become very popular in Japan under what is called *hoshin kanri* (*hoshin* planning or policy deployment). Taking this approach one step further brings the individual's goals and measurements in line with the organization's goals. After all, the best way for an individual to grow within an organization is to increase his or her perceived value to the organization. The performance plan should also focus on the organization's commitment to internal and external customer satisfaction and to developing a strong, effective internal team.

The employee and the appropriate manager should prepare the individual's performance plan; they should work together to understand what assignments the employee has and will be assigned to in the near future (next twelve months maximum). Using the employee job description, the business plan, and input from the individual's customers, they should prepare a list of performance measurements for each of the employee's major projects and activities. As major new projects are assigned, the employee and manager should prepare a new performance plan for the new project. In many cases, this will require that several performance plans be prepared for one individual each year. The job description and input from the individual's customers should be used to define the "meets requirements performance level" for each measurement that will be established.

> **"You take people as far as they will go, not as far as you would like them to go."**
> **—Jeanette Rankin**
> **Pacifist and politician**

The process of aligning organizational objectives as they apply to the individual can be a long, challenging, and difficult one, but it's one that management will find worthwhile.

Avoid using a preprinted performance plan. They are detrimental in the long run. A performance plan should be customized to the individual and the job. The performance plan form should consist of only three columns: the task name, the task description, and the task priority. The rest of the form should be left blank to be filled in by the manager and the employee.

Performance planning for managers usually consists of three major sections. They are management of business issues, technical management, and personnel management.

> **"Executives are expected to construct very comprehensive personal development plans, which detail what they're going to do, for what purpose, by what time frame, and what the measures are that will be used to determine improvement. This approach says average results are no longer good enough. As a result, companies that start down this path will have turnover. Your existing A players will love it. Your non-A players will range from supportive to fearful to disruptive."**
> **—Jon A. Boscia**
> **CEO, Lincoln Financial Group**

PERFORMANCE EVALUATIONS (APPRAISALS)

The ideal time to evaluate an individual's performance is as soon as a job is completed. To take advantage of this timing, the annual performance evaluation should be based upon a series of evaluations that occurred throughout the year. You should do an evaluation each time a project is completed. For long projects (six months or more) evaluations should occur not only at the end of a project but also at key points during the project, thereby allowing the individual to correct errors and eliminate undesirable performance as early as possible. At a minimum, performance evaluations should be scheduled every three months.

> **"It is the responsibility of leadership and management to give opportunities and put demands on people which enable them to grow as human beings in their work environment."**
> **—Sir John Harvey-Jones**
> **Former CEO, Imperial**
> **Chemical Industries**

Feedback should not be limited to the formal performance evaluations. The manager should provide daily feedback that encourages good performance and helps correct unsatisfactory performance. The manager's daily feedback should ensure that there are no surprises at the formal performance evaluation sessions.

Who Should Do Performance Reviews?

"Only the mediocre are always at their best."
—Jean Giraudoux
Diplomat and writer

Employees are in the best position to evaluate their own overall performance. As a result, employees should document their performance compared to the targets that they and management have agreed to. If employees think that they are exceeding requirements, they should explain what was accomplished over and above the required performance. Employees should also record any roadblocks that prevented them from performing as well as they could have and suggest what actions should be taken to improve future performance.

To supplement the individual employee's input, customers of the employee are often asked to evaluate his or her performance from their viewpoint. Using these two types of inputs, the manager should complete a performance evaluation form.

After this form is filled out, the employee and the manager will meet to review it and any other input. During this meeting, they will pay particular attention to any activity in which the employee or the customer rates the employee's performance higher than the manager rates the employee. They will resolve any differences in perception and interpretation of data during this meeting. The manager and the employee will discuss the roadblocks that the employee faced and the suggestions the employee made to improve future performance. The results of these discussions will be recorded on the performance

"We have a responsibility as leaders to raise the performance level of all employees."
—Joe W. Forehand
CEO, Accenture

evaluation short form, and they will develop action plans to help improve the employee's future performance. Also during this meeting, they will develop a list of short-term performance objectives and schedule the next performance evaluation date.

Turnabout is fair play. The appraisal process should provide the opportunity for the employee to make suggestions on how management can contribute to the employee's overall performance. Because the individual's performance is greatly affected by the type of direction and support he or she receives from management, at each evaluation the employee should suggest at least one way that management can change or improve to help the employee perform better.

Annual Performance Reviews

Once a year, the manager will summarize all of the individual reviews to be sure that all of the objectives defined in the performance plan are met. The result of this summary should be reviewed with the employee. This review should run very smoothly because it is simply a summary of many individual reviews.

Organizations that require all annual appraisals to occur at the same time do it so that performance can be considered during the salary planning cycle. Organizations that do this create many problems for themselves. First, because of the heavy additional workload, the manager lets other tasks slip or does them poorly. Second, because of time limitations, the appraisals are poorly prepared and given.

"If you cannot do great things, do small things in a great way."
—Napoleon Hill
Think and Grow Rich

Through the use of many ongoing evaluations, the time required to perform an annual review can be greatly decreased, and they don't all need to be done at the same time. A manager who has twelve employees reporting to him or her can do one a month. Some organizations have refined the process to the point that a total review is conducted only when the employee is recommended for promotion or is being reassigned to a new manager.

The key to this performance evaluation approach is that the manager is never comparing the individual to other employees. The baseline used by the manager is the required performance level as defined by the job description and the employee's customers. A manager could have an entire department consisting of "far exceeds requirements" performers. No longer is there a need for a performance rating distribution that takes the shape of a normal curve because this approach completely ignores the concept of an average performer.

"No one is confused about what is expected, how results will be interpreted, and what the compensation impact will be. It is simple, direct, and effective."
—Jon A. Boscia
CEO, Lincoln Financial Group

One of the high-level key executives who reported to me was being evaluated. We agreed on his performance plan. The objectives were very clear and measurable. I left the approach to reaching these objectives up to him. Through the coming months we discussed his progress toward these objectives and that progress had been slow. At the end of the period, he had missed 80 percent of the objectives by a wide margin. (For example, he missed his sales quota by 95 percent.) As a result, I had to rate him as inadequate. He thought the rating was unfair because he had been working hard and his plans just did not produce the desired results. I agreed that he got an A for effort but an F for performance. The key point here is I didn't tell him what to do or how to meet his performance objectives. I left it up to him, and he agreed that for his salary he would accomplish these objectives. Because he failed to meet these objectives didn't mean I was going to fire him. Quite the contrary; I thought he was capable of being an outstanding performer if he just would be a little more aggressive in closing opportunities. It's often hard to tell a person that he or she is not performing, but you must to be fair to the person so he or she can change and to be fair to the people who are performing well.

"Ideas are a dime a dozen. People who put them into action are priceless."

—HJH

"Exact measurements make work as enjoyable as play because participants have a way to win."
—Charles Coonradt
Management consultant

Don't give up too fast on the poor performers. Help them; don't blame them. Look for the good points and help them to build upon those. Many great people would have been overlooked if someone did not believe in them. A slow start does not mean the individual is a loser. For example:

■ Werhner von Braun failed ninth-grade algebra.

■ Albert Einstein was four years old before he could talk and seven years old before he could read.

■ Haydn stopped teaching Beethoven because he was slow with no musical talent.

■ Walt Disney was fired because he had no good ideas.

Everyone has some good in him or her; it's management's job to find it and cultivate it.

TODAY'S EMPLOYEE

Ann Landers wrote in one of her columns, "Anyone who believes that competitive spirit in America is dead has never been in a supermarket when a cashier opens another checkout line." Yes, people are competitive by nature, but too often they put away that competitive spirit when they enter the organization's front door. They become part of the pack. They're afraid to stand out as individuals. They don't want to be enthusiastic about their jobs because the other employees will think they are strange. But enthusiasm makes the ordinary person extraordinary. All individuals have the same needs that must be fulfilled if they are going to excel at their jobs. They are:

■ *Economic security*. They need to think that they are getting a fair day's pay for a fair day's work.

■ *Personal self-esteem*. They all want to be viewed as value-added to the organization. No one wants to be average.

■ *Personal self-worth*. They need to think that they are contributing to a worthwhile goal.

■ *Personal contribution*. They want to be listened to—to have their ideas heard. They can accept the fact that everything they suggest may not be carried out, but they need a fair hearing.

■ *Personal recognition*. They all need feedback to show that good work is appreciated, and that what they are doing is worthwhile.

■ *Emotional security*. They all need to be able to trust the managers they work for and to believe that the managers will be honest with them.

Only when these six basic needs are satisfied can an individual have a chance at excelling at his or her assigned task(s).

That's Not Fair

Employees don't expect the world to be fair because it isn't. Those who dwell on the unfairness in life use it as an excuse for their lack of drive and success. No matter where you are in the world, there will always be people above you who are not as deserving as you are (in your eyes) and people at your level or below who don't do their fair share. Many people believe that they have more than their fair share of problems. In truth, many people have overcome more obstacles than you will ever face and have become more successful than you will ever be. They have used these obstacles to build stamina and the drive to succeed, to forge a will and personality that are unstoppable. On the other hand, many individuals have had much lighter burdens to carry than you have faced and have failed miserably. No, the world is not fair, but employees accept and understand this fact. All people must make the best use of their talents and opportunities to provide themselves with positive attitudes and a personal dedication and commitment to success. It will make life much easier and more joyful. Look at your cup as half full, not half empty.

The Open-Minded Employee

In today's environment, growth is going to be very limited. Management and employees must look for other ways to stimulate job satisfaction and recognition. Employees must have a very open mind about what is going on around them and how they can contribute. Employees who don't find their jobs interesting are employees who have closed their minds to its possibilities. Employees and managers alike make excuses for their closed minds. Some of the more frequently used excuses are: "We tried that before," "Let's hold it at bay," "Let's give it more thought," "Management would never do it," and "You can't teach an old dog new tricks."

It's time to open your mind and stop using these phrases. Every time you utter or hear one of these popular phrases, it's time to challenge what's going on. Stop putting up roadblocks and detour signs to change and start knocking them down. Ask yourself, "How can I make it work now if it didn't work before?" Ask if it isn't time you tried something new if it's a first-time suggestion. Embrace the positive and cut the legs out from under the negative. You may not always win, but you will never win if you never try.

> "He worked by day
> And toiled by night.
> He gave up play

And some delight.
Dry books he read,
New things to learn.
And forged ahead
Success to earn.
He plodded on
With faith and pluck
And when he won
Others called it luck."
—Unknown author

CAREER BUILDING

Today you are building your career within the organization. The best way to ensure the success of your career is by doing a superb job today. Keys to a successful career within any organization are:

■ Do an excellent job in every assignment you get.

"If you love what you do, you will never work another day in your life."
—Anonymous

■ Make sure you and your manager understand where you want to go.

■ Be willing to make the desired sacrifices.

■ Ask for the opportunity to compete for the desired assignments.

Career Planning

Every individual needs to stop and reflect periodically on how things are going and where he or she wants to go in the future. When it comes to how things are going, the organization's internal measurement system should provide the required information about the job that the individual is performing today. But that is a very short-term look at the employee's career. It provides no input about where the individual is going. From the individual's standpoint, performance appraisals leave two of the most important questions unanswered. They are:

■ Am I progressing at the right speed?
■ Am I heading in the right direction?

It's for these reasons that everyone needs to develop a career plan that plots his or her course to retirement and, often, beyond. Too often, people get so bogged down doing the day-to-day activities that they never stop to determine if what they are doing today will help them to meet their career objectives. A career plan lays out the route that an individual must take to reach his or her personal career objectives. For some people, this career plan can be very simple. For example: "I like what I am doing. I want to do it until I am sixty-five and retire." For others the career plan can be very complex, requiring the person to turn down promotions and more money to gain experience in a new field. For example: "I like being an electrical engineer, but I would like to be the COO of the organization." This may mean that from a career point of view, it may be better for you to take a manager's job in manufacturing at a lower rate of pay rather than the promotion that you are offered. Some jobs don't change; they just disappear. To keep from becoming obsolete, all employees must continually revitalize themselves.

Career planning is a significant part of resource management methodology. The objectives of career planning are:

- Help fulfill the individual's desire to develop his or her potential and grow in the organization.
- Ensure a continuous supply of qualified people as a resource for the future and key leadership assignments.
- Make the best use of the employee's ability now and in the future.
- Enhance the employee's feeling of personal value.
- Provide resources that allow for promotion from within.
- Show that the organization has respect for the individual.

"If a man is called to be a street sweeper, he should sweep streets even as Michelangelo painted, Beethoven composed music, or Shakespeare wrote poetry. He should sweep streets so well that the Host of Heaven and Earth will pause to say, 'Here lives a great street sweeper who did his job well.'"
—Martin Luther King Jr.
Civil rights leader

The difference is distinct between career planning and performance planning. Performance planning addresses the immediate job and its responsibilities. Career planning deals with the individual's skills and preferences for today and for the future. Although the two activities may overlap somewhat, the primary intent is very different. Career planning is a shared responsibility. The basic responsibility rests with the individual. The manager's role is one of giving the employee encouragement, information, and support, and being a reality tester. The organization's role is to develop an environment for personal growth, provide educational support, and promote from within whenever possible.

Accenture has identified six workplace characteristics as critical to satisfying employee career needs:

- Interesting work
- Inspiring leaders
- Flexible work style
- Continuous learning
- A diverse work force
- Competitive rewards

Why is career planning so important when an AON Consulting study, US@work, points out that you can expect to lose half of your workers in the next five years?

Career planning strengthens the employee-manager relationship by placing the manager in a guidance role. It's a useful tool to the employee and the employer in improving the use of the employees and developing the employees' full potential. Without an effective career planning process, the probability is high that the organization will have an underused, disenchanted work force that is prone to making errors and job-hopping.

Building a Bond With Your Manager

No one has more influence over your next career step than your present manager. The relationships you establish with your manager can make or break your career. To have a career-building relationship, you don't have to be a "yes person"; in fact, these types of people are soon discarded as no-value-added individuals by all but the extremely insecure manager. Mark H. McCormack's book, *The 110 Percent Solution* (Villard, 1990), gives this advice to people who want to establish a career-building relationship with their managers:

- *Be loyal.* Disloyalty is a major character flaw that won't be accepted by any manager.
- *Keep the boss informed.* The boss should always know everything that is going on within your span of responsibility.
- *Embrace change, even if you don't understand it.* Managers are measured more and more on how effectively they implement change. Help them with this responsibility. Don't resist change.
- *Respect your manager's time.* Spend your manager's time as you would your own money.
- *Don't tread on his or her turf.* Honor the fact that your manager has divided up the available work into specific job assignments.
- *Follow up quickly.* When your manager gives you an assignment, get it done and out of the way.

These simple rules provide the key building blocks for developing a good relationship with your manager and will apply equally well whether you are an assembly worker or the vice president of a major corporation.

TEAMWORK

It's no longer about me, he, them, or she—it's about everyone working together as a team of professionals, each adding a different dimension to the total effort. The day of the Lone Ranger died when Silver died, and even then his trusted friend, Tonto, was an important part of ensuring that right prevailed over evil. In today's environment organizations can't afford not to take advantage of everyone's ability. The employee who follows orders blindly is a deficit, not an asset. Workers no longer will tolerate checking their minds at the door. They want to contribute to the way things are done. It's been proven time after time that people who take part in planning the work outperform the ones who don't. This is the very reason that organizations that excel build a culture where teamwork thrives. Note the use of the word "teamwork," not "teams." There's a very important difference between teams and teamwork. A team is a group of people who are put together for a specific reason. Teamwork is a condition in which people work to complement each other, not to compete with each other. A culture of teamwork usually starts with building teams that eventually become less and less important than the relationships that are developed in the team.

> "There's a very important difference between teams and teamwork."
> —HJH

To show the difference between teams and teamwork, here's a simple example. A skid is left in the middle of an aisle, causing a safety hazard. To solve this problem using teams, the person who identified the problem would a call a meeting inviting shipping, the department manager who was closest to the aisle, the safety department, and the industrial engineering department. After many phone calls they determined that they would be able to get a conference room and all the people together next Wednesday. At this meeting it was suggested that someone take a picture of the hazard so that the problem could be studied. Industrial engineering agreed to do it. Another meeting was scheduled for the next Wednesday. At this meeting fishbone diagrams were prepared to find the root cause of the problem. The conclusion was that when the stock man rearranged the area, he didn't put the skid back into the storage area. The shipping department agreed that it would talk to the man who was responsible and send him over with a forklift to move the skid out of the aisle. In the meantime three employees had tripped over the skid and hurt themselves, resulting in five days of lost work. Based upon this, the team calculated that the cost savings from their action was forty hours of lost time multiplied by $100 per hour equals $4,000 savings per month or $48,000 per year.

"It's amazing what you can accomplish if you don't care who gets the credit."
—Harry S. Truman

In a teamwork environment the individual who recognized that a skid was left in the aisle would walk over to another employee and ask him or her to lend a hand to move the skid out of the aisle. It would be done right away, eliminating the safety hazard.

Now you may think that this is a ridiculous example—and it is—but things just as ridiculous go on in organizations around the world.

I like Truman's quote above, but I would like to change it to read, "It's amazing what can be accomplished if you don't care who gets the credit, and no one gets the blame."

This is a story about a man who drove his car into a ditch. Upon inspection, he saw that he was so deep in mud that his tires just spun. He saw a farmer out in the field plowing with an old mule and asked for help. After looking the situation over, the farmer said, "Old Tom can pull you out. Yep, Tom can do the job." The farmer connected a rope to the car's front bumper and put Old Tom to the harness. He snapped the reins and shouted, "Ho, Bessy. Pull, Patty. Pull, Jenny. Pull, Tom." And to the man's surprise, Old Tom pulled the car out of the ditch with comparable ease. The man thanked the farmer and put a $10 bill in his hand, asking, "Why did you call out all the other names before you called out to Tom?" The farmer replied, "Old Tom is almost blind. He doesn't mind pulling hard as long as he thinks he is part of a team."

Too many organizations think assigning employees to teams is all that is required. Assigning people to teams is only the starting point. Having teams isn't important. Often teams compete with each other, which has a negative impact on the organization. The excellent organizations foster teamwork, not teams. These are people who take time to help each other, not people who need to have others help them make their decisions. In organizations that foster teamwork, people come together to do a specific task and then disband to do other tasks, be they big or small. Many of the problems are solved without a team meeting.

"See the need and take the lead."

—HJH

CREATIVITY AND INNOVATION

"The Lord gave us two ends—one to sit on and one to think on. Success depends upon which one we use the most."

—Ann Landers

One of the most important resources that all organizations have is their employees' creativity and innovation. All too often this valuable resource isn't developed, and even worse, it's often discouraged. This discouragement doesn't occur intentionally but indirectly through the detailed use of procedures that aren't guidelines but rules and the organization's normally accepted practices. Too often people are put in little job-related boxes that tell them:

- You can't think; you need to do just what you are told to do without question.
- We want you to be creative about the way you do your job, but don't try to be creative with regard to the rest of the organization's activities.
- You can submit your ideas to management, but don't take action on them—that is management's responsibility.

All people are creative when they are born. A small child can play with a Popsicle stick and imagine it to be all sorts of wonderful things—a boat, a friend, a race car, a baby, or a bridge. The list can go on and on; it's all so wonderful at the time. Then the brakes are put on when you start school. School is all about losing your creativity and individuality. It's totally focused on conformity to established rules and predefined concepts, rules such as 1 + 1 = 2 or that little furry animal's name is spelled c-a-t. Why can't you spell it k-a-t? Learn the rules and follow the rules—that's what school is all about. People are taught to be conventional conformists. Children aren't losing their natural creativity, but they are put in an environment where creativity isn't required.

"The demands of our creative abilities have doubled every generation."
—Peter F. Drucker

The Information Age is also killing the creativity of adults. With the vast amounts of information available at their fingertips, people have a real tendency to rely on it rather than developing new creative solutions. Nothing is wrong with getting all the help you can, for everyone needs to learn from the past. But to stop at that point is wrong and it kills creativity. If people had less information available, they would need to be more creative. There is an inverse correlation between creativity and the information and knowledge available. The more information, the less need for creativity. Figure 3.3 is a typical process of need solution thinking.

"It is not possible to solve today's problems with yesterday's solutions."
—Roger Von Oech
President, Creative Think

1. We have a need that we desire to fulfill.
2. We ask ourselves, "Do we know how to fulfill this need?" If we do, we fulfill the need. If we don't, we go to step 3.
3. We do research to determine if someone else has the answer. This can be done in many ways—reading books, going to a Web site, asking friends, anything to gather information and other people's ideas.
4. We ask ourselves, "Did we find an answer to the need?" If we did, we fulfill the need. If we didn't, we go to step 5.
5. We ask ourselves, "Do we really have to fulfill this need?" If the answer is no, then we forget about the need. If the answer is yes, we proceed to step 6.
6. During step 6, we rely on our own creativity and innovation to solve the problem that we haven't been able to solve by using other people's approaches. Often we base our solution on foundations that other people developed.

"You are not limited or tied to the past but have an unlimited sense of what is possible in the future; your mindset is prophecy, not just history."
—Stephen Covey, Ph.D.
Author, *The Seven Habits of Highly Effective People*

7. Were we able to fulfill the need through our own creativity and innovation? If the answer was yes, we solved the problem. If the answer is no, we forget about it.

What is wrong with the cycle in figure 3.3? Too often people give up at step 5. Why? They give up because using their creativity isn't what they have been taught to do and

Figure 3.3 Typical Need Solution Thinking Process

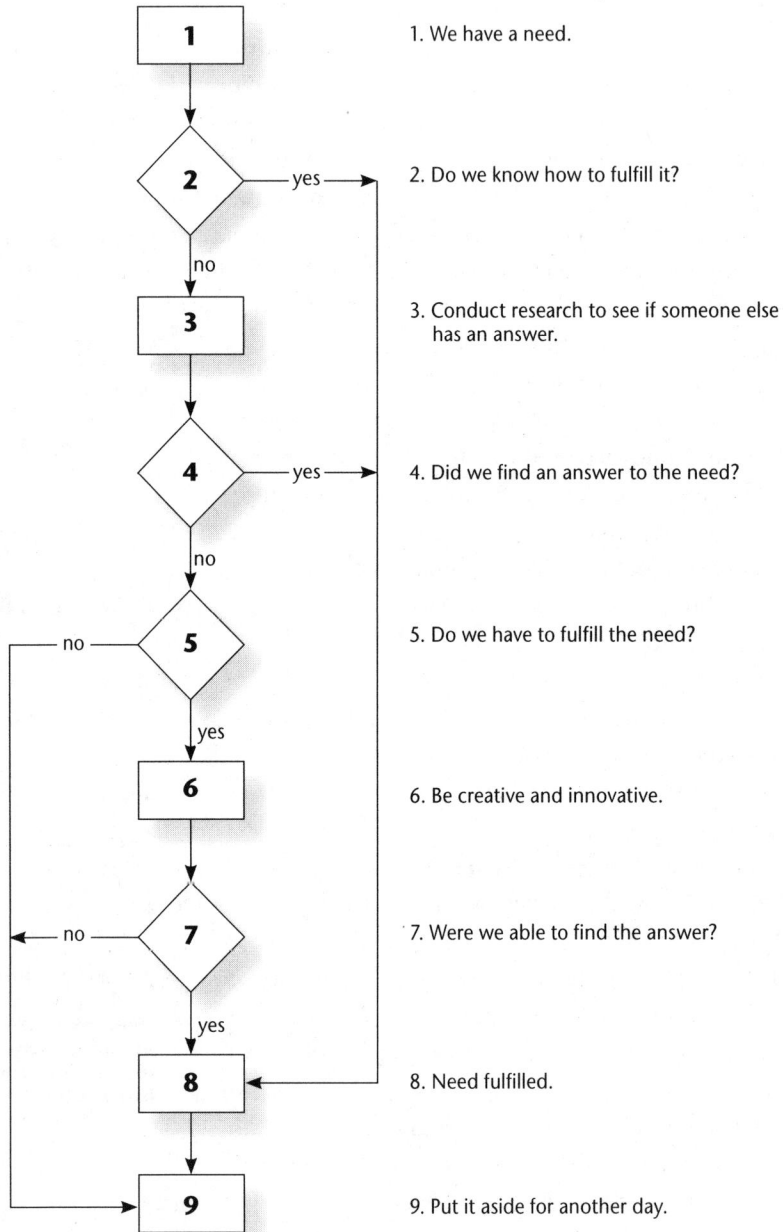

1. We have a need.

2. Do we know how to fulfill it?

3. Conduct research to see if someone else has an answer.

4. Did we find an answer to the need?

5. Do we have to fulfill the need?

6. Be creative and innovative.

7. Were we able to find the answer?

8. Need fulfilled.

9. Put it aside for another day.

because they have too little confidence in their own creative ability. They reason that if all the brightest people in the world haven't been able to find an answer to this need, why would they be able to solve it? To have creative employees, you must build up their confidence in their inborn natural creativity.

The other thing that's wrong with figure 3.3 is that after step 4, when their research has found a solution to the need, people should question if that is the best answer. They should then apply their own creativity to see if they can improve upon the answer that they have.

"Imagination is more important than knowledge."
—Albert Einstein

Creativity provides the spark that motivates an organization and makes it competitive.

Breakthroughs—truly creative approaches—are few and far between. Today creative efforts are more evolutionary than revolutionary. People tend to refine concepts and techniques rather than develop new concepts as Thomas Edison did. This type of creativity is well within the reach of every normal person.

Although being able to think up creative ideas is the first step, organizations must help and encourage their employees to be innovative as well. Creativity without innovation is a waste of effort. Innovation is defined as the "act of converting a creative concept or idea into output."

"Improvement without innovation will sooner or later result in our demise."
—Akira Iwaki
CEO, Iwaki Optical

In the book *The Creativity Toolkit* (McGraw-Hill, 1998), my co-authors and I wrote, "The abilities that are characteristic of creativity can be developed. They include:

- The ability to wonder, to be curious.
- The ability to be enthusiastic, spontaneous, and flexible.
- The ability to be open to new experience, to see the familiar from an unfamiliar point of view.
- The ability to make desirable but unsought discoveries by accident. This is called *serendipity*.

"Unless we are number one, you have to innovate."
—Lee Iacocca
Former CEO, Chrysler Corp.

- The ability to make one more thing out of another by shifting functions.
- The ability to generalize to see universal application of ideas.
- The ability to find disorder, to synthesize, to integrate.
- The ability to be intensely conscious yet in touch with subconscious sources.
- The ability to visualize or imagine new possibilities.
- The ability to be analytical and critical.
- The ability to know oneself, and to have the courage to be oneself in the face of opposition.
- The ability to be persistent, to work hard for a long periods in pursuit of a goal without guaranteed results.

■ The ability to put two or more known things together in a unique way, thus creating a new thing, an unknown thing."

As Walt Disney said, "If you can dream it, you can do it."

The New Economy is really an innovation economy. Innovation is the main thing that sets the good organizations apart from the bad ones. To succeed in the twenty-first century, an organization will have to be creative and innovative; otherwise it will enter into a spiral that will lead it to eventual failure.

"Some men look at things the way they are and ask why? I dream of things that are not and ask why not?
—Robert F. Kennedy

Often things that people read or information that they are provided are faulty and discourages creativity. Some examples of bad information are:

■ "There is no reason for an individual to have a computer in their home." (Kenneth Olsen, president and founder, Digital Equipment Co., 1977)

■ "Computers in the future may weigh no more than 1.5 tons." (*Popular Science* forecasting the development of computer technology in 1949)

■ "Everything that can be invented has been invented." (Charles H. Duell, U.S. commissioner of patents, 1899)

■ "For the majority of people, the use of tobacco has a beneficial effect." (Dr. Ian G. MacDonald, Los Angeles surgeon, quoted in *Newsweek,* November 18, 1963.)

"Require that everyone in your company bring a new idea as his or her ticket to a meeting. The meeting can't start until everybody has punched their tickets."
—Michael Michalka
Author of *Thinkertoys*

■ "I could never convince Ed (W. Edwards Deming) that total quality management is for manufacturing. It works where there is production work and no place else." (Peter Drucker, September 1997)

Managers and parents must be careful in what they say. A simple phrase or simple comment can kill creativity in their employees and children. The following are thirteen commonly used phrases that discourage creativity. I hope you don't use any of them.

■ It won't work.
■ It makes me afraid.
■ We tried that already.
■ That can't be done.
■ It will never work here.
■ Let's be serious.
■ That's ridiculous.
■ What's original about that?
■ How dumb can you be?
■ You obviously don't understand the situation.
■ That's a silly idea.

- That's impossible.
- Who died and left you boss?

The Two Sides of the Brain

> "A new idea is delicate. It can be killed by a sneer or a yawn; it can be stabbed to death by a quip, and worried to death by a frown on the right man's brow."
> —Charles M. Schulz

Visualize your brain as an apartment with two very different people sharing this space. Imagine these roommates are similar to Oscar and Felix from the play *The Odd Couple*. Felix lives in the left hemisphere of the brain. He is well-organized, well-educated, loves lists, does everything exactly as he is supposed to, and never deviates from the plan. He is driven by rules and the clock. He strives very hard to please others and is very disappointed if others don't recognize his efforts.

On the right side of the brain lives Oscar, who is the creative individual. Oscar is unstructured, unorganized, reactive, emotional, and driven by whims. He challenges authority and rejects conformity. He marches to his own drummer and relies on self-gratification to keep him going.

Both Oscar and Felix live in the same apartment and must, therefore, coexist. During the day, Felix rules; Oscar functions like a child, reacting emotionally to outside circumstances. Because Oscar's inputs are radical and reactive, Felix interprets them before they can be put into action. Felix takes Oscar's inputs and tries to put them in order, reshaping them according to Felix's rules for acceptable performance. In this process Felix usually rejects the majority of Oscar's inputs. The ideas that Felix accepts are reshaped so drastically that Oscar cannot recognize them. After years of rejection, Oscar just gives up and stops submitting ideas, content to sit back in the shadows during the day and wait until night, when Felix goes to sleep. When Felix sleeps, Oscar (the right side of the brain) becomes active in your dreams because he isn't held back by Felix (the left side of the brain). When you dream, you have no limitations put upon you.

> "With everyone using the same technology, superior human performance can be the critical variable in separating your company from its competitors."
> —Joe W. Forehand
> CEO, Accenture

You use analytical thinking patterns when you are making judgments and solving problems. This type of thinking pattern lies in the left side of the brain; it is a Felix-thinking pattern.

You use creative thinking patterns when you are developing ways to do something that you have not done before and you can't rely on anyone else's input to tell you what to do. This type of pattern, which is often used to develop new and clever solutions to situations, rests in the right side of the brain; it is an Oscar-thinking pattern.

> "Creativity is not a spectator sport."
> —Anonymous

The following thirteen techniques can be used to increase the effectiveness of your creative abilities:

- Create pictures in your mind and turn these pictures into reality.

"Personal and corporate futures can change if people will once again start tapping into their creative skills, which have sat dormant for so long."

—Michael Jones
Circuit judge

■ Keep your mind open to new ideas presenting new experiences to your senses. Be a keen observer of your environment. Provide the mind with the raw materials that it needs to be creative.

■ Do something creative each day. Set aside a specific time each day to review the creative things that you've accomplished.

■ Define alternative approaches to situations and problems. Don't use a one-track approach and gather data to prove you are right. Focus your creativity on simplifying the old and new approaches.

■ Maintain a questioning attitude. Remember, there's always a better way, and what at first appears to be a roadblock might serve as a stepping–stone stepping-stone to a better future.

"The development of an appropriate system for innovation must be one of the highest priorities. The chief executive officer has to take on a clear role as chief innovation officer, as well.

—John Kao
CEO, The Idea Factory

■ Don't be afraid to take risks. You will never fulfill your true potential if you play it safe.

■ Record your ideas as soon as you get them. Keep a notepad with you at all times.

■ Take time to relax and unwind. Take a long walk or a leisurely hot bath. Play golf or listen to restful music. Try meditation or yoga.

■ Don't accept limiting factors as being unchangeable without challenging them with all your vigor.

■ Gain confidence and enthusiasm by first focusing your creative efforts and ideas on things that are within your control to carry out.

■ Help others be creative by pointing out the strengths, not the weaknesses, of their ideas. The world already has too many devil's advocates. Be an angel's advocate.

■ Find your creative time of day. Some people are morning people; others are evening people. Everyone functions differently. Sample your emotions and creative powers to determine when you are most creative. Then set that sacred time aside to work on developing new concepts.

■ Start today to improve your creative processes. It has been said, "Yesterday is history, and tomorrow is a mystery. Today is a gift. That's why it's called the present."

Creativity Risks

Woody Allen once said, "If you are not failing every now and again, it is a sign that you are not doing anything very innovative." Allen makes a great point here. There is always a risk when you stray from the normal proven path. Creative people aren't successful every time.

Each new creative idea brings along with it a risk of failure, a risk of being criticized, and a risk of not being accepted. It's always easier and safer to say to your boss, "Yes, you have a great idea. I will do it right away" rather than to question his or her approach and suggest other alternatives. To be truly creative, you must be willing to take risks—to risk it all on an idea or belief. Thinking differently (and in some cases acting differently) does involve an element of risk—risk, in the sense that one might be embarrassed, ridiculed, left out, talked about, or whatever else may happen when one stands out from the norm.

"Failure is the opportunity to begin again more intelligently."
—Henry Ford

George M. Allen, retired vice president of research and development at 3M Corp., put it this way:

"You obtain innovation by doing three things:

■ Encouraging innovators

■ Recognizing innovators, and

■ Rewarding innovators.

"Don't feel failure so much that you refuse to try new things. The saddest summary of a life contains three descriptions: could have, might have, and should have."
—Lois Boone
Deputy chair of government caucus

The process of encouraging innovators is never-ending. Push people to stretch beyond their limits—even at the risk of failure. Treat mistakes not as failures, but as learning experiences."

At 3M the company celebrates noble failures. Armand V. Feigenbaum points out that in the best companies, "Innovation and imagination are encouraged, and careers are not penalized if the risks taken do not always succeed."

There is a very strong link between creativity and innovation. Innovation is applied creativity to develop something new or something valuable.

"Creativity is allowing yourself to make mistakes. Art is knowing which one to keep."
—Scott Adams
***Dilbert* cartoonist**

Jim Burke, past chairman of Johnson & Johnson, tells a story about himself when he first started with Johnson & Johnson. One of its products, a children's chest rub, failed, costing the company a lot of resources and money. When Mr. Johnson called Burke into his office, Burke thought he was going to be fired. Instead, Mr. Johnson complimented him for taking a risk, noting: "If you don't take risks, we will never grow."

The Brain Is a Muscle

"Only those who dare to fail greatly can ever achieve greatly."
—Robert F. Kennedy

Your brain is a muscle and like any other muscle in your body, it becomes weak and flabby if you don't use it. Exercising your brain is mandatory if you're going to maintain its effectiveness. When you stop exercising the right side of your brain, you reduce your creative and innovative capabilities. Just as you exercise to flatten your stomach muscles, you must regularly exercise the right side of your brain so that it is toned and ready to react when you need it. Today, more than ever before, people need a regimented program of

"Inspiration is the impact of a fact on a prepared mind."
—Louis Pasteur

continuous exercise to keep the right side of the brain functioning at an acceptable level. Everyone needs to set aside at least fifteen minutes three times a week to exercise and develop his or her creative abilities.

For additional information on creativity and creativity exercises, read *The Creativity Toolkit—Provoking Creativity in Individuals and Organizations*, by Robert P. Reid Jr., Glen D. Hoffherr, and H. James Harrington (McGraw-Hill, 1998).

Tips to Improve Creativity

Here are some tips that will help you and your organization become more creative:

- *Set up a creative exercise schedule.* Document a plan to develop your creative powers. Take a class on creativity. Buy a book such as *Jump Start Your Brain*, by Doug Hall with David Wecker (Warner Books, 1996), to use at your scheduled exercise sections.

"One of the greatest challenges CEOs face is to create a culture continuously accepting of new ideas and new ways of doing things."
—Michael Dowling
CEO, North Shore–Long Island Jewish Healthcare System

- *Learn how to relax.* Stress and tension limit your creative abilities. Use calming exercises such as meditation, respiratory one method (ROM), or self-hypnosis. Sometime just getting away from it all by taking a walk will do it. Take at least seven deep breaths and relax for a few minutes when you feel pressured.

- *Undertake physical preparation.* Physical exercise improves our health, which includes the mind's health, thereby helping you to be more creative. Stretching, tai chi, aerobics, or yoga are recommended approaches.

"The creative response usually happens in a state of relaxed attention."
—Adelaide Bry
Erhard Seminars Training

- *Make creativity a core value.* Keep the importance of increased creativity high on everyone's list. Include it in the individual's performance evaluation. Make it part of your vision statement.

- *Have creative meetings.* Start meetings that address problems with a short creative exercise. Take no more than five to ten minutes. It is well worth the effort because it will set a creative tone for the total meeting.

- *Take time to be different.* Don't hope that you can do the same old thing the same old way and get new results. Go to work by a new route. Go out to dinner at a new restaurant. Make it a rule to meet at least two new people a week. Research what other organizations are doing. Put down that technical manual and read a novel. Continually seek new inputs.

"If we were able to force our brain to work at only half its capacity, we could without any difficulty whatever learn forty languages, memorize the Soviet encyclopedia from cover to cover, and complete the required courses of dozens of colleges."
—W. Ross Adey and Associates

- *Be open-minded.* Don't reject an idea before you have looked at it from all angles. Hold back on your judgments. Help people develop their ideas rather than cut them apart. Be an angel's advocate.

Figure 3.4 Left- and Right-Brain Characteristics

Left	Right
Verbal—words	Nonverbal—pictures
Analytic—step-by-step	Synthetic—holistic
Temporal—sequential	Nontemporal—nonsequential
Rational—reason, facts	Nonrational—no judging
Digital—use of numbers	Analogous—relationships of all
Logical—order	Intuitive—insight, hunches
Linear—sequential	Holistic—patterns, wholeness
Vertical—narrow, sequential	Lateral—broad, many areas

One of the best books for helping you exercise your mind is *Pumping Ions* by Tom Wujec (Doubleday, 1988). Figure 3.4 defines the characteristics that are normally associated with each side of the brain. By reviewing these characteristics, you can easily see what type of exercises you need to use to improve the function of the right side of your brain.

Four Cs summarize the common traits of creative people:

1. Curiosity
2. Confidence
3. Courage
4. Constancy

> "Somehow, I can't believe that there are any heights that can't be scaled by a person who knows the secret of making dreams come true. The special criteria, it seems to me, can be summarized in 4 Cs."
>
> **—Walt Disney**

> "77 percent of CEOs at America's fastest-growing companies say they are more innovative than their competitors."
>
> **—Michael Zey**
> *The Future Factor*

STAFF RESOURCES SUMMARY

> "Why is *equipment* listed on the accounting books as an investment and *people* as an expense?"
>
> —HJH

Management invests a major part of its yearly budget to cover salaries and benefits for its employees. These costs have outrun inflation, and since 1998 the inflation rate has averaged about 2.4 percent per year. During the same period, the employee benefit costs have increased at a rate of 5.3 percent per year, more than twice the inflation rate. Increased health care costs have largely driven this increase. As a result, more of the money that is set aside for employees' salaries and benefits is directed to the benefits side of the equation,

"Half the people are always going to be below average and trying to move up the list. In the capitalist system, that generates creativity."
—George Schaefer
CEO, Fifth Third Bancorp

decreasing the amount in salary increases that the employees receive and thereby reducing their buying power. This runaway increase in the cost of benefits, which in 2006 reached more than 7 percent, must stop as it is having a negative impact on the U.S. economy.

But truly, your people are your most valuable asset and you must invest in them. You can take away my customers and I will find new ones. If my office burns down, I will build a new one. If I spend all my money, I will go out and earn more. But take away my people and I have to close shop.

Your staff truly is not an expense but an investment in the future of your organization. Embrace failure as a learning experience. Train your employees and encourage them to take risks, but don't punish them if they fail; instead, encourage them to learn and try again. 3M celebrates noble failures and you should, too. Always challenge your people to do more than they think they can. Always put more on their plates than they can handle. They never should find a time when they have nothing to do. The sense of urgency should always be with them. John A. Young, former president of Hewlett-Packard and one of the most brilliant CEOs America has ever produced, pushed HP to new and higher objectives. He stated: "In 1979 I launched a new quality campaign by announcing what I called a 'stretch' objective. I asked that our product failure rates be cut to one-tenth their current levels by the end of the decade of the eighties.

Why ask for a factor-of-ten improvement number? If I called for an improvement of only two to one, our people would have done nothing until 1988. They wouldn't have been forced to radically rethink their operating procedures."

Motorola's chief operating officer, William J. Weisz, following HP's example, stated: "In 1981, we developed as one of the top ten goals for the company the Five-Year, Tenfold Improvement Program. This means that no matter what operation you're in, no matter what your present level of quality performance, whether you are a service organization or a manufacturing area, it is our goal to have you improve that level by an order of magnitude in five years."

"Firms themselves know little about the nature and magnitude of the investment they make in human capital, and they know even less about the effectiveness of those investments."
—Brookings Institution report "Unseen Wealth" (2000)

And thus at Motorola, the Six Sigma program was born.

With a very aggressive management campaign you can bring about improvements of 10 percent to 20 percent per year, but if you want to have an order of magnitude change, you have to involve the staff, invest heavily in their skills and capabilities, and then get out of their way so they can excel.

Ask your employees for their ideas, and you'll be surprised at how many bright suggestions you'll get. John K. Hansen, the founder of Winnebago Industries, asked his staff for suggestions that would reduce the weight of its vehicles by putting an open letter in the company newspaper. In the following weeks, suggestions poured in—more than 200 of them—some big and many small that reduced the weight by just a few ounces. However, when they were all put together, they solved a very serious problem for the organization.

Don't ask for help just on a specific problem; ask for help all the time. The owner of the Grapevine Canyon Ranch in Arizona, Eve Searle, asks for and gets a minimum of one suggestion from each employee every two weeks. She holds a meeting every two weeks to share their ideas.

In *Keeping Good People* (Oakhill Press, 1989), Roger Herman provides this list of what is most important to your employees:

- Full appreciation for a job well done
- Feeling "in" on things
- Help on personal problems
- Job security
- Good wages
- Interesting work
- Promotion and growth
- Management loyalty to workers
- Tactful discipline

I would add two more items to Herman's list—trust and understanding. Fulfilling these eleven needs provides the magic for building an excellent staff that will ensure your organization's success.

"Managers who excel are pushed ahead by superb people who work with them, not for them."

—HJH

CHAPTER IV

OUTSIDE RESOURCES

ALLIANCE PARTNERSHIPS

Today organizations can afford to do only the things they do best—their core capabilities and competencies. The rest of the activities are real candidates for outsourcing. In many cases the output costs less and it's usually a much higher level of quality.

In *The Power of Management Capital* (McGraw-Hill, 2003), Armand V. Feigenbaum and Donald Feigenbaum point out that organizations must emphasize "timely integration of joint ventures, mergers, divestitures, and acquisitions with operating and business plans and performance management."

> **"It's not the employer who pays the wages. Employers only handle the money. It's the customer who pays the wages."**
> **—Henry Ford**

Things have changed significantly since the turn of the twentieth century, when Henry Ford set the standard for product best practices in 1905. His concept was complete control and ownership of the total process. It included control over development engineering, the mines that produced the iron ore, the ships that moved the ore, the smelters, the steel mills, the machine shops, the subassembly plants, the final assembly plants, and the distribution systems. It was a time when the individual's worth was based upon how hard he or she worked. People were almost literally slaves to the machines that they were assigned to. I experienced this in late 1950, when my manager at IBM chastised me because I went to the bathroom on company time.

> **"When you outsource to a total-quality-control specialist, he is busy forty-eight weeks a year working for you and a number of other clients on something he sees as challenging. Whereas a total-quality-control person employed by the company is busy six weeks a year and the rest of the time is writing memoranda and looking for projects."**
> **—Peter Drucker**
> ***Fortune*, Jan. 12, 2004**

This approach worked well when the organization paid its employees based upon labor and performance rather than their ideas. Work was divided into small repetitive cycles that unskilled employees could perform with ease. The products were relatively simple and the service industry was a small part of the U.S. economy. Employees spent a lifetime working for a single organization, retiring after thirty-five or forty years of service. Companies such as Endicott Johnson provided 100 percent medical and dental care for their employees. They even built homes that they sold to their employees. It was the time of the company store. The old Tennessee Ernie Ford song, "Sixteen Tons," whose lyrics ran "I owe my soul to the company store," was often more truth than fiction. Loyalty and complete commitment to your organization was a way of life because jobs were very hard to find. People who shifted from job to job were considered unreliable and shunned by other organizations—just as they were in Japan during its "heyday" from the 1970s to 2000. It was a time when apprenticeship programs were the key way to improve an individual's status and income. Only a small percentage of the population went to college, as college degrees weren't needed for most jobs. This system worked well when factory workers accounted for more than 50 percent of the total work force. But today factory workers make up only 14 percent of the work force.

These concepts set some standards that still haven't been beaten. For example, Henry Ford's concepts resulted in the conversion of iron ore into a complete automobile within a seven-day cycle.

Now, early in the twenty-first century, everything is very different. People move freely from organization to organization. Organizations commonly use consultants to bring in specialized, unique skills. Advanced organizations realize that they need to focus their resources on activities that relate to their core competencies. They realize that it's much more effective and efficient to contract out the support activities to organizations that have those skills as core competencies. CEOs are evaluating which activities they can move outside their organizations to where they can be done better, faster, and more cheaply. As a result, organizations are establishing alliance partnerships with organizations that do things such as accounting, sales, human relations, information technology, auditing, and training. ADC Telecommunications outsourced its billing and collection activities to a firm in India. Its CEO, Rick Roscitt, reports, "That function is done on about 15 percent of the U.S.-based rate in India, so the savings for us have been enormous."

"Connectivity is a core competency needed
by individuals and organizations alike."
—HJH

The real key to successful outsourcing is to find an organization whose core competencies are in business processes that complement your noncore business processes. This often provides the organization with higher quality at lower prices. Jack Wilson, CEO of Accenture's business process outsourcing, suggests, "Outsourcing is misnamed. Are you taking a function out or bringing talent in? It depends on how you look at it."

The high-end athletic shoe and apparel industries are good examples. Reebok shoes are designed in Canton, Massachusetts, near Boston. These designs are transmitted electronically to Asia, where prototypes are built. Once Reebok management approves the models, they go into production in countries such as South Korea and China. Reebok has established alliance partnerships with Asian organizations that are willing to dedicate total manufacturing facilities to the Reebok products. These alliance partners are responsible for the total manufacturing cycle, including all interactions with their suppliers. The final boxed shoes are packaged and shipped from Asia directly to the distributors. Reebok realized that its core competencies were in interpreting what would be attractive to its customers, designing the final products, and marketing the products. It selected alliance partners whose core competency was manufacturing athletic shoes, thereby greatly improving quality while reducing the cost of the products.

Organizations in almost all industries have been entering into interorganizational relationships (IOR) in an effort to decrease the cost of improved total performance. A Booz Allen & Hamilton study revealed that since 1987 the number of strategic alliances worldwide has increased by 25 percent per year.

"If you think you can go it alone in today's global economy, you are highly mistaken."
—Jack Welch
Former CEO, GE

Organizations are even looking at their competitors in a very different way today. Competitors are often combining their resources to reduce cycle time and costs to meet a specific customer's requirements. This concept was first proven effective by the U.S. government. The Japanese government expanded this concept to private industry by funding technology-development projects, the results of which could be used by any public or private organization. Given today's complex technology, development costs are a major burden on the organization's resources that can easily cascade into eating all the profits from the products that are created. When three or four organizations try to develop similar products for a similar market segment, it drives up the cost of everyone's products. As a result, competitors are beginning to form alliance partnerships to develop new methodologies. A good example is the alliance partnerships for the development of thin film products. This approach basically divides the development costs by the number of organizations that are participating in the alliance partnerships. These organizations still compete for the market segment, but their competitive advantage now rests in how they apply the technology, not in the basic technology.

More organizations depend upon alliance partners, and they are becoming a very valuable resource. This is particularly true of small- and medium-sized organizations, where alliance partners' personnel often are integrated into the organization as part of their engagement teams. These alliance partners frequently and freely exchange personnel and

"In multibillion-dollar outsourcing deals, you'll find there's a huge effort in the chase, but not much thinking about how you'll run the marriage."
—Rick Roscitt
Chairman and CEO, ADC Telecommunications

methodologies. Some of the alliance partners serve only as a source of potential sales leads. In return for the sales leads, the alliance partner receives a very attractive commission if the sale is made.

Outsourcing is growing year by year. A PricewaterhouseCoopers survey revealed that 72 percent of European organizations are outsourcing financial services, and, in the United

States, 77 percent of them are outsourced. The most commonly outsourced activities are:

- Information technology (IT)
- Systems reporting
- Payroll
- Billing
- Accounts payable

Good outsourcing partners can result in increased revenue generation, not just cost savings. The main reason that organizations outsource is because the outsourcing partner has superior operational expertise. A survey conducted by *Information Week* in 2004 revealed that 47 percent of the respondents stated that operational expertise was the most important reason for selecting an outsourcing partner. Only 35 percent of the respondents selected cost savings as their primary criterion for selection. Carl Ascenzo, the chief information officer (CIO) of Blue Cross Blue Shield of Massachusetts, said that the main reason for its signing a $320 million multiyear contract with EDS was to help move the business forward.

The question is: "Can outsourcing live up to the customer's expectations?" The *Information Week* survey indicated that it has:

- 65 percent met expectations.
- 27 percent haven't met expectations.
- 6 percent exceeded expectations.
- 2 percent were too early to tell.

Dick Le Fave, the CIO of Nextel Communications, who was going to be spending $100 million in outsourcing in the next two years, pointed out the reason he selected EDS. He said, "They bring us a solid, reliable operating environment." (*Information Week*, November 22, 2004.)

IT service has been a big part of outsourcing, and people tend to think it has moved offshore. The truth is that only 19 percent has moved offshore; 5 percent has moved near shore (Mexico or Canada) and 76 percent onshore.

Contrary to common belief, outsourcing doesn't always result in job losses. In the *Information Week* survey, nearly one-third of the organizations that outsourced IT jobs increased the number of IT employees during the same period.

The *Information Week* survey revealed another surprise—when business technology professions ranked IT outsource suppliers, the top seven suppliers were all U.S. organizations. The top IT suppliers, in order of ranking, are:

1. Deloitte
2. Accenture
3. Cap Gemini
4. Unisys
5. Bearing Point
6. Hewlett-Packard
7. CSC
8. Infosys (India)
9. Wipro (India)
10. Tata (India)
11. EPS
12. IBM

Despite the low ratings for the Indian firms, their recent growth has been outstanding. The three firms had an average of 35 percent revenue growth in 2004 compared to single-digit growth in the total industry. It's projected that offshore IT outsourcing will grow almost 250 percent in the next five years.

Outsourcing is a win-win game. It provides poor countries with a way to improve their economies while helping developed countries become more productive and bring products to market faster and less expensively.

SUPPLIERS AS A RESOURCE

"Good suppliers can make even the poorly performing customer look good, but everyone looks bad if the suppliers are bad."

—HJH

The incredible complexity of today's products, the drive to be first in the market, just-in-time manufacturing, and an increasingly quality-conscious global marketplace are causing all manufacturers to re-evaluate the way they do business. Supplier management now applies to many areas other than components and materials. Organizations are outsourcing much of their administrative and support activities, such as human resources (HR), finance, and IT. This approach has made most organizations more dependent upon their suppliers than ever before. Excellent suppliers are no longer a nicety; they are a necessity.

"If your employees are your most valuable resources, your suppliers run a very close second."

—HJH

One clear trend has emerged—the top management teams of leading-edge manufacturers have added supply management to their strategic initiatives. They have channeled major resources into their procurement operations with the mission to manage and develop a supply base that delivers a competitive advantage in availability, quality, delivery, and total cost improvements.

These leading-edge organizations' strategy is to move materials and information faster, better, and more cheaply. These top managers are truly committed to achieving excellence; they realize that it cannot be achieved overnight nor can it be *bought*. Excellence must be developed from within.

At the heart of this proposed supply management process is an experienced cross-functional commodity team with an attitude of teamwork and proactive prevention. The major areas of required responsibilities, qualifications, and activities have been clearly defined. The team performs its responsibilities by linking the organizations' business objectives of quality, cycle-time, and total cost initiatives to the daily activities within the supply base. The linking mechanism is an attitude of a partnering relationship and a "creative purchase agreement" that defines the targets for improvement, the plan to achieve the targets, the supply-customer team, and the performance measure and review process.

Current State Assessment

First the organization needs to do an unbiased review of the present supply management process (SMP). This assessment will provide a picture of the way the SMP works today. It's usually better if people who aren't part of the present process perform the assessment so that they can provide an objective picture. The assessment should look into all sources that supply the organization with any item. The organization's budget is a good starting point for identifying all functions that buy any item. The assessors should prepare a list of functions that pay for services, materials, taxes, parts, assemblies, and so on. Then they can define a list of the items that will become part of the SMP. Very few purchased items should be excluded; typical examples that may be excluded are taxes, electric bills, natural gas bills, and so on. Once it defines the items and the functions that will be included in the SMP, the assessment team must understand how the different supply processes are performed. For example: Do the development lab, the product engineering function, and production control use the same process for procuring parts? If not, how do they differ?

The different processes should be evaluated for items such as:

- How are suppliers selected?
- How are suppliers measured?
- Are good suppliers rewarded?
- How are suppliers involved in the design process?
- How much of the purchase budget goes to each major supplier?
- How well is the system documented?

- Is the SMP in keeping with ISO 9001?
- How good is the process of performance feedback to the supplier?
- How good is the supplier history file?
- Are poorly performing suppliers dropped?
- Who gets supplier interface training?
- What percentage of items go through receiving inspection?
- How well is supplied equipment maintained?
- When and how were the suppliers certified, and how often are they recertified?
- Does the organization report cost to stock?
- How many suppliers are there per item?

This assessment should provide the management team with a view of today's process, its problems, and recommendations on how it should be improved.

What Is Supply Management?

This section discusses a benchmarking study Harrington Institute conducted and summarizes the approaches being applied to supplier management. It includes the underlying principles of operation, some of the key strategies for supplier management, and a list of the important tools and techniques that must be incorporated if the program is to be successful.

History

Since the late 1960s, there has been a transition from the old concept of purchasing as a clerical appendage of management to a newer concept of material management that embraces inventory control, material logistics, distribution, and purchasing. Since the 1980s, this role has been greatly enhanced and labeled "supply management." Companies that have organized for supply management include Motorola, Hewlett-Packard, GE, Xerox, IBM, Solectron, General Motors, Ford, Raytheon, and Rockwell. Most of these companies have been working on developing an SMP and an integrated procurement system that uniquely fits their culture and business needs since the early 1980s. Most companies with advanced SMPs consider them a strategic advantage and will disclose only the basic details. They closely guard their advanced tools and systems.

A key point is that it takes significant resources focused both internally and externally for a long time to achieve world-class status. In general, most companies increased the engineering resources in procurement, but total additional head count decreased.

Benchmark Overview

Common elements found in the leading companies' SMPs are:
- This totally new concept in management involves purchasing, engineering, supplier quality assurance, and the supplier's working together as one team early on, co-located, to foster mutually set goals.

- It's a long-term, win-win partnering for mutual growth and profits.
- A process of concrete, on-site, and frequent mutual help focuses on new product introductions, quality, cycle time, cost reductions, and co-training/learning sessions.
- The supplier is an internal partner and includes its chain of suppliers for early supplier involvement.
- All benchmarked companies state that supply management is a strategic business decision.
- Trends are to centralized price negotiations and decentralized buying.
- Some manage production items and other commodities, while others also manage transportation.
- Single sourcing is OK, but most have two suppliers for capacity and risk reasons.
- Early supplier involvement is practiced carefully.
- Many invest capital into their supplier base.
- Suppliers are given firm, fixed orders covering a month's requirements, never canceled, with a twelve-month rolling forecast.
- All have a credible supplier management system.
- All have "stretched" goals for improving quality, reducing cycle time, and an annual cost reduction target.
- Most have an advanced integrated procurement system.
- All have raised the professional levels of their purchasing staff-engineers, many with advanced business degrees.
- All have reduced their supplier base by as much as 50 percent.
- Most were strongly encouraged by their key customers or competitors. Few started supply management because it was "the thing to do."
- Most are developing partnership relationships.

Companies that are successful in supply management are clear that supply management is not:
- Another fad that will fade away if ignored
- A more sophisticated tool to get suppliers to tow the line
- Golden handcuffs for the supplier
- Smoke-and-mirror dance by top management based upon the same business-as-usual practices
- A "take or else" position

In closing, all benchmark companies came to the following conclusions. Supply management isn't a technology issue—it's a people and communication issue—a mechanism for blending and coordinating the functional areas within the company and the supplier.

Perhaps the biggest problem in implementing supply management, once you obtain agreement to implement it, is that engineers in design, manufacturing, quality, and procurement don't speak the same language.

This is the main reason for developing commodity or supplier teams made up of members from each function. It forces communication and teamwork to get results. It's best to co-locate the teams next to their internal customers and to each other.

It's clear that excellent organizations consider ISO 9001:2000 certification as a minimum requirement to even be considered as a supplier. ISO 9001 by itself is not considered adequate. It will get you into the race to win the contract, but it won't win the race for you.

Most supply relationships start with a requirement that the supplier be certified to ISO 14001 and/or ISO 9001, but this is only a starting point. ISO 9001:2000 is good enough for suppliers that produce commercial commodities such as nuts and bolts, but it isn't good enough if you're going to form a true partnership with the supplier. This requires that the individuals in both organizations get to know each other and establish common objectives. It also requires that the customer gets to know the supplier's process well enough to understand its limitations.

A good supplier should commit to having a continuous improvement process that will more than offset inflation, rising material costs, and rising labor costs. Harrington Institute has negotiated contracts with many suppliers that included a committed cost reduction of 10 percent to 15 percent per year.

Generic Supply Management Model—Ten Steps

You can develop a supply management process using the following ten steps:

1. *Establish a supplier management team.*
2. *Develop an action plan.* A team should start with one supplier or a selected group of suppliers in a pilot effort.
3. *Develop specifications and standards.* Continuous improvement can be achieved only if the customer sets and communicates explicit standards and measures for quality delivery, service, and cost.
4. *Set priorities for product attributes.* A product can have many quality attributes. Important product quality characteristics should be identified on the engineering print. Nonconforming critical characteristics can jeopardize health, safety, or welfare. Nonconforming major characteristics affect product function. A minor product nonconformance, a blemish, affects product appearance.
5. *Determine process control and capability.* Once a commonly understood measurement system has been devised and priorities have been set for product service characteristics, the supplier is asked to submit a process flow diagram and to specify the most suitable locations for tracking quality and testing products. The supplier establishes effective statistical process controls for the designated product quality characteristics.
6. *Measuring performance.* The measurement system indicates how quickly improvements are being pursued. It's a key measure of the commodity team's effectiveness.

7. *Improve continuously.* Continuous improvement means that performance or specification targets have been set and, through time, variation around these targets is gradually reduced.

8. *Take ownership.* Once the customer has initiated the improvement effort, the supplier is encouraged to take ownership of and responsibility for the improvement effort. Only a few suppliers will have the commitment and stamina for the long haul.

9. *Audit performance.*

10. *Continuous improvement.* Start at step one and enhance the supply management process by using more sophisticated tools in each step.

Supplier Ratings

Quality is one of the four supplier performance criteria, the other three being responsiveness, delivery, and cost. A truly comprehensive supplier rating system must include all four.

Many methods exist for calculating an overall supplier performance index, which assigns different weights to the four performance elements through algorithms of varying complexity. In general, though, you should take care not to make the calculations too complex, lest the customer and supplier spend too much time haggling about the exotica of the algorithm and not enough time discussing the underlying phenomena the index is intended to reveal. It's preferable to use a simple weighted-average method for calculating a single rating—if the customer insists on having a single number to represent overall performance—and to provide separate indexes for quality, responsiveness, delivery, and cost performance so that the supplier can see the relative contributions of each.

Each of these four underlying indexes can be complex in itself. In the past, quality ratings were frequently based on simple lot-acceptance rates. In a zero-defects world, however, parts-per-million acceptance rates are more appropriate, but the massive parts inspection required to accurately estimate acceptance rates in parts per million is usually not economical. A quality index based on the results of regular audits of the supplier's process control system may be appropriate. It's also very important that the supplier quality index reflect any problems experienced with the parts after acceptance—problems discovered on the manufacturing line as well as those experienced in the field.

Quality ratings sometimes attach different weights to various types of defects: "critical," "major," and "minor" or "incidental." But incidental defects, such as incorrect or damaged packaging or minor deviations in "nonfunctional" dimensions, can jam up a robot; cause a materials handling system to go haywire; or trigger inordinate amounts of expediting, rework, or other special processing. Thus, it's less realistic to talk about classes of defects. All defects are potentially disruptive in high-efficiency manufacturing processes. Furthermore, the concept of a "minor defect" is philosophically inconsistent with a commitment to zero defects.

The index of delivery performance is usually the easiest to calculate. Specific tolerance limits must be established to define clearly what is meant by "on-time" performance. The simplest system could stop right there, merely rating deliveries as on time or not on time. A more complex system would add varying penalties to shipments based on just how early or late they arrived. (Note that an early shipment is also not on time. Nowadays, an early shipment represents excess inventory, and there may not even be a convenient place to store it.) It's important to note that freewheeling change in a customer's delivery demands necessarily creates havoc with suppliers' ability to maintain good delivery ratings through no fault of their own.

A supplier cost index can be a very difficult and somewhat arbitrary thing to develop. An index comparing several suppliers' prices to that of the lowest-cost supplier sounds attractive, but this can lead to accidental revelation of confidential supplier data. In addition, the trend toward fewer suppliers makes such an index less important. Another approach would be to base the cost index on how well the supplier performs against a schedule of planned cost reductions if such provisions are contained in a long-term contract. For companies with good cost-estimating skills, the best solution is to compare actual prices to estimated costs as an index of supplier cost performance.

One very practical problem in developing a composite supplier rating system is that the necessary data are usually spread among several organizations. Even if all the data are contained within an integrated computer network, the programming to bring it all together can be very tricky. The lesson here is to try to keep the rating system pretty simple, especially if the number of suppliers is very large.

As the customer-supplier relationship becomes increasingly more important, the communication systems are continuously evolving to include much more than these three basic elements. Narrative and graphic reports that include things such as responsiveness, in-line fallout, and field performance are prepared regularly. They also include comments from all departments that have anything to do with the supplier. Departments such as quality assurance, product engineering, accounting, purchasing, shipping, manufacturing, accounts payable, and so on provide monthly input that goes directly to the supplier. Software products, such as Performance 360 sold by Market Answers, sets up Internet collabri-card (superscript) automatic systems that acquire data from enterprise resource planning (ERP) or workflow; each month the key stakeholders for each supplier answer a predetermined set of questions related to the product. It then prepares a comprehensive report that is transmitted directly to the supplier. The supplier uses the same system to respond to the problem and to define its corrective action. The summary of all the supplier activities is then presented to all the relevant management within the organization in a form that is designed for their specific need.

"Today acceptable supplier management systems are measured in percentage of suppliers that have provided perfect compliance for the last twelve months."

—HJH

Managing the Supply Chain

Most organizations need to train some of their employees to manage their supply chains. A typical five-day supply-chain management class would include subjects such as the ones in the following course outline.

- Introduction to supply chain management
  - ☐ Supply-chain management process overview
  - ☐ Value and benefits to key stakeholders
  - ☐ Functional supply chains
  - ☐ Integrated supply chains
  - ☐ Supply chain networks

- Supply chain management strategy
  - ☐ Alignment with corporate strategy
  - ☐ Analyzing the competition
  - ☐ Driving supply chain decisions
  - ☐ Analyzing core competencies
  - ☐ Outsourcing
  - ☐ Aligning the global supply chain

- Managing the supply chain
  - ☐ Value drivers
  - ☐ Key performance indicators (KPI)
  - ☐ Balanced scorecards
  - ☐ Network configuration
  - ☐ Product design
  - ☐ Process design
  - ☐ Inventory control
  - ☐ Performance metrics

- Supply chain information technology
  - ☐ Enterprise resource planning (ERP)—aligning operations with strategy
  - ☐ Synchronization

- ■ Continuous improvement and the supply chain
  - ☐ Continuous improvement
  - ☐ Just-in-time manufacturing
  - ☐ Lean organization
  - ☐ Lean supply chain
  - ☐ Approaches to quality and reducing variation
  - ☐ Quality tools and the supply chain
  - ☐ Certification

- ■ Implementing and sustaining change
  - ☐ Challenges to effective supply chain implementation
  - ☐ Barriers to effective supply chain management
  - ☐ Success factors—sustaining the gains

- ■ Demand management
  - ☐ Introduction to demand management
  - ☐ Sales and marketing role
  - ☐ New product introduction
  - ☐ Product life cycle
  - ☐ Product management
  - ☐ Understanding forecasting
  - ☐ Listening to the customer

- ■ Effective process and product design
  - ☐ Design for the customer
  - ☐ Design for manufacturing
  - ☐ Design for service
  - ☐ Design for logistics
  - ☐ Design for supply chain

- ■ ERP systems
  - ☐ ERP infrastructure
  - ☐ Data management
  - ☐ Information technology and the supply chain

- ■ Technologies for competitive advantage
  - ☐ Using technology for real-time visual management
  - ☐ Advanced technologies
  - ☐ Radio frequency identification

- Manufacturing planning and control systems
  - ☐ Business planning
  - ☐ Sales and operations planning
  - ☐ Master scheduling
  - ☐ Material requirements planning
  - ☐ Production activity control
  - ☐ Capacity management

- Transportation and logistics
  - ☐ Warehousing
  - ☐ Warehouse management systems
  - ☐ Transportation
  - ☐ Transportation management systems
  - ☐ Global logistics—pulling it all together

- Supply-chain relationship management
  - ☐ Understanding supply-chain relationship management
  - ☐ Aligning the supply chain processes

- Customer relationship management (CRM)
  - ☐ Understanding customer relationship management
  - ☐ CRM technology

- Supplier relationship management (SRM)
  - ☐ Understanding supplier relationship management
  - ☐ SRM technology

- The extended enterprise
  - ☐ Understanding the roles and values throughout the supply chain
  - ☐ Building collaboration
  - ☐ Driving improved supply chain performance
  - ☐ Barriers to the fully integrated supply chain

- Enhancing supply chain performance with information technology
  - ☐ ERP and the supply chain
  - ☐ Electronic data transfer and standards
  - ☐ Performance enhancement systems

■ E-commerce
  □ The Internet and supply chain management
  □ The supply chain and e-business
  □ Back-to back strategies
  □ Going directly to the customer

SUPPLIER RESOURCE SUMMARY

A few key points you should always keep in mind:
■ Select a few very good suppliers.
■ Work with them so they understand how your operation works.
■ Understand the suppliers' needs and be sure they understand your needs.
■ Have the suppliers provide you with plans on how they're going to improve their outputs through time. Then measure the improvements.
■ Expect them to make a fair profit from working with you.
■ Have well-defined and well-used communication channels.
■ Make the quality of your input to the suppliers as good or better than the outputs you expect from them.

Some suppliers you cannot control. Energy is a good example. The cost of a barrel of crude oil has soared since 1998. (See figure 4.1.) The cost of this required resource has a major impact on business costs; these rising costs must be passed on to the consumer both

Figure 4.1 U.S. First Purchaser's Crude Oil Price ($/Barrel)

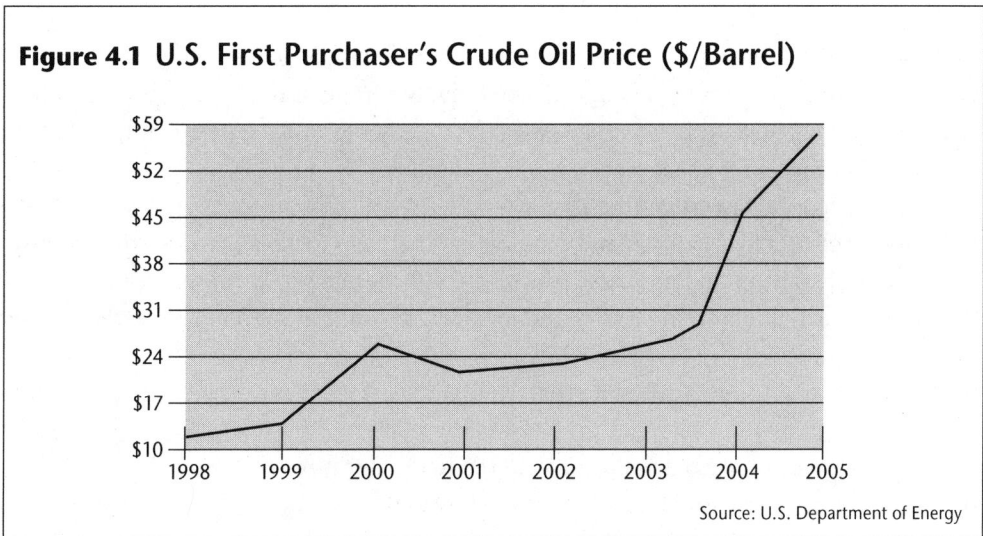

Source: U.S. Department of Energy

directly and indirectly. This has resulted in a decrease in consumer spending, which leads to a lower demand for products and services.

Just because you can't control all of your suppliers doesn't mean that you can't manage the supply chain suppliers that are competing for your business.

> "In customer-supplier relationships, both partners need to go 60 percent of the way."
> —HJH

SUPPLIER MANAGEMENT

One clear trend that has emerged in today's environment is increased focus on supply chain management, in which the supplier plays a central role. Top management teams of the leading-edge organizations have added supplier management to their strategic initiatives. They have channeled into their procurement operations a mission to develop and manage a supplier base, so that it provides a competitive advantage in availability, quality, delivery, and cost. Since the 1980s, interface with the supplier has been greatly enhanced and labeled as "supply management." Companies that have organized for supply management include Motorola, Hewlett-Packard, Xerox, IBM, Solectron, General Motors, Ford, Raytheon, and Rockwell. Most of these companies have developed a supply management process (SMP) and an integrated procurement system that uniquely fits their culture and business needs. Most of these companies with advanced SMPs consider them a strategic advantage and will disclose only the basic details. They closely guard their advanced tools and systems.

Some of the common elements found in the excellent organizations' SMPs are:

- This totally new concept in management involves purchasing, engineering, supplier quality assurance, and the supplier's working together as one team early on, co-located to foster mutually set goals.
- It's a long-term, win-win partnering for mutual growth and profits.
- A process of concrete, on-site, and frequent mutual help focuses on new product introductions, quality, cycle time, cost reductions, and co-training/learning sessions.
- The supplier is an internal partner and includes its chain of suppliers for early supplier involvement.
- All benchmarked companies state that supply management is a strategic business decision.
- Trends are to centralized price negotiations and decentralized buying.
- Some manage production items and other commodities, while others also manage transportation.

- Single sourcing is OK, but most have two suppliers for capacity and risk reasons.
- Early supplier involvement is practiced carefully.
- Many invest capital into their supplier base.
- Suppliers are given firm, fixed orders covering a month's requirements, never canceled, with a twelve-month rolling forecast.
- All have a credible supplier measurement system.
- All have "stretched" goals for improving quality, reducing cycle time, and an annual cost reduction target.
- Most have an advanced integrated procurement system.
- All have raised the professional levels of their purchasing staff-engineers, many with advanced business degrees.
- Most were strongly encouraged by their key customers or competitors. Few started supply management because it was "the thing to do."
- Most are developing partnership relationships.

Most supply relationships start with a requirement that the supplier be certified to ISO 14001 and/or ISO 9001, but this is only a starting point. ISO 9001:2000 is good enough for suppliers that produce commercial commodities such as nuts and bolts, but it isn't good enough if you're going to form a true partnership with the supplier. This requires that the individuals in both organizations get to know each other and establish common objectives. It also requires that the customer gets to know the supplier's process well enough to understand its limitations.

A good supplier should commit to having a continuous improvement process that will more than offset inflation, rising material costs, and rising labor costs. Harrington Institute has negotiated contracts with many suppliers that included a committed cost reduction of 10 percent to 15 percent per year.

Supplier measurements and rating systems have also changed drastically. In the 1970s organizations measured and reported to their suppliers the percentage of lots that were rejected. In the 1990s, quality is only one of three supplier performance criteria. The other two are delivery and costs. A truly comprehensive rating system must include all three.

Many methods exist for calculating an overall supplier performance index, which assigns different weights to each of the three performance elements through algorithms of various complexities.

> "Today acceptable supplier management systems are measured in percentage of suppliers that have provided perfect compliance for the last twelve months."
>
> —HJH

OUTSIDE RESOURCES SUMMARY

The way resources are used has changed. In the 1920s, Ford owned everything that was needed to produce the Model T—starting from the mines that dug the iron ore out of the mountain, to the smelter, to the machine shop, to the subassembly, to final assembly. Today's organizations have realized that they must concentrate on what they do best and build a set of alliance partners and suppliers that can do the other jobs better, faster, and less expensively than they can. This approach from complete control to indirect control has greatly increased the need for fast, effective communication between suppliers, alliance partners, and organizations. Methodologies such as supply chain management and other IT enablers have stepped up to meet this challenge, minimizing the total risk.

At the end of the supply chain is the external customer. You may not think of the external customer as one of your organization's resources, but you must agree it's one of the organization's assets. Management around the world has now realized that it's much less expensive, by a factor of ten to one, to keep the customer it has than to go out and find a replacement customer. This realization has changed the way organizations interact with their present customers. They are looking at the lifetime value of the customer, not just the transactional value. Customer survey results have come to be as important as profit-and-loss statements. Fast, effective corrective action on customer problems is now a requirement to keep your customers buying your services and products. Empowering your first-line service employees with a means to handle unhappy customers is a must. The level of customer dissatisfaction doubles each time a customer has to speak to another individual to get his or her problem resolved. If a customer brings a quart of milk back to a food store claiming that it's sour, why would you question it? Why would your employee smell it or taste it? That's telling the customer that you don't believe he or she is truthful. For the sake of $1.55 you're risking your customer's future business, which is worth about $135 per week times fifty-two weeks times thirty-five years or $245,700.

Marketing strategies must address keeping your present customer base and then consider attracting potential new customers.

"It just came to me that our extremely large federal debt
is the result of buying from the lowest bidder."

—HJH

CHAPTER V

SUPPORT TECHNOLOGY RESOURCE MANAGEMENT

"IT is an enabler, not the answer."
—HJH

TECHNOLOGY ON THE MOVE

The effective use of technology to handle repetitive, time-consuming activities is essential for reducing costs and cycle time while improving quality and morale. In the last twenty years computer technology and its supporting software have transformed people's lives in their homes and businesses. Who ever would have guessed forty years ago that computers would be standard fixtures in most homes? Who would have guessed that three- and four-year-olds would be using computers as toys? Who would have guessed that people would depend more on a computer to send and receive mail than they depend upon the U.S. Postal Service? When the movie *2001: A Space Odyssey* came out, people liked the idea of talking to the computer (HAL) and having it do the work, but they thought that it was just science fiction, or at least a long, long way into the future. Well, today I'm writing this book by dictating to my computer, and it's typing, punctuating, and checking grammar, all without my help. It's 2006 and technology has far surpassed the vision of the early science-fiction writers. HAL now fits on a lap and soon will be carried in a shirt pocket.

Technology has collapsed the world into local neighborhoods. I've been involved in projects in which we designed a product on the East Coast of the United States, sent the specifications electronically to India to do the programming, and within the same day sent the programs to our simulation laboratory in London. London performed the required testing and transmitted the test results back to the design team so that it could work with completed results sixteen hours after it prepared the design concept. That's a single twenty-four–hour cycle from the design to test the output with no overtime and no second- and third-shift operations.

> "E-business and the Internet mean a business model and a way of managing, not just the application of technology."
> —Armand V. Feigenbaum
> President and CEO,
> General Systems Co.

Technology has also broken down the walls that surround the office by allowing employees to work out of their homes, saving travel time and reducing the costs of expensive office space. For example, when Ernst & Young in San Jose, California, moved to the home-office concept, it was able to reduce its office space by more than 50 percent. Many managers' basic concern with the home-office concept is that they have no control over how the employee is spending his or her time. They question whether the employee is home working or playing with the children or out buying groceries. The real question is, "Does it make any difference when the employee does the company's work?" The answer is no. If it's best for employees to do their work starting at 9 p.m. after the house has quieted down, they should have that option. Management needs to measure results, not the time of day that the individual employee is working to accomplish those results. As long as the employees complete their assigned tasks on time, within budget, and produce a high-quality output, it shouldn't matter what days of the week or what hours of the day they work. But for you managers who don't trust your employees, software can track what each employee accomplishes during each hour of the day. This allows complete accountability even in this virtual working environment. A typical software product that accomplishes this is sold by Virtual Enterprise Solutions of San Jose, California.

It wasn't long ago that bar codes were state-of-the-art, but that technology is fast being made obsolete with radio frequency identification (RFID) and collaborative compliance services (CCS). Exxon Mobil Speedpass and E-Z Pass use this technology. Imagine going into Safeway, removing a can of Campbell's chicken noodle soup from the shelf, and putting it into your shopping cart. With this simple act, an electronic scanner automatically checks out the product and deducts the cost from your debit card. In the background, a radio signal notifies the stockroom that one can was removed from the shelf and notifies Campbell's that one can of chicken noodle soup has been sold by that specific Safeway. When sufficient quantities of the soup have been sold, as specified by Safeway, Campbell's automatically delivers a replacement supply. This is all possible with RFID. For example, Wal-Mart required all its major suppliers to convert to RFID labeling on products delivered to Wal-Mart in 2005; it required that all its other suppliers convert by 2006. As of this writing, suppliers are behind schedule in meeting this goal, but they're making progress. The conversion will result in millions of dollars in savings for Wal-Mart and its suppliers through better inventory management, reduced workloads, and reduced pilfering. It will also improve customer satisfaction by eliminating those long waits in checkout lines; eventually, checkout clerks will be able to scan items without removing them from customers' carts. It's estimated that Wal-Mart will save $8.35 billion a year as a result of using RFID. Reduced labor costs from not having to scan the bar codes of incoming goods accounts for most of the savings. This technology will also help Wal-Mart solve two of its major problems—out-of-stock items and products lost as a result of theft (shrinkage).

Larry Kellam, former director of supply-network innovation at Procter & Gamble, stated, "Reducing out-of-stock products by 10 percent to 20 percent could boost [Wal-Mart's] annual sales by anywhere from $400 million to $1.2 billion." (Source: *Fortune Magazine*, November 10, 2003.)

TECHNOLOGY MOVERS

Technology and software have changed and will change business profiles in many different ways. Typical technology tools are:

- Customer-relationship management (CRM)
- Project portfolio management
- Simulation modeling
- Data warehouse
- Business to business
- Business to customer
- Material requirements planning (MRP)
- Knowledge management software
- Portals
- Web sites
- Distance learning
- Automated testing
- Automated production
- E-commerce
- Database management system
- SAP (systems, applications, and products in data processing)
- RFID

> **"We discovered that ROI was so high because companies have begun to scope out very specific goals and purchase only those applications that helped the companies do what they wanted to do."**
> **—Mary Wardley**
> **VP, IDC, CRM Applications Research**

A recent International Data Corporation (IDC) study of CRM implementation revealed that the returns ranged from 16 percent to 1,000 percent.

The IDC study revealed that only 7 percent of the return was technology-related; 93 percent was the result of understanding the process before IT was applied.

These technologies have penetrated almost every facet of the excellent organization's business. You might question if it's worth all the additional costs and bother. Often the technology is outpacing the employee's ability to install and use it. Theoretically, it all sounds extremely good, but practically it often outruns the organization's ability to effectively change the culture and get the required employee buy-in. On the other hand, if your competitors are using all this modern-day technology and you don't follow, or better still, lead the trend, you are giving your competitors a very significant advantage.

Technology Examples

Microsoft reported the following typical savings from the use of some of its software products:

- Saks saved more than $1 million in payroll and increased productivity by 40 percent while decreasing response time from forty-five to eight seconds.
- E-College installed a contact server and call-center solution and realized an annual ROI of 1,700 percent.

The South African Revenue Service (SARS) fixed its fragmented taxpayer information database by installing Siebel's Public Sector Single View of the Taxpayer solution. This provided it with a completely integrated multiple-taxpayer system that generated the following results:

- Paid for itself within two months
- Saved $12 million per week
- Provided more accurate tax assessments, fewer data entry errors, and faster response to inquiries
- Reduced time to collect taxpayer information from three weeks to fifty seconds

Overland Storage, a supplier of hardware and software solutions that serviced more than 75,000 customers, had no single repository for integration of call and support information. None of the organization's databases were linked. Superior customer service and support was crucial to the organization's ongoing growth. As a result, it installed Epicor Software's Clientele Customer Support to improve customer care, sales support, technical support, internal repair, and quality of software and hardware. It measured these improvements:

- ROI of 278 percent in one year
- Inventory reduction of 28 percent
- 5 percent to 15 percent improvement in customer satisfaction
- 16 percent improvement in first-time fixes
- 9 percent improvement in contract renewals

Use of the *Reader's Digest* customer service Web site was growing fast. An outside supplier handled the work. To answer the questions, it needed to search as many as twenty different databases. It was taking too long to respond to its inquiries and the quality of some of the answers was questionable. The company installed RightNow's SmartAssistant, which provided *Reader's Digest* with an integrated self-service knowledge base. It even scanned incoming e-mail inquiries and suggested answers. As a result, *Reader's Digest* saw the following improvements:

- 35 percent improvement in agent productivity
- 35 percent reduction in processing time
- 360-degree view of its customers and their history

United Asset Coverage (UAC) streamlined its customer service and sales representatives processes and installed Oracle's E-Business. The results were:

- 205 percent first-year ROI
- $3.4 million recovered annually in savings and revenue
- Invoice cycle time reduced from one week to two days
- Billing questions now answered in one call

EMI Industries focused on streamlining its customer communications and installed Siebel's e-Business Applications. The results were:

- 25 percent savings in verifying delivery information
- 10 percent reduction in overtime
- 10 percent reduction in inventory
- 75 percent resolution rate on the first call
- 90 percent time savings in resolving accounts receivable inquiries

iQ Net Solutions focused on its customer-relationship processes. It streamlined these processes and installed Microsoft CRM. The results were incredible:

- 234 percent ROI within five months
- Much greater commitment servicing customer needs

How Much Should We Rely on Technology?

> "Technology is not a magic bullet—if you fire technology at poorly constructed sales, marketing, or service processes, you will only end up doing inefficient and ineffective activities faster than ever before. Successful CRM often requires some serious process redesign."
> —Jim Dickie
> Partner, CSO Insights

Robert Cole, professor at the University of California at Berkeley, conducted an extensive study on how Japan and the United States were using technologies such as enterprise resource planning (ERP) and CRM. He reported that the United States was using ERP and CRM 500 percent more than Japanese organizations. Few of the Japanese organizations were using CRM and ERP, while these software packages were used extensively throughout the United States. He believes the reason for the difference was that there was a low measurable return on investment from ERP and CRM, causing Japanese organizations not to incorporate these software packages, while U.S. organizations justified using these packages based upon both direct and indirect benefits that they received.

Cole also reported that only 11 percent of the Japanese organizations had full-time chief information officers (CIOs) while 56 percent of the U.S. organizations had full-time CIOs. He also reported a vast difference in IT departments' participation in strategic planning. In the United States 51 percent of the organizations included IT while only 14 percent of the Japanese organizations did.

IT must play an important role in improving the processes within an organization. But remember, it's just one of the many tools available to you. Your best approach to process improvement is simplification. Then, and only then, should you bring in IT to do the repetitive jobs.

CAPABILITY MATURITY MODEL

Capability maturity model (CMM) is an approach accepted worldwide to improve the performance of organizations that build and maintain IT facilities. Carnegie Mellon's Software Engineering Institution developed it with input and assistance of major software development companies throughout the world. Its eighteen major areas of software engineering processes include more than 300 different practices. (*Note:* CMM is now referred to as "capability maturity model integration," or CMMI, but the following information still applies.) Unlike ISO 9001:2000, which was designed to set minimum standards, the CMM is a progressive model that's designed to give an organization milestones to mark its continuous journey to improvement. This journey consists of five distinct levels. They are:

■ Level 1—Initial: Unpredictable and poorly controlled; all organizations that haven't been evaluated are considered to be at level 1.
■ Level 2—Repeatable: Can repeat previously mastered tasks; at level 2 the basic management systems and controls are in place. IT projects are usually successful in terms of cost, schedule, and requirements. This is at the ISO 9001 certification level.
■ Level 3—Defined: Processes are characterized and fairly well understood; all of the key software processes are well documented, understood, and followed.
■ Level 4—Managed: Processes are measured and controlled; at this level all of the key processes have measurement points defined. Data are collected at these points and used to ensure success of the projects.
■ Level 5—Optimizing: Level 5 is a state of continuous process improvement; to maintain level 5, the organization must continuously demonstrate that it is improving. Few organizations have reached CMM level 5, and most of them are in India.

Each level of CMM adds additional important software and management practices specific to that maturity level. They are called key process areas (KPAs). (See figure 5.1.)

The application of technology and software approaches is enormously complex. It has to be a balanced mixture of technology, processes, and people. They all have to intermarry so that they are in complete harmony. The Systems Security Engineering organization has

Figure 5.1 CMM Levels/Key Process Areas

CMM levels	Key process areas
1. Initial	Key process areas not defined
2. Repeatable	Software quality assurance
	Software configuration management
	Document control
	Software subcontract management
	Requirements management
	Software project planning
	Software project tracking and oversight
3. Defined	Training programs
	Intergroup coordination
	Peer reviews
	Integrated software management
	Software product engineering
	Organization process focus
	Organization process definition
4. Managed	Software quality management
	Quantitative process management
5. Optimizing	Defect prevention
	Process change management
	Technology change management

developed a procedure for implementing CMM called SSE-CMM. This is an outstanding way to make best use of your technology resources. Its Web site is *www.sse-cmm.org*.

Be a smart buyer of software. Check out at what level on the CMM scale the seller's development processes are. Think twice before you buy from anyone who hasn't reached a minimum level 3.

IT PLANNING

"The time has come for us to shift from the 'T' in IT to the 'I.' It's time to learn the balance if there's to be information focus."
—Peter Drucker
Author and consultant

Because most of an excellent organization's future success is highly dependent upon technology, it's very important that it has a well-defined approach to managing its information technology resources. A nine-phase approach to managing this resource is effective.

■ Phase I—Planning for managing the technology resource

☐ Use the business plan to develop the requirements.

☐ Meet with internal and external customers to understand their needs, wants, and how they will use the output.

☐ Develop the organization's system architecture.

☐ Define what technologies and methodologies will be used.

☐ Develop the data standards.

☐ Define the technology organization's infrastructure.

☐ Define the standards and control.

■ Phase II—Deployment

☐ Perform needs assessments for internal and external organizations.

☐ Work with internal organizations to prepare value propositions.

☐ Set priorities for the workload.

☐ Select the supplier the organization will work with and the technologies.

☐ Define the data life cycle.

☐ Define the organization's support system.

☐ Pilot the support systems.

☐ Deploy the support systems.

■ Phase III—System controls and security

☐ Install a document control system.

☐ Define the data security strategies and what data are available to which people.

☐ Test to ensure controls and security work correctly.

■ Phase IV—Operations (storage and retrieval)

☐ Define the different databases (repositories).

☐ Set up procedures to control the way the data are collected and added to the databases.

☐ Set up procedures to retrieve and report information that is stored in the different databases (warehouses).

☐ Develop procedures that define by whom, when, and how data are deleted from the different databases.

■ Phase V—Facilities and network operations management

☐ Develop procedures that define how and who will manage the facilities, which may include distributed and network facilities.

■ Phase VI—Set control measurements related to the way services are provided. Having effective key performance indicators that reflect internal and external customer requirements are essential to providing excellent service.

- Phase VII—Develop information-sharing and information centers infrastructure facilities
  - ☐ Establish the internal and external communication processes, including the preparation and distribution of any needed publications.

- Phase VIII—Measure the effectiveness of the systems
  - ☐ Conduct regular audits of the technology systems.
  - ☐ Conduct regular surveys of the customers to define their level of satisfaction and future needs. These surveys should also define when services should be made obsolete.

- Phase IX—Continuous improvement
  - ☐ Use CMM as a guide for continuous improvement activities.
  - ☐ Stay abreast of technology development so that the excellent organization can stay ahead of the competition. This is absolutely essential.

To continue discussing how to improve your use of IT wouldn't meet the objectives of this book. It's sufficient that you recognize the magnitude of the impact that technology has on your organization and that you realize it's a major organizational resource that can become obsolete very quickly if you don't keep pace with the rapidly changing

> **"IS [information system] organizations with no strategy for blending internal and external resources to achieve 'best-in-class' staffing will incur 25 percent higher labor costs than those that do."**
> **—Gartner Research**

technology. As a result, you must have a very active program in place to maintain this very costly, but very valuable, resource. It may be best for you to outsource the IT activities if they're not one of your core competencies. As much as 60 percent of IT work in the United States is now outsourced to a CMM-certified supplier because it costs less and is done on schedule a higher percent of the time.

SUPPORT TECHNOLOGY RESOURCE SUMMARY

> "IT can't make up for poor management."
> —HJH

Too often people get carried away with the wonderful things that technology can do for the organization. They end up relying on IT to fix their problems. They install CRM systems and believe that they will correct their customer-related problems. The truth is IT will not correct the problems. It can help you manage the situation, but it's the processes that allow the situation to occur. IT can't make up for untrained, unmotivated, poorly directed people who are using obsolete, overly cumbersome, bureaucracy-laden processes. IT can't make up for poor management. It can help define problems and disseminate information faster than manual systems only if the people in the organization are willing to use them. An e-mail gets to a person in seconds when a memo takes days, but if the receiver doesn't open the e-mail and react to it, the IT advantage is lost. In many cases IT has made people lazy and take more time. People have a tendency to wait until the last minute to do things because they can deliver them in minutes, not in days as when they

"Data decay at a steady rate: After 18 months, everything's out of date. Unless you're taking action, your data's getting worse."
—Kermit Yensen
CEO, The Massini Group,
***Customer Relationship Management*, December 2004**

use conventional systems. I've seen e-mail bouncing back and forth for days on a problem that could have been solved in five minutes with a simple phone call. Technology has changed our business lives. Now my cell phone rings at 2 a.m. with a call from Dubai, and I am expected to answer it. It evens follows me into the bathroom. I set aside the first part of every day, seven days a week, to read and answer the sixty-two to a hundred e-mails that came in during the last twelve hours. That's two to three hours of my productive time, taking away from whatever else I need to do that day. I cannot imagine getting 100 letters in a single day or even in a week.

Technology has its advantages and disadvantages, but it's a lot like waging a war. If your enemy is using automated rifles and bazookas, you can't win by using bows and arrows. It may be costly to supply your people with the required technology to keep up with your competition with no increase in sales, but if you don't invest in the better systems, your competition will have a significant business advantage.

"IT is needed to keep market, not to grow market."

—HJH

CHAPTER VI

FINANCIAL MANAGEMENT

"In business, profits aren't the only thing, but it's hard
to think of what's more important."

—HJH

Financial capital is a critical resource for all organizations. Those that manage this resource well have a high probability of achieving excellence in their operations. It doesn't matter how good you are in the other four pillars. If the organization isn't good at financial management, the organization will fail. More organizations go out of business for financial reasons than any other reason by a factor of three to one.

**"Profit is like oxygen—
essential for our survival,
but not the reason for our
existence."**
—Lance Secretan
Reclaiming Higher Ground

THE ROLE OF THE CHIEF FINANCIAL OFFICER

Financial management is concerned with raising, using, and investing financial capital. How successfully chief financial officers (CFOs) perform these three basic tasks usually determines the success or failure of the organizations they lead. The role of the CFO is no longer limited largely to internal financial control. The external aspects of the job are equally, if not more, important. Savvy CFOs take the latter seriously because they realize that managing the organization's relations with the outside world—the banks, brokerage firms, investment houses, fund managers, the SEC, rating agencies, the press, shareholders, and so on—is supremely important to the financial health of the organization. An important aspect of financial management is risk management.

Changes brought about by globalization and changes in the structure of capital markets and financial intermediaries have radically altered the role of the modern CFO in recent years. The instruments available to the CFO to raise capital and invest corporate cash are increasingly numerous and complex. The New Economy, driven by the Internet and electronic media, has far-reaching implications for the way corporate finances are raised and invested.

To be successful, the CFO must possess significant insight and knowledge about currency and interest-rate products as well as risk management options available in the market. An in-depth knowledge of these instruments will not only enhance an organization's creditworthiness; it will improve its profitability.

Today's CFO has access to a variety of financial instruments to hedge risks. These include currency and interest rate swaps, forward contracts, futures and options, currencies and commodities, and many other derivatives. Effective use of these risk management instruments can produce great returns for the organization and build value.

Most organizations have business interests outside their home countries. Large organizations can no longer afford to ignore markets outside their borders. Globalization has opened new frontiers for business organizations willing to go after opportunities in both emerging and developed countries all over the world. While this presents exciting profit opportunities, it also introduces significant risks that the CFO must manage. Although risk management products provide value, they may not offer the most effective hedging strategy for many clients. In some instances, access to longer-term risk management products may be possible, but it would entail an organization's posting collateral in ways that could be costly.

> **"The accounting scandals weren't all bad. Yes, they shook investor confidence. But they're also driving overdue changes in financial reporting."**
> **—Gregory J. Millman**
> *The Chief Executive,* **January–February 2003**

The process starts with the identification and measurement of the risk arising from an organization's exposure to financial price movements. The next step is to select an appropriate hedging mechanism to mitigate the assessed risk and cover the associated cost.

To generate revenues, organizations must incur operating expenses. They also must invest money in real estate, buildings, equipment, and in working capital to support their business operations.

The CFO's Investor Mindset

The modern CFO must have an investor mindset. He or she must think and act like an investor, which means taking into account what the investor in the organization's stock wants. (See figure 6.1.) The size of the investor population in the United States has more than doubled in the past two decades. These investors' attitudes, needs, and concerns are of critical importance to the CFO, who has to worry not only about how to raise debt and negotiate with banks and financial intermediaries but also about the shifting, and sometimes psychological, behaviors of the average stockholder. To have an investor mind-set:

■ *The CFO must focus more on the economic reality of the business than its accounting reality.* As every CFO knows, financial statements prepared by accountants don't necessarily reflect the economic reality of the organization. Accounting that is governed by the Generally Accepted Accounting Principles (GAAP) is a conservative discipline. It's backward-looking and can tell you only what happened to the organization in the past. The CFO, however, must make investor decisions based on the current and future economic reality of the business. Financial officers who spend too much time poring over the past performance of the organization, as captured by its accounting records, cannot be effective or visionary leaders in the New Economy. This new reality acknowledges the value of an organization's intangible assets, such as patents and trademarks as well as the special know-how and reputations of the executive team. These valuable intangibles are not recognized under GAAP, which measures results in terms of net profits. The savvy CFO must measure results by the business's cash flows, too. Today excellent organizations are reporting both GAAP data and economic value-added (EVA) data.

"We very deliberately choose to report both GAAP and EVA results—GAAP for reasons of consistency and comparability with our peers, and regulatory compliance. But we believe EVA is ultimately the best economic representation of our business performance."
—**Michael Volkema**
CEO, Herman Miller

GAAP reports provide a view of the past, and EVA data provide you with the information needed to manage the organization and determine its true worth.

- *The CFO must look forward and recognize the time value of money.* One of the most important responsibilities of the CFO is to allocate financial resources to capital investments, which are necessary for the survival and growth of the business. In making such investment decisions, the CFO must fully recognize that "time is money" and use discounting methods that reflect the present value of future streams. CFOs often spend time and effort analyzing sunk costs, or expenses that are already incurred or transactions that have already taken place. That's a wasted effort, which adds no value to the future of the business. Warren Buffet, the guru of value investing, stated that the intrinsic value is the present value of future expected performance. Capital budgeting is about making choices and selecting investment options that give maximum value to the organization. It's extremely important that such analysis exclude considerations based on what has already been invested.

- *The CFO must account for the cost of lost opportunities when making financial decisions.* The concept of opportunity cost, which is well founded in economic theory, comes in handy for financial management, too. Financial officers must worry as much about missing attractive opportunities for resource allocation as managing existing opportunities. In a dynamic economic environment, not investing in the right project at the right time can cost an organization heavily in lost business opportunities, market share, or even a leadership position in its industry. Financial management must be a central part of the organization's business strategy.

- *The CFO should understand the risk/return concept very well.* This requires that return on investment follows the risks assumed. No investment, by definition, is risk-free because no one can be absolutely certain about the future, and investing is basically about assessing future performance by making assumptions about how certain factors will behave. Some of these factors, such as the way the economy may behave, can't be controlled by the CFO or the executive team. Therefore, there will be an element of risk in each financial decision. The objective should be how to mitigate that risk and not how to eliminate it. The intuitive relationship between the risk and the return provides useful guidance to

Figure 6.1 Examples of Areas in Which Organizations Should Think Like Investors

Investing	Raising capital
Capital budgeting	Bank credit
New products	Selling bonds
Cash management	Selling equity
New technology	Leasing
Plant closing	Securitization
Mergers and acquisitions	Factoring

financial officers. Appropriately pricing the risk involved in any financial transaction is not only critical to the success of the transaction; it also forces the financial manager to realize that managing risk is central to effective financial management. Walter Wriston, former chairman of Citibank, wrote, "We read in our newspapers and even business magazines solemn words about "risky investments" *and* "risky loans" from writers who do not seem to realize that these phrases are as redundant as talking about a one-story bungalow." The fact is all investments and loans are risky because their value is dependent on calculated guesses about future performance.

■ *The CFO must understand the value of diversification of portfolio as a risk management tool.* Successful organizations seek to diversify both the sources of the capital they raise and the investments they make. The New Economy has empowered CFOs in many ways. They now have access to practically all markets in real time. They have powerful financial tools and models to guide them in their analysis. They can make investments in major international markets online. All of these capabilities provide the organization a wide range of diversification opportunities all over the world.

■ *The CFO must focus on value creation.* As a manager of the financial resources of the organization, the CFO serves as an agent of the shareholders because his or her decisions must all be targeted to creating corporate value and thus enhancing the shareholders' interests. Decisions about declaring dividends or plowing funds back into the organization must be guided by what is in the best interest of the investor/shareholder. That decision isn't always easy to make and unless the financial officer considers all possible investment opportunities open to the organization, he or she can't establish an optimum dividend payout. Knowing the alignment of management and owners of the organization is useful to creating value.

■ *The CFO must make investment decisions based on reliable information and analysis.* In today's e-economy, senior executives, including CFOs, are bombarded with an overload of information. They need to sift through a huge pile of data to make informed investment decisions. The organization's knowledge management system must accommodate this need and provide reliable and analytical inputs to the financial officer.

Project Financing

Organizations everywhere use various forms of project financing to raise capital for their expansion or modernization programs. The past two decades have brought a huge increase in global interest in project finance as a tool for investment. Project finance is a technique used to structure new investment around a project's own operating cash flow and assets without recourse to sponsor guarantees. It's a way to reduce investment risk and raise capital at a low cost. Without sufficient expertise in project finance and the skills to alleviate associated risks, CFOs won't succeed in today's competitive business environment.

CFO and Corporate Governance

Financial management continues to play a key role in corporate governance. Financial executives have growing responsibilities to ensure financial transparency in all aspects of the business operation. These days, after the scandal of Enron and others, government regulatory institutions as well as credit rating agencies all pay closer attention to the way organizations present information to the public. It's a sign of tightened regulation that CEOs are required to attest to the accuracy and credibility of the financial information produced by their organizations. They can no longer relegate that responsibility to the financial officers of the organization alone. Keeping good books makes good business sense. It's also a legal necessity that can mean the difference between sustainable growth and bankruptcy.

EXCELLENT ORGANIZATIONS' FINANCIAL MANAGEMENT

Although this discussion has concentrated on the CFO's activities and responsibilities related to financial management, they play only a small part in the total financial management system. The CFO's role in financial management is similar to the chief quality officer's (CQO) role in the organization's quality management system. Both executives are the watchdogs for their disciplines, helping to set objectives, provide direction, and measure results, but the real financial and quality management is performed by all the other parts of the organization.

> "Accounting's function is to signal to potential suppliers of capital and labor the productive capacity of an organization, so that capital can flow to its most productive uses. But the productive capacity of an organization is no longer revealed by its financial statements."
> —Ira Solomon
> Head, Department of Accountancy, University of Illinois, Urbana-Champaign

Excellent organizations have instilled into the hearts of each and every person the feeling of personal responsibility for maximizing the use of the organization's finances. They instill into all employees a feeling that each dollar they spend is like their own money. They prepare all employees to look at alternatives each time they make a decision that has a financial impact. Their employees automatically ask questions such as, "Is it cheaper and just as effective to rent a car or take a taxi?"

The excellent organization trains its people how to prepare accurate estimates. A good estimate doesn't include too little or too much money. Annual natural work teams' (departments') budgets should be accurate to plus or minus 3 percent. The manager's performance plan should include a line item related to the accuracy of his or her financial estimates and financial management. The same is true for return-on-investment estimates, in which a plus or minus 5 percent accuracy is acceptable.

"Given a choice between building your business on large debt or facing a firing squad... choose the firing squad. There's a chance the firing squad might miss."
—Unknown auditor

Just as a chief quality officer can't ensure the quality of the organization's output, the CFO can't ensure that the organization's finances are managed properly. Financial management is everyone's job, not just the CFO's job.

TYPICAL RATIOS

The following is a list of typical ratios that are used to measure an organization's performance.

- Investment ratios
  - ☐ Long-term liabilities to capital = Long-term liabilities
    - ▲ Current assets—current liabilities
    Note: Points out the possible need for future borrowing

  - ☐ Earnings per share = Profit attributable to shareholders
    - ▲ Number of shares issued
    Note: Used to measure profit performance

- Performance ratios
  - ☐ Return on capital = Return rate
    - ▲ Capital employed
    Note: Measures the effectiveness of the way an organization is using its core financing

☐ Return on sales = Revenue
  ▲ Sales
  Note: Measures how successfully the organization is using its core financing

☐ Capital turnover = Sales
  ▲ Capital employed
  Note: Measures the relationship between sales and core financing

■ Performance ratios
  ☐ Capital turnover performance = Net sales
    ▲ Capital employed
    Note: Used to evaluate management effectiveness regarding sales in relation to assets employed

  ☐ Debtors to working capital = Debtors
    ▲ Current assets—current liabilities
    Note: Measures the dependence of working capital on receivables

  ☐ Gross profit to net sales = Gross profit
    ▲ Net sales
    Note: Used to measure the productivity of sales

  ☐ Return on capital employed = Net profit before taxes
    ▲ Capital employed
    Note: Measures the earnings of a sufficient return on investment in assets to ensure perpetuation of the investment/profit/investment cycle

  ☐ Creditor turnover = Creditors × 365 days
    ▲ Costs of goods sold expressed in days
    Note: Measures supplier bill-paying cycle time

  ☐ Marketing, G & A (general and administrative) = Marketing, G & A expenses
    ▲ Expenses to net sales—Net sales
    Note: Measures if the amount spent on administration is out of line with sales

  ☐ Debtor turnover = Debtors × 365 days
    ▲ Sales revenue expressed in days
    Note: Measures internal credit and collections efficiency

☐ Net sales to fixed assets = Net sales
   ▲ Net fixed assets
   Note: Measures how effectively the organization is investing its fixed assets

☐ Net sales to working capital = Net sales
   ▲ Working capital
   Note: Measures the demands placed upon working capital to support sales

☐ Return on sales = Group profit before taxes
   ▲ Net sales
   *Note: Meas*ures the profit per item sold; it's the best measure of overall organization effectiveness

These ratios may seem a little confusing to some people, but it's essential that every manager understand them and use them to adjust his or her work plan.

FINANCIAL MANAGEMENT SUMMARY

The mighty dollar, yen, euro, pound, ruble—whatever you call it—has been the primary business driver since the beginning of time and rightly so. You go into business to make money. People all need it to buy food, clothing, medicine, shelter, books, and much more. They go to work and sell their lives, minute by minute, hour by hour. The people who invest their time and money in the organization have a right to make a fair return on their investment. Organizations that do a poor job of managing their finances cannot and should not stay in business.

All managers must be good financial managers, spending each dollar as though it were their own. All employees must be misers about how they spend their time to be sure that the organization is getting its money's worth out of the progress that's made. Ask yourself, "Would you pay someone else what you are getting to do the job that you are performing?" If the answer is "no," then look for ways to add more value to the organization. Be sure you know what you are costing the organization. It's a lot more than your salary. Often the variable cost—insurance, benefits, equipment, space, direct support-related costs, and so on—is more than two times the individual's salary.

This chapter was purposely kept short. It could have covered how all managers must be trained to understand how to control their financial obligations and how to prepare and manage a budget. It could have covered how to get financial help from venture capitalists to start an organization. It could have covered how to handle bankruptcy. It could have covered the best way to use surplus money. It could have covered ways to reduce income tax. Instead, it takes a look at only some of the issues that are important in managing an organization's finances. It doesn't attempt to make CPAs out of readers. This will disappoint some and make others happy. If you fall in the latter group, you should buy yourself a book on financial management. And if you're among the former, you no doubt already have the book the "happy" reader should reach for next.

> "Money is the root of all evil, unless you are cold, hungry, or sick; then it is the beginning of hope and happiness."
> —HJH

(*Note:* Chapter 6 was prepared by Abdul Rahman Awl.)

CHAPTER VII

OTHER RESOURCES

A number of resources that have to be managed in all organizations still remain to be addressed. For example:

- Products and services
- Property/brick and mortar
- Equipment
- Investors
- Inventory
- Customers

All of these are extremely important and I could write a book, or at least a chapter, on each of them, but to keep this section from getting too robust, I will comment on just these six items.

> "More important than our people are our products and services."
> —HJH

PRODUCTS AND SERVICES

A product or service is a key asset. Selecting the product/service is critical to the success of every organization. You can have outstanding people doing outstanding work producing a product of superb quality and go bankrupt if there isn't a market for the output. You're not going to have a successful business manufacturing amplifier tubes for TV sets or manufacturing mustache wax no matter how good your employees are or how hard they try. Having the right product available at the right time is key to any organization's success. Being too early or too late is very costly.

Marketing Resources

It's equally important to know when to remove or change your output. All the money and effort invested in research and development (R&D) is directed at developing marketable assets. The art of understanding where to invest your R&D spending and to know when to replace the present offerings is all part of resource management.

Marketing's primary role is to work with future, potential, and present customers to identify their future needs and to nurture and romance the customer to the point that they are excited about buying the organization's products and services. Marketing has let most organizations down by performing poorly in the following areas:

- Poor forecasting
- Lack of accountability
- Inadequate follow-through

Poor Forecasting

Marketing's responsibility is to identify future products, target-cost structures, relevant market windows, and volume. The high failure rate of new product introduction is a testimonial to the poor job that it's doing. Inaccurate market forecasting has caused a lot of equipment to be underused, or at the other extreme, put the organization in a position in which it can't meet customer demands. Companies such as Campbell's Soup won many awards for its innovative products, most of which didn't sell when presented to the general public. In the 1980s poor market forecasting led IBM to pour most of its R&D resources into mainframe development instead of PC development, resulting in its losing the lucrative PC market.

Not only are marketing's projections of quantity bad, but its analyses of when and how long the product window will be open are also faulty. Marketing must better understand and project the technological developments related to the industry, the competition's strategy, and customers' changing expectations, because product obsolescence and R&D funding is highly driven by these projections.

Lack of Accountability

The management team in most organizations accepts marketing's poor performance as being a way of life; management has been made to think that marketing is an art, not a science. It's a guessing game, like throwing darts at a dartboard. Marketing projections that are plus or minus 20 percent, 30 percent, or 40 percent are accepted without discussion. Marketing must be held accountable for its projections. A management system must be put in place that compares actual to marketing forecasts in areas such as:

- Marketing product requirements to released engineering specifications
- Sales volume for six, twelve, and eighteen months
- Completeness of input into the engineering specifications
- Accuracy of the support costs projections

Follow-Through

Marketing functions have a tendency to develop their market forecasts and throw them over the wall to engineering, never being held accountable for their adequacy and accuracy. As a result, frequently the final product isn't aligned with the marketing definitions. Marketing should be responsible for following through and ensuring that products/service specifications agree with its input, or at a minimum, meet the requirements set forth within its input.

Other Functions

Other functions also have a lot to do with providing high-quality products and services, functions such as R&D, manufacturing, sales, customer-call centers, and so on. But this chapter is limited to marketing because it has the biggest opportunity to improve, more than any other function in most organizations, and it has done the least to improve.

PROPERTY: BRICK AND MORTAR

Property is the facilities you invest in, your buildings, offices, and stores. It represents your image to the outside world. The organization may have started in a garage in back of the house, but that's not the image most organizations want to present to the general public. Clean, well-organized facilities that are customer- and employee-friendly are a must for all excellent organizations. One Japanese company was doing a supplier survey and observed a crack in a bathroom window. Based on this, the company believed that management didn't take good care of things and so didn't buy from the supplier. Although you may have departments that are completely dedicated to facility maintenance, maintenance has to be made everyone's responsibility. Have your employees use what the Japanese call the 5S method:

- *Seiri*—Sort things out; keep only needed items.
- *Seiton*—Put things in order, organize them, ready to use.
- *Seiso*—Keep things neat and clean.
- *Seiketsu*—Clean after use; leave everything in running order.
- *Shitsuke*—Practice discipline; follow standards.

Of course, property management includes careful consideration about location and whether you buy, lease, or sell the facilities.

By consolidating data centers, IBM was able to reduce information technology (IT) spending by 31 percent—that was a total savings of more than $2 billion. In the late 1980s and early 1990s, small organizations were the trend. Today small groups are giving way to large organizations because business leaders realize that consolidation is less expensive and more effective.

EQUIPMENT MANAGEMENT

Organizations have much of their resources tied up in equipment. This includes things such as computers, software, desks, milling machines, cars, trucks, telephone systems, and so on. Having the right equipment can make the difference between success and failure, but having good equipment isn't the total answer to equipment management. It must be maintained and used. The employees must be empowered and trained to do basic ongoing maintenance to the equipment they use. The maintenance department then can focus on major breakdowns and complex maintenance procedures. This is a very effective way to help keep equipment in top running order. Use of equipment in which you have a major investment is critical to operational effectiveness. Having appropriate maintenance and calibration recall systems are a must. Your equipment must be operationally ready or you are losing money. In one recent study, Harrington Institute found that because of equipment downtime, the company's line was working at only 72 percent of its potential capacity.

INVESTORS

Organizations are formed because someone has a good idea that will fulfill a customer's need, but that's only the starting point. Without people and organizations that believe in the idea to the point that they are willing to invest their hard-earned money, nothing can happen. The investors, who believe in what the organization is trying to accomplish, represent one of the most valuable resources that the organization has. Many of these investors are pension funds or retired individuals; in the case of retired investors, they depend on the organization to generate sufficient profit so they can pay for their food and housing. This means that the organization must make effective use of their money to ensure that their return on investment is greater than it would be in a no-risk investment such as a bank account, greater than the inflation rate, and better than they could get by investing in another organization with equivalent risks. This requires management to maintain an excellent communication system that keeps the investors well informed with honest and factual information. It requires management to price its product and services so that they generate a profit, which allows the organization to pay attractive dividends and causes the stock price to rise at a rate that is greater than the Standards & Poor's index.

Too many organizations forget about how important dividends are to their investors. They give raises to the employees and big increases to the managers. They even cut prices to make the customer happy. But they forget the people whose money they are using. Dividends should go up at the same rate as the executive's salary. IBM is a good example of this bad practice. When things got tough in the 1990s, it cut its dividends by 75 percent.

Now that things are good again, it hasn't restored the dividend level, although it's paying its executives a lot more money. The result is that the employees, who worked for IBM for thirty to forty-five years and put 10 percent to 15 percent of their pay into stock every week so that the dividends would give them a good living standard when they retired, are now receiving just 25 percent of what they were planning on. This has resulted in a very significant drop in IBM's retirees' living standard.

INVENTORY MANAGEMENT

Inventory management is the skill of minimizing the cost and risk of incoming, in-process, and final goods inventory. Inventory is a costly part of every organization's operation. It represents the costs of the materials and labor that go into producing the inventory, plus the cost of the floor space that the inventory occupies. Inventory costs also include the costs of the money that was used to produce the item. These very high costs have driven organizations to develop a number of inventory reduction approaches. Among them are one-minute-process changeover, single minute exchange of die (SMED), *kanban,* total productive maintenance (TPM), lean, cellular manufacturing, *poka-yoke, kaizen* blast, just-in-time production flow, single unit build, and build to order. Much of the effort to date has been directed at reducing in-process inventory. Toyota Motor Corp. led the auto industry in just-in-time. Just-in-time is good, but controlling finished goods inventory is even more important. When Toyota was having its suppliers deliver components to its assembly line every day to keep in-process inventory down, it had thousands of cars sitting in U.S. receiving docks that it couldn't sell. If you're going to have inventory, it's best to have it at the component level, rather than in finished goods, because your investment is much less.

Although low levels of inventory are desirable, low inventory levels also represent a very significant exposure to risk. Out-of-inventory costs run in the billions of dollars per year for U.S. companies. Larry Kellam, former director of supply-network innovation at Procter & Gamble, notes that reducing out-of-stock products by 10 percent to 20 percent could boost its annual sales by anywhere from $400 million to $ 1.2 billion.

Another disadvantage of low inventories is that any disruption in the supply chain can shut down an organization because of parts shortages. One trucking strike in Germany cost the country 3 percent of its yearly gross national product. With the increased trends in single-source suppliers, a fire or a strike or a natural disaster such as a flood can quickly shut down its customers.

The challenge for inventory management is to keep the correct balance between customer demands, inventory costs, and risks related to the supply chain. This is a delicate balance that requires a well-designed risk and cost analysis.

CUSTOMERS AS A RESOURCE

You can't overlook the organization's customers as an important part of the organization's resources. Too often organizations get so involved in finding new customers and growing their market share that they take their present customers for granted. It's estimated that the cost of finding a new customer is ten times the cost of keeping the current customers satisfied. For example, suppose an organization has 1,000 customers and it wants to grow by 10 percent, the average cost to obtain a new customer is $400, and the past retention rate has been 80 percent with no special focus on the present customers. This would mean that, if there were no change in the customer relationship strategy, the sales force would need to acquire 300 new customers—200 customers to make up for the loss of current customers and 100 to make up for the 10 percent growth in sales. That would be a total of 300 new customers at $400 each for a total cost of $120,000. If the sales force invested $40 in each current customer, it would cost $40,000 to keep the current customers and another $40,000 to gain the additional 100 new customers for a total of $80,000, which is a $40,000 (50 percent) reduction in cost.

> "Amazons and the Priceline. coms of the world have developed an enormous franchise in a very short amount of time because they started with the customer and what the customer needed."
> —**Nigel Morris**
> **President and COO,**
> **Capital One Financial Corp.**

Customer care requires a consistent and methodical yet creative approach that will turn customer outreach into collaborative innovation. This means that you need to go beyond having satisfied customers to making them loyal allies.

Excellent customer-care processes result in excellent customer-satisfaction results. Four key groups often have been overlooked in an organization's improvement programs. They are:

- Sales
- Marketing
- Customer call centers
- Customer service centers

> "The best hedge against uncertainty is to be close to the customer."
> —**Rosabeth Moss Kanter**
> **Harvard Business School**

Most improvement processes have focused on products, development engineering, suppliers, and manufacturing. The products are important, but equally and perhaps even more important are the service processes that directly interact with the organization's customers. Organizations lose more customers over poor service than over poor products. These four customer-interface groups play the single most important role in obtaining and keeping customer satisfaction levels high.

Four major characteristics are prevalent in all excellent organizations. They are:

- They have a well-defined service strategy, which highlights the real priorities of their customers.

- Their front-line employees like people and are interested in them. They make a good assessment of the customers' current situations, their frames of mind, and their needs.
- They have developed customer-friendly systems. Their systems are designed for the customers rather than for the organization.
- They keep their commitments to their customers. They have follow-up systems to ensure that any commitment made to the customer is met on schedule.

Only two activities count in any organization:
- Making things
- Selling them

All employees who are not directly involved in these two areas must be mindful that their jobs are supportive of these two activities.

If your customers don't think they are being served as well as they could be, they will move on to another supplier. A typical organization will lose 10 percent to 30 percent of its customer base each year, while an excellent organization will lose less than 5 percent.

Customers look to these four customer-care groups to provide them with excellent service, as though they were the only customer that the organization has. You might hate to stand in line waiting to check in at the airport, but when you get to the counter, you want the attendant to be friendly and to take all the time necessary to process your reservation and explain what you need to do to make your flight. These conflicting customer attitudes present a serious problem for the organization and also a very important challenge. Customers expect five things each time they contact any one of these four critical groups. They are:
- Accuracy
- Timeliness
- Responsiveness
  - Caring
  - Polite
  - Knowledgeable

> "The average business loses 15 percent to 35 percent of its customers each year due to poor sales or customer service."
> —**David B. Puglia**
> **Vice president, Aspect Communications/Microsoft**

- Reliable service (dependability)
- Clean, neat, attractive tangibles
  - Physical surroundings
  - Personal appearance

The sum of all the customers' perceived positive and negative evaluations of all their contacts with an organization defines the customers' perception of organizational excellence. Unfortunately, negative experiences are weighted twenty times more heavily than positive experiences. Understanding the customer's perception is critical to providing high levels of customer satisfaction. It's not enough to provide excellent service—the customers must perceive it as excellent. They need to be *wowed* by the experience. They need to feel that this is an organization that knows them, respects them, and values them as a preferred customer.

> "Ultimately, your goal is to enhance the lifetime value of your most profitable customers and leverage what this brings to your company."
> —Joe W. Forehand
> CEO, Accenture

Every executive team plays a very important role in customer perception. What it does, what it says, and where it says it are all-important. Microsoft's executive team stays close to its customers by making sales calls. That includes the CEO and COO. Robert J. Herbold, retired CEO of Microsoft, stated, "It [executive sales call] signals that the customer is very important, and that, consequently, the customer says, 'Wow, that's an organization that is clearly viewing me as a valued customer.'"

> "Information about the outside is obsolete quickly, especially today when technologies crisscross, and markets and distribution channels change four times a week. The only way you can get outside information is to go out with your customers."
> —Peter Drucker
> Author and consultant

Jeff Bezos, founder of Amazon.com, sends e-mails to customers asking them to respond to him personally with their thoughts. Richard Branson, president of Virgin Atlantic Airlines, comes to Gatwick to apologize for late flights. The chairman of EMC, Dick Egan, spends more than 50 percent of his time with the organization's customers. These are just typical examples of how the executive team needs to lead the customer-care process.

The excellent organization consistently provides surprisingly good service to its external customers. To provide surprisingly good service, you must have surprisingly good people. What characteristics make up an organization that develops "surprisingly good people" resources?

- Properly selecting employees
- Providing superb training
- Securing competitive equipment
- Developing great communication with management and even better communication with customers
- Selecting management that is concerned about the employees and their needs
- Hiring employees who are concerned about their customers' needs and expectations
- Developing honest and straight-talking managers
- Promoting the understanding that customers may not always be right, but they are never wrong
- Developing managers who understand that employees aren't the problem but they can be part of the solution
- Preparing clear, understandable definitions of customer expectations and feedback systems that measure the degree of compliance

- Hiring managers who solve problems and don't place blame
- Hiring managers who build people and don't use them
- Setting targets that challenge the individual
- Promoting the belief that you are never good enough
- Establishing a reward system that recognizes surprisingly good service

This requires all organizations to invest heavily in training all employees, with even more emphasis on the individuals who make up these four customer-care groups. (For example, Marriott spends more than $20 million a year training employees who interact with its customers.) At a minimum, all employees should receive forty hours of training per year.

A study conducted by the White House Office of Consumer Affairs found that customers who complain about products and services are more likely to do business with companies that upset them than the individuals who don't complain. If a complaint is resolved, between 54 percent and 70 percent of people would do business with the company again. This reaches 95 percent if the customer thinks that the complaint is resolved expeditiously. It's likely that satisfied customers will tell five more people about the product or service, while dissatisfied customers spread the word to an average of twenty-four other potential customers.

It's very important that you really consider the impact that you have on a customer and the organization's future whenever you take exception to a customer's complaint. The cost of losing a current customer usually has a much greater impact on the organization than providing the customer with a new product. For example:

- The lifetime costs of losing a customer in the auto industry runs $180,000.
- The yearly costs of losing a customer in the supermarket industry are $4,800.
- The yearly costs of losing a customer in the appliance industry are $210.
- The yearly costs of losing a customer in the banking industry are $110 per year in profit.

> "Don't ask, 'Is everything OK?' Instead ask, 'What's
> the one thing I could do better next time?' "
> —HJH

It's easy to see that supermarkets should seldom question a customer complaint about a product the customer claims is faulty. *An organization mustn't just handle complaints; it must go out of its way to encourage complaints and to solve them.* Studies prove that less than 5 percent of people who are unhappy with products and services complain to the organization. The other 95 percent—the silent majority—just walk away from these products in favor of the competition. The organization's objective should be to double the number of complaints it receives, not because the products and services perform worse than before, but because the communication system has improved significantly and has broken down the customers' reluctance to share their thoughts with the organization. A restaurant owner shouldn't ask a customer, "Was there anything wrong with the meal?" or "How was the meal?" What the owner should say is, "Can you suggest any way that we can improve our service or food?" A question such as this doesn't put the customer in a position in which he or she is complaining but instead is actually being helpful by offering advice and suggestions.

> **"We look every month at the customers we lose. To me those mean that we failed in the relationship."**
> **—Alexandra Lebenthal**
> **President, Lebenthal & Co.**

Members of the sales team must be motivated and competitive. They must be individuals who are driven to win and truly enjoy working with people. An old saying goes, "Give me a person who is in debt and I will show you a great salesperson." This may be true, but it can be overdone. In excellent organizations the sales personnel are highly motivated and driven to meet quotas, but they are also rewarded for ensuring that the products and services that they sell truly represent value to their customers. For this very reason, many of the excellent organizations have decreased the emphasis on sales commissions and refocused their reward systems based on customer satisfaction.

In the movie *Miracle on 34th Street*, Macy's Santa Claus sends customers to Gimbels when Macy's didn't have what they needed or when Gimbels had it at a better price. You may reason that this happens only in the movies, but the concept is a legitimate approach to building customer loyalty.

Attitudes in the sales forces of organizations classified as "excellent organizations" are very different from those in typical organizations. Figure 7.1 provides a list of characteristics of the old type of sales force that is prevalent in most organizations and the new type of sales force that is prevalent in excellent organizations.

> **"You'd be surprised how much outside information about customers and noncustomers companies simply do not have, and in many cases, cannot get. And yet, you don't make your decisions on what goes on inside your company; you shouldn't, at least."**
> **—Peter Drucker**
> **Author and consultant**

The discussion to this point has primarily focused on sales. Marketing, customer-call centers, and customer-service groups also have an equal potential to detract or contribute to high levels of customer satisfaction. All four groups require equal focus on performance improvement and customer satisfaction for the organization to excel. For the sake of brevity, improvement activities for the other three groups won't be discussed in detail. But some of the more effective tools that focus on maintaining customer resources and that those interface groups should have in their toolboxes are:

- Customer-relationship management (CRM) software
- Customer surveys
- Business to customer (B2C) software
- Balanced scorecard
- Indirect poor-quality cost measurement system

Figure 7.1 Old Versus New Styles of Sales Forces

Old style of sales force	New style of sales force
Does what needs to be done	Knows the whole business
Knows the product	Knows the customer's business
Every sale is unique.	Every sale is based upon the standard process, modified to the customer.
Works hard to look good.	Makes the organization look good. Takes pride in the organization.
Resists any type of measurements	Uses measurements to benchmark activities
Monetarily motivated	Performance motivated
Sells the products	Sells solutions
Gets new customers	Keeps the proven customers
Changes job often	Long-term commitment
Sells the product even if it is not the best answer for the customer	Helps the customer find the best answer even if it is another organization's product
Finds ways to beat the system	Changes systems that are bottlenecks to progress
Heavy-handed selling	Haggle-free buying
Measured by number of new sales	Measured by customer retention

- Knowledge management
- Complaint handling (corrective action tracking) systems
- Peer reviews
- Customers as part of the design process

"Buying the CR solution—that's the 1 percent. Making it work is the 99 percent."
—Jon Anton
Director of Benchmark Research, Purdue University Center for Customer-Driven Quality

Ford's former chairman Donald E. Petersen put it this way, "If we are not customer-driven, our car won't be either." The past chairman of Premier Industrial Corp., Morton L. Mandel, stated, "To us, customer service is the main event."

Customer Lead or Customer Followed

Excellent organizations cannot afford to wait until the customer has a need and then fill that need. Excellent organizations have to be able to project what is possible and then create the market. They must be well ahead of their customers, offering new and exciting products that their customers never even dreamed about. No one asked for the Sony Walkman, VCRs, electric lights, minivans, or the World Wide Web. Customers ask for their present needs. They seldom have the technical know-how to realize what is possible. The excellent organization has to have the vision of the future and bring that vision to reality. This is what wows the customers.

"The way customers are getting serviced is completely changing."
—Greg Gianferte
CEO, Right Now Technologies

As a result of Dow Corning's change to a customer-oriented focus, revenue growth reached the double digits. This transformation reinforced four points:

- A change in business strategy must be reflected in every aspect and every level of the company.
- Success is no longer about technology leadership or cutting-edge products alone.
- Success requires achieving a competitive advantage even if it disrupts the status quo.
- Companies must redefine success and regularly reinvent the business—in good times and bad.

"The customer cannot articulate unmet and emerging needs. If you ask them, 'How do you improve this?' you generally end up with incremental improvement. So it's very important to start with game-changing ideas internally and then go validate or prioritize them with the customer."
—Jay Desai
Institute of Global Competitiveness

(Source: Charles Butter, *Customer Relationship Management*, June 2004.)

Winning and Losing Customers

International customers are attracted to your organization for four reasons, in the order shown in figure 7.2.

Product and service capability is driven by using the latest technology and using present technology in more creative ways. Trust is based upon experience and reputation. It reflects the faith that the customer has in your ability to meet your cost, schedule, and performance commitments. Price today ties in directly with value. Customers are looking at getting the best performance at the least cost. Quality reflects more than just the initial view of the products and services they buy. It reflects the quality of the total organization, the reliability of its products, and the capability of its sales and service personnel. You lose customers for the same four reasons that you attract them, but in a different order.

Figure 7.2 Win Customers/ Lose Customers

Win customers	Lose customers
1. Capabilities	1. Trust
2. Trust	2. Quality
3. Price	3. Capabilities
4. Quality	4. Price

"Of all your resources, your present customers are one of your most valuable resources."
—HJH

All Customers Are Not Equal

Theoretically, all customers are equal, and good always wins over evil. But everyone knows that isn't true. In the movie *Where the Boys Are,* two girls come into a restaurant and ask for two cups of hot water. When the waiter arrives, they add ketchup to the water, get some free crackers, and enjoy the soup and crackers while watching the boys pass by. When they ask for a second cup of water, the restaurant owner says, "Yes, but do me a favor. Tomorrow go to my competitor across the street."

All businesses have customers that cost them more to service than they pay for. You would like these customers to go to your competitors. On the other hand, you have customers who stay with you and allow you to make a reasonable profit each time they buy from you. As consultants, Harrington Institute sees this all the time. Customers and potential customers want free information all the time. They want very detailed proposals and then take the information provided and do it themselves. Here is a typical example. A customer asked the institute to turn in a proposal to do a benchmarking study. The customer came back stating it liked the proposal but would like more detail about how the study would be conducted. We provided a detailed process flow. It then came back to say that before the executive team would approve the proposal, it had to have a typical agenda for a meeting with a benchmarking partner. We supplied this and then the customer said that to get the proposal approved, it wanted to know the names of the organizations that we would visit. We provided this information and then we were told the project was put on hold for the time being. Later we found out that the customer conducted the benchmarking study without our participation. This doesn't sound ethical, but this is the way many organizations operate. It's important that you select your customers carefully. You probably don't want 10 percent of the market, and your competition is trying to unload it. Robert Cole of the University of California at Berkeley has offered the following relationship theory:

■ Try to attract customers you can keep.
■ Try to keep the customers you attract.
■ Try to attract high-value customers.
■ Try to turn your customers into salespeople.

Murray Raphel, co-author with Neil Raphel of *Up the Loyalty Ladder* (HarperCollins, 1995), developed the following customer-relationship grid. (The object of any organization is to move from a suspect to an advocate customer.)

1. Suspect customer
2. Prospect customer
3. Customer
4. Repeat customer
5. Loyal customer
6. Advocate customer

OTHER RESOURCES SUMMARY

You've gotten this far into the book only to find no discussion of the many key resources that must be managed if an organization is going to excel. However, to keep the book to a reasonable length, I decided to just highlight some key points about each of these other resources. Subjects such as products and services, investors, inventory management, and suppliers all would require separate books to cover how to manage them in an excellent manner.

"You can manage and design the customer's experience— or the customer will do it for you."

—Wendy Close
Research director,
Gartner Group,
CRM Magazine, **Dec. 2004**

For example, the products and services section of this chapter primarily discussed marketing's role in defining the future voice of the customer. It didn't address how R&D takes these inputs and transforms them into a design, and then how reliability engineering evaluates them to ensure they reflect the life cycle needs of the stakeholders, and then how the industrial engineer converts these drawings and development models into a production line that is capable of mass-producing millions of them at minimum cost while improving the quality of the delivered products. Nor did it cover the sales force that converts this huge investment into cash that can be poured back into the organization to pay its suppliers, investors, and employees for the resources that they have provided. And finally, it didn't address the field support staff that keeps the product functioning when errors escape the internal processes. The focus was on marketing because it doesn't get the attention it needs to really excel in most organizations. Management seems to accept mediocrity from marketing and sets lower standards of performance for this department than it does for other departments within the organization, but in the product's cycle, marketing is the starting point and if it doesn't excel, the rest of the activities have two strikes against them before they start.

CEOs say that it's the customer who pays the bills, but the investors start the cycle, and if you don't take care of them, the organization collapses even faster than when it loses its customers. Is it any wonder that management feels a primary obligation to take care of these investors?

Each and every one of these other resources are critical to the success of your organization, for without them it is not a matter of excelling but a matter of existing.

"All resources are important. If you neglect any of them, the organization's foundation will be weakened and the most beautiful house will collapse."

—HJH

CHAPTER VIII

STRATEGIC PLANNING

> "The nice thing about not having a strategic plan is that you can't
> be off course if you don't know where you're going."
>
> —HJH

We've talked about only a few of an organization's resources and assets. We could go on to discuss at greater length money, equipment, inventory, customer goodwill, facilities, patents, and so on, but let's get down to the heart of managing the organization's resources.

Looking at the varied types of resources, you may wonder, "What approach can be used to manage all of the organization's resources?" That's a good question. The answer is an old, tried, and proven tool that most organizations use, although not very effectively. It's strategic planning. The basic purpose of the strategic plan is to define how the organization will use its resources to optimize its value added to all of its stakeholders—well, at least to the stockholders and management. The resource plans are called many things—*business plans, strategic plans, operating plans, budgets, annual plans,* and so on. It doesn't matter what you call it; the objective of these plans is to define how to optimize the use of the limited amount of resources that are available to the organization. They are intended to put the organization in the best possible position to compete in this complex, changing world. They should align the organization's resources toward a common business objective that sets the organization apart from its rivals. And all organizations have rivals. Even government agencies are finding that they need to be competitive or their work is farmed out. The plan must include the organization's change management plan discussed in Pillar III, change management excellence. The real purpose of your strategic (business) plan is to determine the external focus of your organization in terms of customer service and value provided, along with identifying the areas in which the organization must excel to be successful. A well-crafted plan can provide the road map to success and let each person know how he or she can contribute to the results. The strategic plan provides an opportunity and a stimulus that encourage creativity, communication, and mobilize the

> "More than 90 percent of effectively formulated strategies don't get successfully implemented. . . . In the Middle East and Asia, we estimate the failure rate of the best strategies to be between 70 percent and 90 percent. . . . Although 60 percent to 70 percent of top management understood their strategy, when it came to middle management, the figure dropped to about 40 percent—and less then 10 percent for line employees."
> —Advait Kurlekar
> Director, Cedar Consulting

efforts of the total organization. It provides competitive insight in your business field and develops buy-in and commitment to the organization's short- and long-term objectives. A good strategic plan involves everyone, from the boardroom to the boiler room.

Resource plans are most commonly called *business plans* or *strategic plans*. To be in tune with common practice, we'll use the term *strategic plan*. A strategic plan must be based upon future needs, not past performance and experiences. Sure, you learn from experience and take it into consideration, but the past shouldn't limit your plan. Your strategic plan must be determined by the external environment and management's best knowledge about how the environment will change. These considerations should include things such as:

"CEOs and boards of directors are learning that human resources can be one of your biggest game changers in terms of competitive advantage. The success of strategy rests in people's execution."
—Dennis Donovan
Executive VP, Human Resources, Home Depot

- The choices that will be presented to the customer
- What old, new, and potential competitors will be offering
- Demographic changes
- Advances in related knowledge and technology
- New rulings from government and other players
- Ecological changes
- Public sentiments

The problem that most organizations face today is that management prepares a strategic plan, updates it one or more times a year, shares it with just a privileged few, and then files it away in the corporate vault so that competitors won't be able to get their "dirty little hands" on this strategic document. That's all well and good, but it keeps the strategic plan from accomplishing its true objective of uniting the organization and focusing on a set of common goals (see figure 8.1). The truth is that your competition probably has a good idea of what's in your strategic plan; your employees are the ones you're keeping in the dark. A good business plan involves everyone in the organization. You should communicate all but a very few sections of the plan to all employees. You might have to hold back something such as acquisitions, limiting that part to a small group of people, but you should make 99 percent of the plan available to your employees and proactively communicate it to the entire staff.

THE THREE OBJECTIVES OF STRATEGIC PLANNING

"While selecting some cold medications in the drugstore, I noted: Some are quick acting while others are long lasting. It makes you think, 'Do you worry about the present or the future?'"

—HJH

Planning is an activity defining objectives and selecting the most appropriate means of reaching these objectives before taking action.

Strategic planning is a process by which the executive team of the organization defines the future of the organization and defines the actions required to achieve the desired future state.

Long-range planning is defined as a multiyear plan that is an extrapolation of current business trends. It's based upon anticipating the future and preparing accordingly. In this case, the organization's strategic planning helps it create its own future.

Tactical planning, sometimes called "operational planning," addresses how the job gets done and sets specific measurable objectives and milestones that the individual units within the organization should achieve during the next one to three years. It's important that the tactical plan be based upon the strategic plan.

The strategic planning process must consider three questions:

- Where is the organization going?
- What is the future state environment?
- How are we going to get there?

> **"Planning . . . is anticipatory decision making. It is a process of deciding . . . before action is taken."**
> **—Russell Ackoff**
> **Professor, Wharton Business School**

Strategic planning is much more than just envisioning processes. It requires well-defined goals and objectives. The organization must define its present state and the desired future state. Then based upon the gap between these two states, the organization can develop an action plan to make the transformation during a specific time period. This requires development of intermediate targets that are milestones along the road to the future state. These progress points should be aggressive but realistic, objective, and obtainable.

The process of self-examination, the confrontation of different choices, the setting of priorities, and openness to change characterize successful strategic plans. Too often excellent strategic plans are prepared and then put on the shelf to be dusted off every six months. This approach is a waste of effort. A strategic management process must support the strategic plan. Strategic management is defined as the day-to-day implementation of the strategic plan. This leads to the development of a tactical plan for carrying out the strategic plan for the first one to three years of the plan. This tactical plan should become the heart of the annual business plan, because the strategic planning process should provide the organization with its core priorities and guidelines for virtually all of its day-to-day management decisions. By connecting the tactical plan to the annual business plan, you ensure adequate resources are assigned. The tactical part of the strategic plan should take the form of a formal project or projects, and you should develop work breakdown structures for each strategy. The pressure of day-to-day tasks can easily push aside the strategic planning strategy if it isn't continuously reinforced. This is why you must use an excellent project management software package such as PMOffice (IBM's new product) to manage the implementation of the strategic plan. Task reminders must be brought automatically to the attention of the individual assigned to the task. These reminders should highlight overdue tasks and point out those that are due to be completed in the near future. The individual assigned to the task should be able to easily update the status of these tasks. An escalation process must be designed into the system to highlight to the executive management team when tasks fall behind schedule so it can readjust priorities.

What does a good strategic plan do for the organization?

- It enables the organization to unleash the energy of the organization behind a shared belief and vision.
- It provides a forum to address strategic issues, discuss alternatives, and decide on actions to be taken in a specific time period.
- It increases the capability of the organization to carry out the strategic plan on a timely basis.
- It develops a better understanding of the operational environment.
- It develops a better understanding of the organization's customers and its capabilities and limitations.

"People are not on the same page regarding the top priorities. They really aren't. It's amazing how confused and distracted and misdirected so many people are."
—Stephen Covey
The Seven Habits of Highly Effective People

Harrington Institute's normal approach to strategic planning is to develop the environmental change assumptions and then define the organization's business drivers. For each of these business drivers, we would work with the organization to develop a statement that defines the present condition (the as-is condition). We then would develop for each of the business drivers a vision statement that defines the

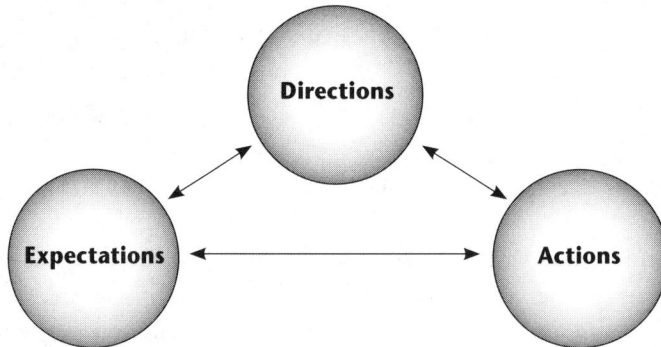

Figure 8.1 The Three Purposes of Business Planning

Directions

Expectations

Actions

Figure 8.2 Objectives, Document, and Person Responsible

Objectives	Document	Person Responsible
1. To set direction	Mission statement	Top management
	Value statements	Top management
	Organization vision statements	Top management
	Strategic focus	Top management
	Risk analysis	Top management
	Critical success factors	Top management
2. To establish expectations	Objectives	Top management
	Goals	Middle-level managers
3. To define actions	Strategy	Middle- and first-level managers
	Tactics	First-level managers and employees
	Budgets	First-level managers
	Performance plans	First-level managers and employees

desired future state (to-be condition). Once we understood the difference between the two states, we would define the present problems related to that business driver and the road-blocks to moving to the desired future state condition. Once these problems and obstacles had been identified, we would select the tools to make the required transformation.

The three main objectives of preparing a strategic plan are:

- To set direction
- To establish expectations
- To define actions

Each of these purposes is accomplished by a number of related outputs. The three purposes combined produce twelve major outputs. (See figure 8.2.)

> "For full effectiveness all work needs to be integrated into a unified program for performance."
> —Peter F. Drucker
> Author and consultant

Setting Direction

No one disputes the major role that top management plays in setting direction. That's why the top management team is held responsible for preparing the outputs related to the setting-direction part of the strategic plan. Six major outputs set the direction for most organizations.

Mission Statement

The mission statement defines the type of business that the organization is in. Some organizations call it a purpose statement or the central reason why they are in business. It should define exactly what product or services the organization provides and include guidelines that define what products and services are within and outside the organization's scope. For example, McDonald's mission statement is: "To satisfy the world's appetite for good food, well served, at a price people can afford." As you can see, this mission statement is short, clear, and concise, as a mission statement should be. Typically a mission statement is prepared when an organization is founded and changes only if there's a drastic change in the makeup of the product or service that the organization provides.

The mission statement for Boston Scientific is as follows: "Boston Scientific's mission is to improve the quality of patient care and the productivity of health care delivery through the development and advocacy of less-invasive medical devices and procedures. This is accomplished through the continuing refinement of existing products and procedures and the investigation and development of new technologies that can reduce risk, trauma, cost, procedure time, and the need for aftercare."

Value Statements

Value statements provide a set of operating and managing rules that are the basis for the moral and cultural operation of the organization. Think of it as the "employee's bill of rights." Value statements serve as the rules that are never broken nor compromised. They are also called *operating principles, guiding principles, basic beliefs,* and *operating rules.* Here are some typical examples.

Ford's values can be briefly summarized as follows:

■ Quality comes first.
■ Customers are the focus of everything we do.
■ Continuous improvement is essential to our success.
■ Employee involvement is our way of life.
■ Dealers and suppliers are our partners.
■ Integrity is never compromised.
■ People are the source of our strength.
■ As our products are viewed, so are we viewed.
■ Profits are required to survive and grow.

Texaco defines its values as:

■ Establish the self-image that we can be the best.
■ Require profit accountability of all managers.
■ Set up objectives that affect the good of the organization.
■ Instill a sense of urgency to do it today.
■ Know where the problem is and solve it.
■ Challenge how we have always done it.
■ Develop heroes and reward success.

Owens/Corning Fiberglass's guiding principles are:
- Customers are the focus of everything we do.
- People are the source of our competitive strength.
- Involvement and teamwork is our method of operation.
- Continuous improvement is essential to our success.
- Open, two-way communication is essential to the improvement process and our mission.
- Suppliers are team members.
- Profitability is the ultimate measure of our efficiency in serving our customers' needs.

Toyota Motor Corp.'s guiding principles are:
- Honor the language and spirit of the law of every nation and undertake open and fair corporate activities to be a good corporate citizen of the world.
- Respect the culture and customs of every nation and contribute to economic and social development through corporate activities in the communities.
- Dedicate ourselves to providing clean and safe products and to enhancing the quality of life everywhere through all our activities.
- Create and develop advanced technologies and provide outstanding products and services that fulfill the needs of customers worldwide.
- Foster a corporate culture that enhances individual creativity and teamwork value, while honoring mutual trust and respect between labor and management.
- Pursue growth in harmony with the global community through innovative management.
- Work with business partners in research and creation to achieve stable, long-term growth and mutual benefits, while keeping ourselves open to new partnerships.
  (Established in 1990, revised in 1997; translation from original Japanese.)

Boston Scientific's values are as follows:
- As our company grows and our technology advances, the following values are the unchanging guides for how we conduct our business:
  - To provide our people with a strong understanding of our mission and shared values.
  - To think like our customers and work hard on their behalf.
  - To pay relentless attention to business fundamentals.
  - To bring a commitment to quality and a sense of urgency to everything we do.
  - To rely on one another, to treat each other well, and to put the development and motivation of our people at the top of our priority lists.
  - To encourage innovation, experimentation, and risk taking.
  - To recognize bureaucracy as an enemy and not allow it to inhibit our good sense and creative spirit.

□ To provide shareholders with an attractive return through sustained high-quality growth.

□ To recognize and reward excellence by sharing Boston Scientific's success with our employees.

IBM is taking a different approach to developing a new set of values. Sam Palmisano, IBM's CEO, presented a draft set of values to 300 executives and to 7,000 IBM employees using focus groups to get their inputs. They then had what they called a "value jam," in which all 316,000 IBM employees were invited to take part in an online discussion with Palmisano.

IBM's operating principles are that an organization, like an individual, must build on a bedrock of sound beliefs if it is to survive and succeed. It must stand by these beliefs in conducting its business. Every manager must live by these beliefs in making decisions and in taking actions.

The beliefs that guide IBM activities are expressed as IBM principles.

■ *Respect for the individual.* Our basic belief is respect for the individual, for each person's rights and dignity. It follows from this principle that IBM should:

□ Help employees develop their potential and make the best use of their abilities.

□ Pay and promote on merit.

□ Maintain two-way communications between manager and employee, with opportunity for a fair hearing and equitable settlement of disagreements.

■ *Service to the customer.* We are dedicated to giving our customers the best possible service. Our products and services bring profits only to the degree that they serve the customer and satisfy customer needs. This demands that we:

□ Know our customers' needs, and help them anticipate future needs.

□ Help customers use our products and services in the best possible way.

□ Provide superior equipment maintenance and supporting services.

■ *Excellence must be a way of life.* We want IBM to be known for its excellence. Therefore, we believe that every task, in every part of the business, should be performed in a superior manner and to the best of our ability. Nothing should be left to chance in our pursuit of excellence. For example, we must:

□ Lead in new developments.

□ Be aware of advances made by others, better them where we can, or be willing to adopt them whenever they fit our needs.

□ Produce quality products of the most advanced design and at the lowest possible cost.

- *Managers must lead effectively.* Our success depends on intelligent and aggressive management, which is sensitive to the need for making an enthusiastic partner of every individual in the organization. This requires that managers:
  - ☐ Provide the kinds of leadership that will motivate employees to do their jobs in a superior way.
  - ☐ Meet frequently with all their people.
  - ☐ Have the courage to question decisions and policies; have the vision to see the needs of the company as well as the operating unit and department.
  - ☐ Plan for the future by keeping an open mind to new ideas, whatever the source.

- *Obligations to stockholders.* IBM has obligations to its stockholders whose capital has created our jobs. These require us to:
  - ☐ Take care of the property our stockholders have entrusted to us.
  - ☐ Provide an attractive return on invested capital.
  - ☐ Exploit opportunities for continuing profitable growth.

- *Fair deal for the supplier.* We want to deal fairly and impartially with suppliers of goods and services. We should:
  - ☐ Select suppliers according to the quality of their products or services, their general reliability, and competitiveness of price.
  - ☐ Recognize the legitimate interests of both supplier and IBM when negotiating a contract; administer such contracts in good faith.
  - ☐ Avoid suppliers' becoming unduly dependent on IBM.

- *IBM should be a good corporate citizen.* We accept our responsibilities as a corporate citizen in community, national, and world affairs; we serve our interests best when we serve the public interest. We believe that the immediate and long-term public interest is best served by a system of competing enterprises.

> **"The values can never be compromised, but the business results have to be delivered. We don't compromise on either."**
> **—William C. Weldon**
> **CEO, Johnson & Johnson**

As you see, they are sound beliefs, and a theme of excellence weaves throughout all of them.

Call them what you will; it makes no difference. What does make a difference is to be sure that your managers and employees understand them and live up to them. Nothing will do more harm to an organization than to have grand value statements that the management does not live by and enforce.

Organization's Vision Statement

The organization develops a vision statement to paint a picture of how it wants to position itself ten to fifteen years in the future. Top management usually prepares the organization's vision statement. It primarily focuses on the organization's output and how its customers and the rest of the world perceive the organization. The vision statement must be able to express an energizing picture of the future in terms of market presence and customer interface, and it must have enough realism to it to make it aggressively believable.

Jack Welch, former CEO of General Electric, stated, "Leaders—and take everyone from Roosevelt to Churchill to Reagan—inspire people with clear visions of how things can be done better. Some managers, on the other hand, muddle things with pointless complexity and detail. They acquaint it with sophistication, with sounding smarter than anyone else. They inspire no one." Father Theodore Hesburgh, former president of the University of Notre Dame, stated, "The very essence of leadership is that you have to have a vision. It's got to be a vision you articulate clearly and forcefully on every occasion. You cannot blow an uncertain trumpet."

Too often organizations prepare unrealistic vision statements using phrases such as the best, the largest, and the most profitable. Each of these phrases can apply to only one organization in the organization's field of competency. Much better are phrases such as world class, recognized as a leader, one of the best. For example, CNN's vision statement could read: "To provide firsthand news from all around the world as it is happening, customized to each country's interest and needs."

The following is Toyota's global vision for 2010, which it calls "Innovation into the Future—A Passion to Create a Better Society:"

- Through "*monozukuri*—manufacturing of value-added products" and "technological innovation," Toyota is aiming to help create a more prosperous society. To realize this, the company is challenging the themes:
  - ☐ Be a driving force in global regeneration by implementing the most advanced environmental technologies.
  - ☐ Create automobiles and a motorized society in which people can live safely, securely, and comfortably.
  - ☐ Promote the appeal of cars throughout the world and realize a large increase in the number of Toyota fans.
  - ☐ Be a truly global company that is trusted and respected by all peoples around the world.

  (Announced in April 2002.)

"The factory of the future will have only two employees, a man and a dog. The man will be there to feed the dog. The dog will be there to keep the man from touching the equipment."

—Warren Bennis
Professor of Business Administration, University of Southern California

Strategic Focus

All successful organizations have the ability to identify four key areas of strategic focus that are characterized by the following:

■ Technologies or functions that the organization has that define its specific areas of excellence

■ Activities that are most valued by their customers

■ Areas that the organization is especially good at

■ Areas that will distinguish the organization from its competition

Through the years, these strategic focus factors have been labeled under many names. The most common are:

■ *Core competencies*. The technology and product skills that underline an organization's product or service (for example, Sony's skill at miniaturization)

■ *Core capabilities*. The business processes that visibly provide value to the customers (for example, Honda's dealer-management process)

■ *Strategic excellence positions*. Unique and distinctive capabilities that are valued by the customer and provide a basis for competitive advantage (for example, Avon's distribution system)

Call them what you will, but to excel, the organization must focus its resources on improving these key attributes to ensure that the organization keeps ahead of its competition in these critical areas. The organization can farm out everything else that it does, but it must preserve its leadership role in these strategic focus functions. Typically, the strategic focus is defined by top management and looks five years in the future.

Risk Analysis

A lot of things can go wrong—changes in the business environment can occur outside the organization's control. People who prepare the business plan must be like chess players; the best chess players not only plan their moves far in advance, but they also seek moves that offer them the greatest flexibility to take advantage of future unexpected events. The organization must be flexible enough to take advantage of and deal with unanticipated internal and external events. Typical risks that must be considered are:

■ Competitive initiatives

■ Too many initiatives

■ Sponsor situations

■ Customer needs

■ Business economics

■ Supply problems

■ Industry trends

Figure 8.3 The Seven Phases of a Risk Management Cycle

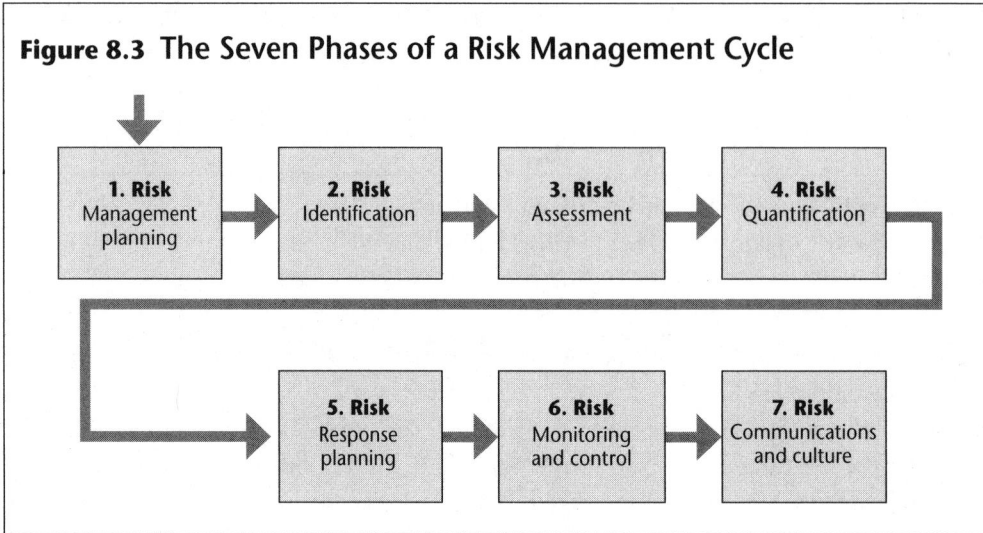

1. Risk Management planning	**2. Risk** Identification	**3. Risk** Assessment	**4. Risk** Quantification
5. Risk Response planning	**6. Risk** Monitoring and control	**7. Risk** Communications and culture	

- Stock market fluctuations
- Wars
- Government rulings

Figure 8.3 shows the seven phases that make up the risk management cycle.

Successful risk management ensures that your organization will identify, analyze, and respond to risk. In global organizations the element of risk can be greater because of team members from one country assuming that things can be done the same way in another country as at home. This puts the onus on the senior manager to validate plans in the country where they will be executed. An experienced global leadership team can minimize these risks as it develops the expertise to trap faulty assumptions early in the strategy planning sessions. Communications plays a big role in minimizing internal risk based on poor planning and false assumptions. Good communications also play a big role in understanding and planning the management of external risks over which the team has no control, such as weather and fluctuations in currency exchange rates.

Murphy's law—anything that can go wrong will go wrong—is not necessarily accepted as widely in some countries as it is in North America or the United Kingdom. The denial of risk's negative outcomes tends to arise in certain cultures in which all decisions are made by top management, and corporate belief in excellence allows little room to admit that errors can and do occur.

Critical Success Factors

These are defined by top management and look forward two to three years in the future. It includes the traditional strengths, weaknesses, opportunities, and threats (SWOT) analyses. Preparing a vision statement requires the executive team to look outside of the box and take an unconstrained strategic perspective. It's also important that the vision be linked back to today's reality by specifically focusing on the things that could affect or prevent the successful implementation of the plan. The critical success factor defines the assumptions on which the plan is based. These can vary all the way from insufficient funding to lack of market growth. Critical success factors perform the service of identifying obstacles that need to be addressed if the plan is to be successfully carried out. They often create several additional strategies that are incorporated into the strategic plan. Often critical success factors are translated into risks for which mitigation plans need to be prepared. By identifying these critical success factors and monitoring them closely, the probability of successfully carrying out the strategic plan is greatly improved. The organization needs to view these obstacles as additional challenges, not as obstacles that can't be overcome.

Establishing Expectations (Measurements)

> **"Strategies without metrics are only wishes."**
> —**Charles Phillips**
> **Co-president, Oracle**

This category consists of two parts, business objectives and performance goals. The words *objectives* and *goals* seem to have different meanings to different organizations. Some organizations believe that you set objectives and develop goals to support the objectives as measurements along the way. Other organizations look at goals as a higher-level measurement and objectives as the milestones along the way to meet the goals. Let's define both based upon *Merriam-Webster's Collegiate Dictionary*.

- *Objective*—something toward which effort is directed: an aim or end of action
- *Goal*—the end toward which effort is directed; the terminal point of a race

As you can see, they both are end points, so in reality they can be used interchangeably. The key is the word that defines what kind of goal or objective they are. In this discussion, business objectives are the higher-level measurement, and performance goals are the milestones along the way to reach the business objectives.

To start this part of the planning cycle, you should perform a SWOT analysis. SWOT stands for:

S = *Strengths*
W = *Weaknesses*
O = *Opportunities*
T = *Threats*

> **"Plan ahead. It wasn't raining when Noah built the Ark."**
> —**Anonymous**

Strengths are what the organization is good at and what sets the organization apart from other organizations. Typical strengths could be a big part of the market share, brand recognition, experience, competent staff, and so on.

Weaknesses are things that other organizations do better and things the organization is not prepared to handle. Typical weaknesses could be lack of resource funding, understaffing, poor commitment, high turnover rate, poor quality, and so on.

Opportunities are the things that the organization could take advantage of to make it stronger and improve its performance. Typical examples of opportunities are to install total quality management (TQM), expand into China, acquire another organization, provide a new service, use a new technology to make the product faster, and so on.

Threats are things that could happen that would have a negative impact on the organization and the strategic plan. Typical examples of threats are new government laws, increased gas prices, strikes, suppliers that go out of business, not being able to hire the right skilled people, increased interest rates, new competitors' products, increased competition from developing countries, products in development failing to perform to requirements, and so on.

You will note that both strengths and weaknesses are factors that are internal to the organization. Opportunities and threats are mostly external to the organization. You should analyze your data in a matrix such as the one in figure 8.4.

Figure 8.4 SWOT Matrix

Internal factors / External factors	Strengths 1. 2. 3. Etc.	Weaknesses 1. 2. 3. Etc.
Opportunities 1. 2. 3. Etc.		
Threats 1. 2. 3. Etc.		

This matrix allows you to analyze how each of the strengths supports the opportunities and how the strengths offset each of the threats. Likewise it allows you to define how the weaknesses have a negative impact on each of the opportunities and how these weaknesses increase the likelihood of the threats becoming a reality.

Business Objectives

These are prepared by top management and approved by the board of directors. They define what the organization wants to accomplish in the next five to ten years. They provide a big-picture focus that is usually not quantified. For example, Hewlett-Packard (HP) sets "stretch objectives" to reduce all of its product failure rates to one-tenth of their current value in a ten-year period, while Motorola sets more aggressive objectives of a ten times improvement in quality in all parts of its business, both service and manufacturing, in a five-year period. Typical business objectives would be:

- To sustain your profitability, which funds your growth
- To exhibit product leadership across your entire product line to excel in technology, value, and quality

- To grow with the industry
- To be the most effective at everything you do
- To be the low-cost producer, the low-cost seller, and the low-cost administrator
- To quantify the impact that all major decisions have upon the organization's stakeholders

As you can see, these types of business objectives are not quantified but are quantifiable. For example, to grow with the industry can be quantified; if the industry grows at a rate of 15 percent in a given year, the organization should grow at least 15 percent during the same year.

> **"In 1997 we added a growth-oriented objective: Grow earning-per-share by 10 percent a year across the cycle (planning cycle)."**
> **—William Slavropoulos**
> **CEO, Dow Chemical**

It's very important that you communicate the business objectives to each and every employee within the organization and that you continuously report back to all employees any progress related to each of these business objectives. Good business objectives not followed, measured, and reported are just scraps of paper that are no good to anyone.

In the early 1960s, John F. Kennedy set an objective to put a man on the moon by the end of the decade. He didn't know how it would be done or how much it would cost. He knew there were a lot of problems that needed to be solved—technical, financial, and political. He just set the objective and defined the end date. Then he left it up to others to define intermediate goals and strategies. He stepped back and got out of the way so that others could do their thing, but he never lost interest or stopped following the project. Everyone knows what the result was—before the end of the decade, Neil Armstrong took his "giant leap for mankind."

Objectives set by management define what and when major accomplishments should be achieved. Once that is done, get out of your employees' way so they can get the job done. Don't think that you need to have all the answers in advance of setting the organization's objectives.

In the early 1980s John Young, then president of Hewlett-Packard, set an objective to improve all of HP's products by ten times in ten years. That's a 1,000 percent improvement! Engineers and management were overwhelmed with the task. They told him it couldn't be done the way they were working. John's reply was, "Now you got the idea."

Performance Goals

These have two key elements: First, they specifically state the target for improvement, and second, they give the time interval in which the improvement will be accomplished. They usually have short- (one year) and long-range (five years) targets. (For example, your short-term goal might be to have 80 percent of your customers rate you as "exceeds requirements" or above by the end of this year, and your long-term goal would be to have 70 percent of your customers rate you as "outstanding" within the next five years.) Each year middle managers should develop a set of short-range performance goals that are reflected in the department's budget. Top management should review and approve these goals to be sure that they support the business objectives and are aggressive enough.

A survey of 23,000 people conducted by Harris Interactive reported the following:

- 37 percent of the people clearly understand what their organization is trying to achieve and why.
- Only 20 percent are enthusiastic about their team's and organization's goals.
- 15 percent think the organization fully enables them to execute key goals.
- Only 20 percent fully trust the organization they work for.

Defining Actions

The third part of the strategic plan is the most important of the three. The best-laid plans will go astray if they are not implemented. This is the weak part of many strategic plans. A lot of work goes into preparing the strategic plan, but they aren't effectively carried out in some organizations and have very little impact upon the way the organization functions. It's easy to plan, to define what someone else should do, but making it happen requires a lot of work, sweat, and dedication. The defining-action phase of the strategic planning process is designed to focus the organization's resources on the expectations that top management has set and the board of directors has agreed to. Four outputs define how the organization's resources will be used to carry out the strategic plan. They are:

"The new line is making sure people strategies are aligned with the business strategies so you can execute and get to where you want to go."
—Susan Meisinger
CEO, Society for Human Resource Management

- Strategies
- Tactics
- Budgets
- Performance plans

Strategies

Strategies are defined as the approaches that will be used to meet performance goals. They are developed by the first-line manager. They are approved by middle management. They define specific programs, initiatives, and decisions that will require allocation of resources. *Merriam-Webster's Collegiate Dictionary* defines *strategy* as "the art of devising or employing plans or stratagems toward a goal." They define what is going to be done, not how it is going to be done. (For example, you will sign alliance partnerships with a software firm that produces resource management software, or you will redesign three of your critical processes that have the biggest impact upon cycle time.) Strategies often stay constant for a number of years. In fact, you should make every effort to keep the strategies up to date without making major changes. Dropping one strategy to pursue another strategy in a different direction often prevents the original strategy from meeting its objectives and wastes many resources.

Tactics

The dictionary defines *tactics* as "the art or skill of employing available means to accomplish an end." In this case, tactics are the detailed plan that defines how the resources will be used to carry out the strategy. They are developed jointly by the first-line manager and the employee who will be implementing them. They normally are detailed down to the activity level but not down to the task level; they fall short of a complete work breakdown structure. The tactics are updated at least once a year and change frequently. Tactics become very personal to the first-line manager and the employee because they define a major part of the coming year's endeavors.

Performance Plans

Of course, performance plans should be based upon the agreed-to tasks required to support the department's strategy. These performance plans provide a more detailed description of the contribution that an individual is expected to make to complete the tasks that the department has set for the coming year. For more complex, creative assignments (for example, those of engineers, programmers, project managers, designers), a detailed work plan supplements the performance plan. Basically, performance plans define the major activities that each employee will be assigned to accomplish, what acceptable performance is for each activity, and when they should be completed. Each individual activity is further weighted as a percentage of the total activities that the employee is assigned. The sum of the individual weighting should equal 100 percent. It's absolutely imperative that both the employee and the manager agree to the performance plan. It must also be in complete harmony with the department's task, tactics, and strategies. The performance plan defines the individual's commitment of resources to each of the department's tactics and to other assigned maintenance activities.

Budgets

> "Before you can start to focus on performance, you need a common language and measurement system."
> —**Gary Loveman**
> **CEO, Harrah's Entertainment**

A combination of the department's tactics, the performance plans, and last year's experience make up the inputs that an effective budget is based upon. It's easy to see why budgeting is the last activity in the strategic planning process. No budget should be prepared before the department's strategy, tactics, and performance plan are complete. If for some reason the budget is reduced, then the department's strategies, tactics, and performance plans must be redone to reflect this decrease or increase in resource allocation. The problem that many organizations face is that the annual budget is prepared by adding to last year's actual expenditures a percentage for inflation, plus additional costs related to any new assignments. This is a sure way to lead the organization into mediocrity. The budgeting cycle should always be a bottoms-up cycle based upon the department's strategies, tactics, and commitments. In addition, management should expect a 10 percent minimum reduction in maintenance activities from year to year based upon normal improvements in productivity. The budget should be very specific for the next twelve months and detailed for the following twenty-four months. I like to tell each employee the amount of money that is being set aside to cover his or her costs for the coming year. I find the employee is often surprised at what he or she costs the organization.

Calvin London, vice president of INO Therapeutics, reported in *Quality Progress* (August 2002) the following savings for an Australian company that used a good strategic plan for a two-year period:

- Sales revenue up 25 percent
- Export sales over budget 30 percent
- Reject rates down 81 percent
- Average unit throughput up 37 percent
- Overtime cost down 10 percent
- Lost time injuries down 87 percent

The strategic plan is not top management's plan or the president's plan. If you receive a paycheck, it's your plan. Top management may define the overall game plan, but it's up to each of you to do your part to make it work. You may not agree with the plan; you may even question if it will work. But once the plan is put in motion, you have a responsibility to do everything you can do to make it work. Top management cannot do the job by itself; it requires the whole team to work in harmony to accomplish the tasks required to make the plan a success.

Community Strategic Planning

The strategic planning process applies to the public and private sectors equally. The national government now is requiring it from all units. Figure 8.5 is a typical example of how a community transforms goals into action.

(*Source:* Frank Voehl, *Operating System Guidebook,* ASQ Quality Press, 2001.)

Figure 8.5 Transforming Goals Into Action

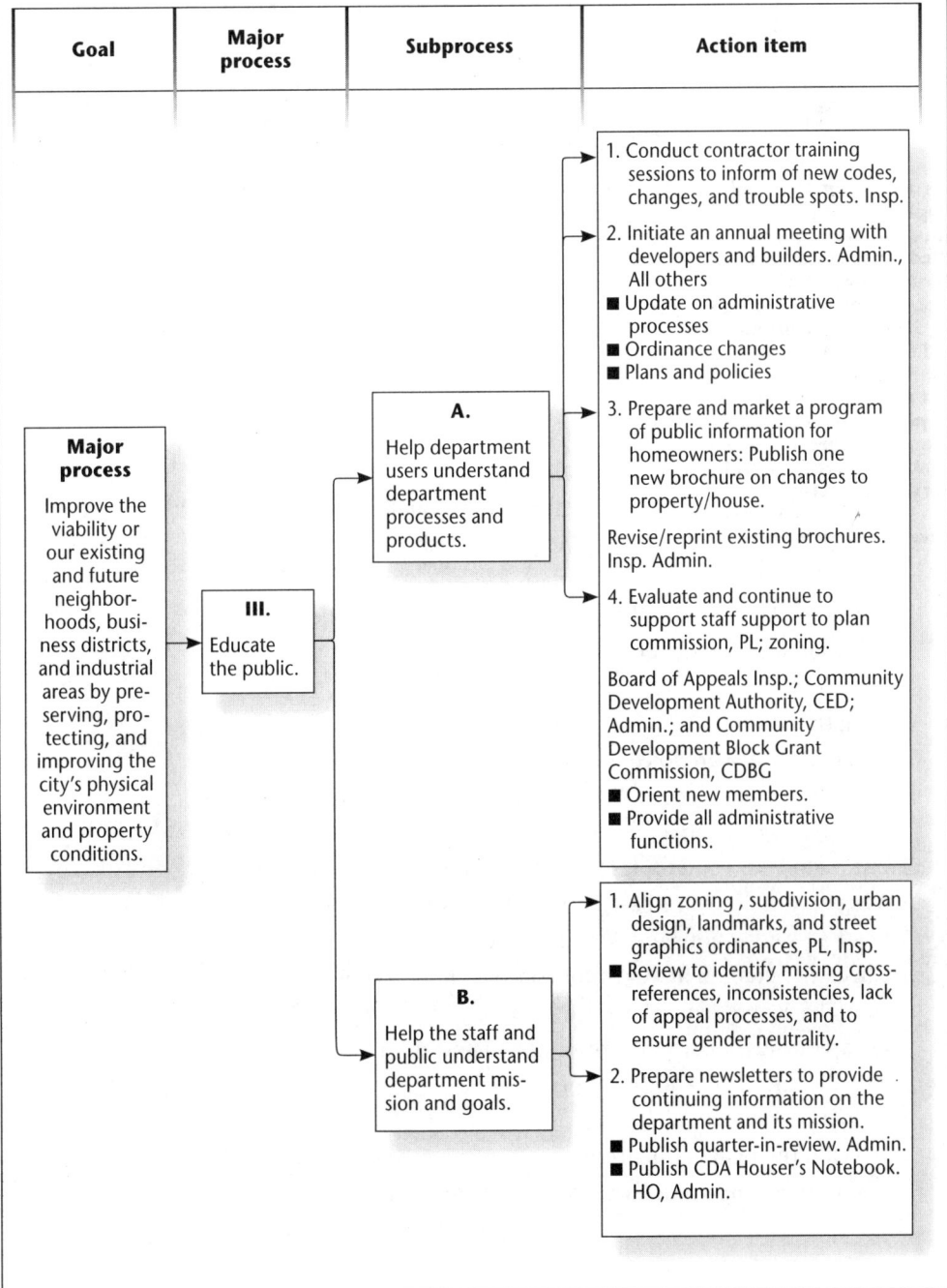

Goal	Major process	Subprocess	Action item

Major process

Improve the viability or our existing and future neighborhoods, business districts, and industrial areas by preserving, protecting, and improving the city's physical environment and property conditions.

III. Educate the public.

A. Help department users understand department processes and products.

B. Help the staff and public understand department mission and goals.

1. Conduct contractor training sessions to inform of new codes, changes, and trouble spots. Insp.

2. Initiate an annual meeting with developers and builders. Admin., All others
   ■ Update on administrative processes
   ■ Ordinance changes
   ■ Plans and policies

3. Prepare and market a program of public information for homeowners: Publish one new brochure on changes to property/house.

   Revise/reprint existing brochures. Insp. Admin.

4. Evaluate and continue to support staff support to plan commission, PL; zoning.

   Board of Appeals Insp.; Community Development Authority, CED; Admin.; and Community Development Block Grant Commission, CDBG
   ■ Orient new members.
   ■ Provide all administrative functions.

1. Align zoning , subdivision, urban design, landmarks, and street graphics ordinances, PL, Insp.
   ■ Review to identify missing cross-references, inconsistencies, lack of appeal processes, and to ensure gender neutrality.

2. Prepare newsletters to provide continuing information on the department and its mission.
   ■ Publish quarter-in-review. Admin.
   ■ Publish CDA Houser's Notebook. HO, Admin.

STRATEGIC PLANNING SUMMARY

"If you don't have a compass, you'll never know
if you're sailing in the wrong direction."

—HJH

**"The issue is that the task
of implementing strategy
is time-consuming and
riddled with vested interests,
ambiguity, even lack of
acceptance of the strategic
plan. Strategy documents
remain isolated. . . . 85
percent of top management
teams spend less than one
hour per month to discuss
strategy; 95 percent of the
typical workforce doesn't
understand strategy."
—Advait Kurlekar
Director, Cedar Consulting**

Frank Voehl, president of Strategy Associates, summarizes the planning process as follows:

- Preliminary tasks
  - ☐ Complete market research and analyses.
  - ☐ Clarify key matters relating to products/services.
  - ☐ Form the basis of the management team.
  - ☐ Prepare a strategic plan as a framework for a detailed plan.
  - ☐ Decide the central purpose of the plan and its target audience.
  - ☐ Find professional advisers to assist with the planning.
  - ☐ Acquire any software tools needed to help prepare the plan.
  - ☐ Research and compile a list of possible recipients of the plan.
  - ☐ Ascertain any specific needs of likely key recipients.

- Writing the plan
  - ☐ Create a framework for the plan, for example, a table of contents.
  - ☐ Identify possible appendices, attachments, and so on.
  - ☐ Estimate page lengths for each key section.
  - ☐ List main issues and topics to be covered within key sections.
  - ☐ Assign work programs based on the framework and lists.
  - ☐ Draft all key sections in a logical sequence.
  - ☐ Check the preliminary draft for completeness and plug gaps.
  - ☐ Stand back and take a detached overview of the draft.
  - ☐ Let an outsider or adviser critique the latest draft.
  - ☐ Redraft, fine-tune, and spell-check.
  - ☐ Write the executive summary.
  - ☐ Develop the plan's conclusion.
  - ☐ Get an independent assessment of the final draft.

- Reviewing the plan
  - ☐ Is the plan nicely presented—bound, pages numbered, and so on?
  - ☐ Has the plan been spell-checked in its final form?
  - ☐ Is the plan's length appropriate to its purpose?
  - ☐ Have the business's (funding) needs been clearly stated?
  - ☐ Does the plan's summary stimulate interest?
  - ☐ Have all key questions been anticipated?
  - ☐ What likely objections remain unresolved?
  - ☐ Will the plan provoke the desired responses?

Too often an organization devotes a great deal of effort and thought to the strategic plan once a year and then sets it aside until it's dusted off the next year. If this is the case in your organization, don't waste the time and effort. Let the executives play golf instead; it will do more for the organization. Your plan should be a living vibrant thing that is used daily to ensure everyone is marching to the same drummer.

The critical features of a successful strategic plan include:

- Visible leadership commitment
- Regular reporting and sharing of results
- Widespread sharing of the plan throughout the organization
- Well-understood linkage between individual performance and business success
- Willingness to change
- Adapting from experience

> "When you complete the plan, you are 5 percent of the way to your goal. The real challenge is in implementing it."
>
> —HJH

CHAPTER IX

STAKEHOLDER MEASUREMENTS

WHAT TO MEASURE?

Armand V. Feigenbaum points out that excellent organizations have an "effective relationship of measurements—financial, operating, and others—to each other and the company's strategies and plans." An integral part of every strategic plan is an effective measurement system that reflects the needs of all the organization's stakeholders. These measurements are used to evaluate progress compared to the strategic plan and also to measure the plan's impact upon all of the stakeholders. At times the strategic plan will fill some individual stakeholder's needs but will be in direct opposition to another stakeholder's needs. For example, investors want the organization to cut costs so that dividends will increase. This is often accomplished by reducing or laying off personnel. The employees, on the other hand, want job security. It's obvious that these two desires are in direct opposition to each other.

You must first define who the stakeholders are for your organization, and then you can contact all of them to define what they would consider organizational improvement. Typical public business stakeholders would be:

- Management
- Investors
- Customers
- Suppliers
- Employees
- Employees' families
- Communities/humankind

> "My ability to manage our performance was undermined by my inability to measure it."
> —Gary Loveman
> CEO, Harrah's Entertainment

The following is a list of the top five ways each of these stakeholders might measure organizational improvement.

- Management
  - ☐ Return on assets
  - ☐ Value added per employee
  - ☐ Stock prices

- ☐ Market share
- ☐ Reduced operating expenses

- ■ Investors
  - ☐ Return on investment
  - ☐ Stock prices
  - ☐ Return on assets
  - ☐ Market share
  - ☐ Successful new products

- ■ Customers
  - ☐ Reduced cost
  - ☐ New or expanded capabilities
  - ☐ Improved performance
  - ☐ Ease of use
  - ☐ Improved responsiveness

- ■ Suppliers
  - ☐ Increased return on investment (supplier)
  - ☐ Improved communications/fewer interfaces
  - ☐ Simplified requirements/fewer changes
  - ☐ Longer contracts
  - ☐ Longer cycle times

- ■ Employees
  - ☐ Increased job security
  - ☐ Increased compensation
  - ☐ Improved growth potential
  - ☐ Improved job satisfaction
  - ☐ Improved morale

- ■ Employees' families
  - ☐ Less time at work
  - ☐ Increased job security
  - ☐ Increased salary
  - ☐ Improved benefits
  - ☐ Improved working conditions (safety)

- Community/humankind
  - ☐ Employment of more people
  - ☐ Increased tax base
  - ☐ Reduced pollution
  - ☐ Support of community activities
  - ☐ Safety of employees

> **"If you are not keeping score, you're only practicing."**
> **—Tom Malone**
> **President, Milliken**

THE BALANCED SCORECARD

The balanced scorecard (BSC) provides an effective way to evaluate if all the stakeholders' concerns and interests have been addressed in the annual strategic plan.

The BSC is a conceptual framework for translating an organization's strategic objectives into a set of performance indicators distributed among four perspectives: financial, customer, internal business processes, and learning and growth. Additional measurements are often included to cover the requirements of all the organization's stakeholders. Indicators are maintained to measure an organization's progress toward achieving its strategic objective; other indicators are maintained to measure the long-term drivers of success. Through the BSC, an organization monitors both its current performance (finances, customer satisfaction, and business process results) and its efforts to improve processes, motivate and educate employees, and enhance information systems—its ability to learn and improve.

Basically there are two types of organizational measurement, financial measurement and nonfinancial measurement.

- Financial measurements are dependent variables and are retrospective or lagging indicators.
- Nonfinancial measurements are independent variables and are leading indicators of change.

> **"Very few senior executives have asked the question, 'What information do I need to do my job?' in part because they've all been brought up with the accounting information that they understand. But the other type of information system, they don't understand."**
> **—Peter Drucker**
> **Author and consultant**

In the present environment, rapid learning, agility, and flexibility provide an organization with a bigger competitive advantage than the rapidly changing technology methodologies provide. Therefore, it's very important that you consider these items as you develop the organization's measurement systems.

What is the BSC? In the early 1990s, Robert Kaplan and David Norton developed a new approach to strategic management, which they named the "balanced scorecard." They recognized some of the weaknesses and vagueness of previous management approaches, and the BSC approach provides a clear prescription as to what companies should measure to "balance" the financial perspective with other requirements.

The BSC is a management system (not only a measurement system) that enables organizations to clarify their visions and strategies and translate them into action. It provides feedback around both the internal business processes and external outcomes to continuously improve strategic performance and results. When fully deployed, the BSC transforms strategic planning from an academic exercise into the nerve center of an enterprise.

Kaplan and Norton describe the innovation of the BSC as follows:

> "The balanced scorecard retains traditional financial measures. But financial measures tell the story of past events, an adequate story for Industrial Age companies for which investments in long-term capabilities and customer relationships were not critical for success. These financial measures are inadequate, however, for guiding and evaluating the journey that Information Age companies must make to create future value through investment in customers, suppliers, employees, processes, technology, and innovation."

The BSC is a system. This means that it's made up of a number of related processes. Organizations that look at BSC as just a reporting and measurement system tend to get a much lower return on their investment than those that use it to drive their total improvement efforts. An effective BSC system contains the following elements:

- It sets priorities for stakeholder requirements based upon the organization's strategy objectives.
- It identifies the processes that are the key drivers for the priority stakeholders' requirements.
- It creates metrics for the processes that are at the top of the list.
- It creates aggressive goals for the key metrics.
- It creates action plans designed to improve the priority processes.
- It measures and tracks improvement in these key process metrics.
- It provides the stakeholders with continuous feedback on what progress is being made to improve these key process metrics.

A key part of a BSC system is process improvement and control tools such as:

- Process redesign
- Process reengineering
- Quality function deployment
- Organizational change management
- Benchmarking
- Poor-quality cost
- Area activity analysis
- Statistical process control

- Error proofing
- Failure mode and effects analysis

The BSC suggests that you view the organization from five major perspectives and that you develop metrics, collect data, and analyze them relative to each of these perspectives:

- *Customer.* Measurements that reflect how the organization appears to its external customers
- *Internal business processes.* Measurements of the internal processes that are used to determine if the strategy objective and external and internal customers' expectations are fulfilled
- *Financial.* Measurements to ensure that the financial performance of the organization is accurately presented to the investors, management, government, and other interested stakeholders
- *Learning and growth.* Measurements designed to review the degree of improvement in intellectual capital and retained knowledge
- *Organizational governance.* Measurements that reflect the need of stakeholders whose needs have not been covered in the first four perspectives

These five perspectives are all interrelated and driven by the strategy plan and the organization's vision. (See figure 9.1.)

The Customer Perspective

Recent management philosophy has shown an increasing realization of the importance of customer focus and customer satisfaction in any business. These are leading indicators: If customers aren't satisfied, they will eventually find other suppliers that will meet their needs. Poor performance from this perspective is thus a leading indicator of future decline, even though the current financial picture may look

> "I recommend that every organization develop a stakeholder information system—a feedback system or database on what shareholders, customers, employees, communities, suppliers, distributors, and other parties want and expect."
> —**Stephen R. Covey**
> *Principle-Centered Leadership*

good. When developing metrics for satisfaction, you should analyze customers in terms of the kinds of customers and processes for which you are providing the product or service.

The Business Process Perspective

This perspective refers to internal business processes and provides data regarding the internal business results against measures that lead to financial success and satisfied customers. To meet the organizational objectives and customers' expectations, organizations must identify the key business processes at which they must excel. Then they must monitor those key processes to ensure that outcomes are satisfactory. Internal business processes are the mechanisms through which performance expectations are achieved. Metrics based

Figure 9.1 The Balanced Scorecard Key Measurements

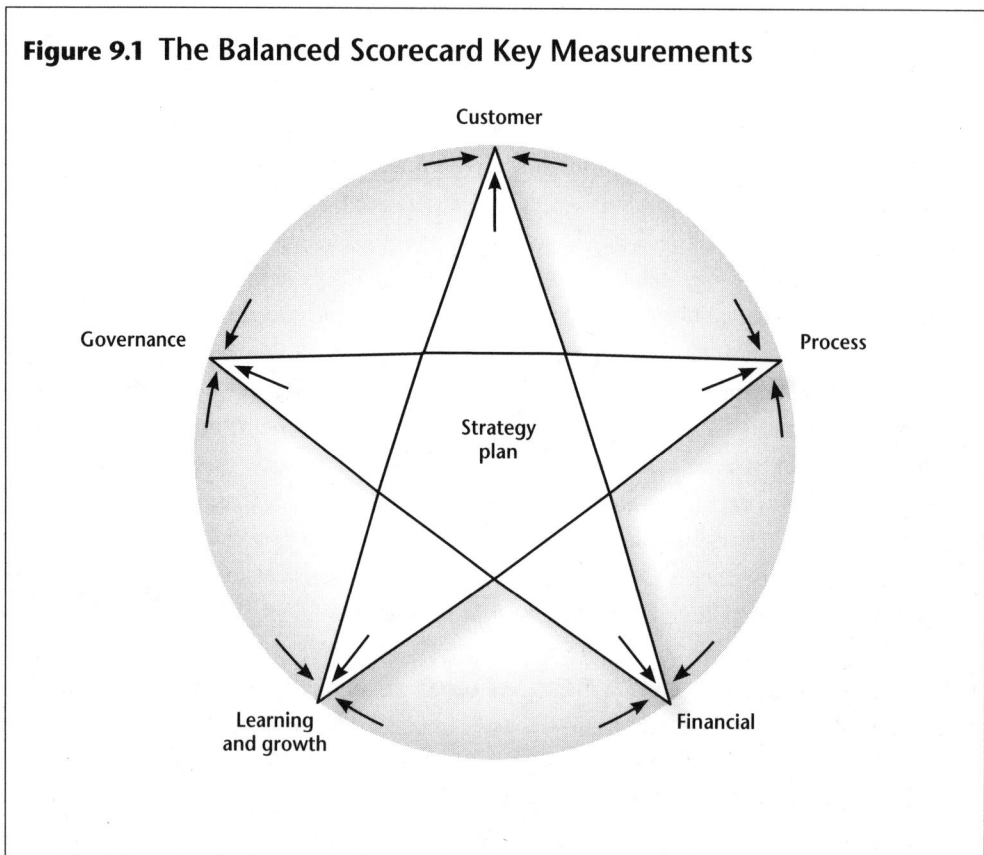

Customer

Governance

Process

Strategy
plan

Learning
and growth

Financial

on this perspective allow the managers to know how well their business is running and whether its products and services conform to customer requirements.

These metrics have to be carefully designed by those who know these processes. With organizations' unique missions, these aren't something that can be standardized. In addition to the strategic management process, there are two kinds of business processes:

- *Mission-oriented processes.* These are processes that are used to provide output that goes directly or indirectly to the external customer. For example, the process of an external auditor's performing an ISO 9001 audit deals directly with the external customer. A subassembly process that produces an assembly that goes in a car is a mission-oriented process.

- *Support processes.* These are processes that are designed to support only internal customers (for example, the payroll process). These processes are more repetitive in nature and hence are easier to measure and benchmark using generic metrics.

Financial Perspective

Private-sector financial objectives generally represent clear long-range targets for profit-seeking organizations operating in a purely commercial environment. Financial considerations for public organizations have an enabling or a constraining role but will rarely be the primary objective for business systems. Success for such organizations should be measured by how effectively and efficiently these organizations meet the needs of their constituencies. In government, this perspective captures cost efficiency, delivering maximum value to the customer for each dollar spent.

Kaplan and Norton don't disregard the traditional need for financial data. Timely and accurate financial data will always be a priority, and managers will do whatever necessary to provide it. In fact, often there's more than enough handling and processing of financial data. The creation of a corporate database should allow more of the processing to be centralized and automated. But the point is that the current emphasis on financials leads to the "unbalanced" situation with regard to other perspectives. Perhaps there's a need to include additional financials-related data, such as risk assessment and cost-benefit data, in this category. Public sectors' national units should be measured with metrics such as percent of GNP consumed and cost per person serviced.

The Learning and Growth Perspective

This perspective includes employee training and corporate cultural attitudes related to both individual and corporate self-improvement, and it captures the ability of employees, information systems, and organizational alignment to manage the business and adapt to change. Processes will succeed only if adequately skilled and motivated employees, supplied with accurate and timely information, are driving them. This perspective takes on increased importance in organizations that are undergoing radical change. To meet changing requirements and customer expectations, employees may be asked to take on dramatically new responsibilities and may require skills, capabilities, technologies, and organizational designs that were not available before.

In a knowledge-worker organization, *people*—the major repository of knowledge—are the main resource. In the current climate of rapid technological change, it's becoming necessary for knowledge workers to be in a continuous learning mode. Organizations often find themselves unable to hire new technical workers and at the same time show a decline in the training of existing employees. On the other hand, people leaving the organization take with them knowledge that has never been documented and that requires years to replace.

This leading indicator of "brain drain" must be reversed. One way is to put metrics into place to guide managers in focusing funds for training where they can help the most. In any case, learning and growth constitute the essential foundation for success of any knowledge-worker organization.

Kaplan and Norton emphasize that "learning" is more than "training"; it also includes things such as mentors and tutors within the organization, as well as that ease of communication among workers that allows them to readily exchange experiences and to get help on a problem when they need it. It also includes technological tools—what the Baldrige criteria call "high-performance work systems." One of these is a knowledge management system and another is the organization's intranet.

Organizational Governance

In today's competitive environment all of the organizations' stakeholders have options. Investors have the option of investing in organizations where they expect to get the largest return on their money. Suppliers have the choice of selling to the customers who want their product and are willing to pay a fair price for it. Employees today feel freer about moving from one organization to another as organizational loyalty has given way to personal desires. Communities have the responsibility to commit their limited resources (infrastructure, money, etc.) to organizations that will provide the greatest value to their constituents.

After studying many successful and unsuccessful BSC implementation efforts, Harrington Institute has defined a seven-phase process that includes all of the best practices and minimizes the rest of the failures. They are:

1. Set BSC project goals.
   - Adopt the BSC program.
   - Perform initial planning.
   - Develop the communications plan.
   - Define the education plan.
   - Prepare a project plan and budget.
   - Approve the project plan and budget.

2. Perform assessment and align strategy.
   - Customize the assessment plan.
   - Conduct the assessment with internal/external customers/suppliers.
   - Analyze the results.
   - Prepare the assessment report.

3. Define improvement opportunities.
   - Identify stakeholders.
   - Relate stakeholder segments to the business plans.
   - Define the stakeholders' needs.
   - Define performance gaps.
   - Set gap priorities.

4. Define process drivers.
   - Identify which process drives the priority gap.
   - Set priorities for internal processes.
   - Assign process owners.
   - Define process metrics that will close gaps.
   - Set improvement goals.
   - Define operating system.

> **"Modern businesses depend upon measurements and analysis of performance. Measurements must derive from the company's strategy and provide critical data and information about key processes, inputs, and outputs."**
> **—The Baldrige Criteria Booklet**

5. Install the BSC system.
   - Adopt model and guidelines for critical success factors.
   - Develop measurement-system training requirements.
   - Perform competitive intelligence (i.e., research the business environment a firm operates in to influence its emerging strategy for business development).
   - Build the measurement system framework.
   - Build the indicators.
   - Develop issues and problems in BSC measurement system.
   - Prepare a structure tree for changing the system.

6. Business process improvement.
   - Benchmark the key processes.
   - Begin process reengineering.
   - Begin process redesign.
   - Create fast action solution teams (FASTs).
   - Perform area activity analysis.

> **"I am looking for a dashboard that would group key performance indicators and give me the ability to double-click on a key metric and drill down to see where the problem areas are, as opposed to wading through a sea of data."**
> **—Jeff Ferguson**
> **Past CEO, Marriott Senior Living Services**

7. Reassess BSC priorities.
   - Perform process and project evaluation.
   - Continue to benchmark best practices.
   - Perform remedial training and system enhancement.
   - Measure overall progress and replicate bright ideas.

Excellent organizations such as Cisco Systems, Dell, and GE have employed an executive "dashboard" of performance indicators that they use to manage and control the organization. The BSC brings additional dimensions to these dashboards. All organizations must develop robust dashboards that provide the executive team with the status of the organization at a glance.

KEY PERFORMANCE INDICATORS

One of the key questions in business management is, "How will the decision makers know whether the business is performing according to plan?" It's important that performance standards—also known as key performance indicators (KPIs)—are in place and that a feedback mechanism is also in place to deliver information on results back to the decision makers.

A common weakness in an entire performance management system is failure to measure the right things. What the "right" things are is a debatable point: It's up to the decision makers in your company to decide, based on what's important to them, the business, and their employees' reward systems.

What follows is a list of 101 performance measures, any of which could be right for your company.

Financial perspective
■ Total assets ($)
■ Total assets/employee ($)
■ Revenues/total assets (%)
■ Revenues from new products or business operations ($)
■ Revenues/employee ($)
■ Profits/total assets (%)
■ Profits from new products or business operations ($)
■ Profits/employee ($)
■ Market value ($)
■ Return on net assets (%)
■ Value added/employee ($)
■ Return on total assets (%)
■ Return on capital employed (%)
■ Profit margin (%)
■ Contribution/revenue or contribution margin (%)
■ Contribution employee ($)
■ Cash flow ($)
■ Shareholder equity/total assets or solvency (%)
■ Return on investment (%)
■ Total costs ($)

Customer perspective
■ Number of customers (#)
■ Market share (%)
■ Annual sales/customers ($)

- Customer lost (# or %)
- Average time spent on customer relations (#)
- Customers/employee (# or %)
- Sales closed/sales contacts (%)
- Satisfied-customer index (%)
- Customer-loyalty index (%)
- Cost/customer ($)
- Number of visits to customers (#)
- Number of complaints (#)
- Marketing expenses ($)
- Brand-image index (%)
- Average duration of customer relationship (#)
- Average customer size ($)
- Customer rating (%)
- Customer visits to the company (#)
- Average time from customer contact to sales response (#)
- Service expense/customer/year

Process perspective

- Administrative expense/total revenue (%)
- Processing time, out payments (#)
- On-time delivery (%)
- Average lead time (#)
- Lead time, product development (#)
- Lead time, from order to delivery (#)
- Lead time, suppliers (#)
- Lead time, production (#)
- Average time for decision making (#)
- Inventory turnover (#)
- Improvement in productivity (%)
- Information technology (IT) capacity (central processing unit, or CPU, and sequential access storage device, or SASD) (#)
- IT capacity/employee (#)
- Change in IT inventory ($ or %)
- IT expense/administrative expense (%)
- Emissions from production into the environment (#)
- Environmental impact of product use (#)
- Cost of administrative error/management revenues (%)
- Contacts field is error-free (#)
- Administrative expense/employee ($)

Renewal and Development/Research Perspective

- R&D expense ($)
- R&D expenses/total expenses (%)
- IT development expense/IT expense (%)
- Hours, R&D (%)
- R&D resources/total resources (%)
- Investment in training/customers (#)
- Investment in research ($)
- Investment in new product support and training ($)
- Investment in development of new markets ($)
- Direct communications to customer/year (#)
- Patents pending (#)
- Average age of company patents (#)
- Suggested improvements/employee (#)
- Competence development expense/employee ($)
- Satisfied-employee index (#)
- Marketing expense/customer ($)
- Employee's view (empowerment index) (#)
- Share of employees below age X (%)
- Nonproduct–related expense/customer/year ($)
- Ratio of new products (less than X years old) to full company catalog (%)

Human resources perspective

- Leadership index (#)
- Motivation index (#)
- Number of employees (#)
- Employee turnover (%)
- Average employee years of service with company (#)
- Average age of employees (#)
- Time in training (days/year) (#)
- Temporary employees/permanent employees (%)
- Share of employees with university degrees (%)
- Average absenteeism (#)
- Number of women managers (#)
- Number of applicants for employment at the company (#)
- Empowerment index (#)
- Number of managers (#)
- Share of employees less than 40 years old (%)
- Per capita annual cost of training ($)

- Full-time or permanent employees who spend less than 50 percent of work hours at a corporate facility (#)
- Percentage of full-time permanent employees (%)
- Per capita annual cost of training, communication, and support programs ($)
- Number of full-time temporary employees (#)
- Number of part-time employees or nonfull-time contracts (#)

(This section on performance measurements is an excerpt from the paper, "Translating Strategic Intent Into Action and Budgets," by Marek Gitlin of the Corporate Training Warehouse.)

Appendix B provides a list of measurements for nonmanufacturing departments. Appendix C shows a typical total KPI report for the ABC Co. without targets or minimum performance requirements defined as they should be.

SETTING IMPROVEMENT PRIORITIES

As previously discussed, the BSC methodology is designed to provide a system that will aid the organization in meeting its strategic planning goals and objectives. Of course, this requires that the strategic plan consider the needs and requirements of all the organization's stakeholders. For the purpose of this discussion, assume that all of the stakeholders were considered when the organization developed its strategic plan. For more information on developing plans, read my book, *Total Improvement Management* (McGraw-Hill, 1995).

The approach recommended here is significantly better than the use of causal loop diagrams that are used in BSC strategic maps. It uses the basic concept defined as quality function deployment (QFD). QFD is defined as "a structured process of taking the 'voice of the customer,' translating it into measurable customer requirements, translating the customer requirements into measurable counterpart characteristics, and developing these requirements into every level of the product and manufacturing process design and customer service process." For more information on QFD, see my book *Performance Improvement Methods* (McGraw-Hill, 1999).

This approach will proceed through two levels:

- *Level one:* analysis of the different strategies and relationship to the different stakeholder requirements
- *Level two:* analysis of the different stakeholder requirements related to the organization's processes

In setting priorities, you first need to look at the stakeholders and define the priorities that the organization places on each stakeholder. The quick answer to this is that they are all equally important, but in reality, that's not the case. For example, if you don't satisfy your investors and they take away their backing, the organization goes out of business and all of the stakeholders lose. If it's a public agency and it's not funded, it can't service any of the stakeholders. Figure 9.2 shows a typical stakeholder's priority list.

Investors were selected as the number one priority because the organization committed to them first to provide a good return on their investment. Customers were given second priority because only by providing the customer with what they expect can the organization survive. The management was given third priority because it's responsible for setting strategic direction and overall performance of the organization. Employees were given fourth priority because without them the organization cannot provide

Figure 9.2 Weighting of Stakeholders

Stakeholders	Priority	Weighting
Investors	1	10.0
Customers	2	9.5
Management	3	9.0
Employees	4	8.0
Suppliers	5	7.0
Community	6	6.0
Special interest groups	7	5.0

any output. Suppliers were given fifth priority because their input is essential to producing the organization's output. The community was given sixth priority because it provides much of the infrastructure that the organization needs. The special interest groups were given last priority because the organization must consider its obligation to society.

Next, you need to develop a weighting factor for each customer. A ten-point scale works well. The number one–priority stakeholder gets a value of ten. Then go to the lowest-priority stakeholder (special interest groups) and ask the question, "Compared with the number one-priority stakeholder, how important is it to meet this stakeholder's requirements?" In this case, say you believe it's twice as important to meet the investor's requirements as it is to meet the requirements of the special interest groups. As a result, you give the special interest group a weighting of five. This sets the range (10–5) for the weighting factors for all of the stakeholders. You use the same approach to weight all of the stakeholders. The weighting factor for each stakeholder must be less than the one that is the next-highest priority and more than the weighting factor for the lowest-priority stakeholder. (See figure 9.3.)

The next thing you must do is list five to ten priority improvement items for each of the stakeholders and set priorities for them. In this case, all of the items are important, so instead of ranking them numerically, group them as follows:

■ Critical
■ Very important
■ Important

Give *critical* items a three-point weighting, *very important* two points, and *important* one point. Drop any that are not important. Figure 9.3 defines the top five improvement measures for a typical organization's stakeholders.

Based upon the analysis performed in figure 9.3, you can now rank the stakeholders' requirements in their order of importance to the organization. (See figure 9.4.) (N = non-functional, and F = functional)

The next challenge you need to address is what processes support the strategic plan. For the sake of this discussion, assume the following activities make up the strategic plan.

- Transfer the products in Plant 1 to your Mexican alliance partner.
- Subcontract out all accounting responsibilities.
- Develop a new product that is two times faster than the present product.
- Acquire Company X to add to your product line.
- Install total quality management (TQM).
- Install a BSC system.
- Install a customer-relationship management system.

Now define the impact the strategic plan has on each of the stakeholders' requirements. (See figure 9.5.) This discussion will address only three stakeholders: investors, employees, and customers. In a real analysis, all stakeholders would be considered. To perform this analysis, you must prepare a matrix similar to figure 9.5. To keep it simple, only the first five of the seven strategic action items are analyzed to determine their impacts on the stakeholders. A ● indicates that there is a positive impact. A ▲ indicates that there was some impact. A ○ indicates that there is little or no impact and an "N" indicates that there is a negative impact. A weighting of three is given to ● for a very positive impact, a weighting of one to ▲ for some impact, no points to ○ for no impact, and -3 to "N" for a negative impact. Then multiply each requirement's weighting factor by the impact weighting factor. For example, for strategic action plan number one's impact on "return on investments," the requirements weighting factor is thirty times an impact factor of three, which equals a total weighting factor of ninety.

By summing up the total weighting factors for each stakeholder, you can evaluate the total impact on each stakeholder. For example, for strategic action plan number one the total weighting factor is:

Investors:	930
Employees:	-144
Customers:	228
Total:	1,014

Figure 9.3 Weight of the Five Top Improvement Requirements by Typical Stakeholders

	Stakeholder's ranking	Ranking weight	Requirements' weighting factor
Management's measurements of improvement	9.0		
■ Return on assets		3	27.0
■ Value-added per employee		3	27.0
■ Stock prices		2	18.0
■ Market share		1	9.0
■ Reduced operating expenses		2	18.0
Investors' measurements of improvement	10.0		
■ Return on investment		3	30.0
■ Stock prices		3	30.0
■ Return on assets		2	20.0
■ Market share		2	20.0
■ Successful new products		1	10.0
Customers' measurements of improvement	9.5		
■ Reduced cost		3	28.5
■ New or expanded capabilities		2	19.0
■ Improved performance		3	28.5
■ Ease of use		1	9.5
■ Improved responsiveness		2	19.0
Suppliers' measurements of improvement	7.0		
■ Increased return on investment (supplier)		3	21.0
■ Improved communications/fewer interfaces		2	14.0
■ Simplified requirements/fewer changes		1	7.0
■ Longer contracts		3	21.0
■ Longer cycle times		2	14.0
Employees' measurements of improvement	8.0		
■ Increased job security		3	24.0
■ Increased compensation		3	24.0
■ Improved growth potential		3	24.0
■ Improved job satisfaction		2	16.0
■ Improved morale		1	8.0
Community/mankind's measurements of improvement	6.0		
■ Employment of people		3	18.0
■ Increased tax base		2	12.0
■ Reduced pollution		2	12.0
■ Support of community activities		1	6.0
■ Safety of employees		3	18.0
Special interest groups' measurements of improvement	5.0		
■ Improved environment		3	15.0
■ Women in management		3	15.0
■ Improved job security		2	10.0
■ Reduced pollution		3	15.0
■ Safety of employees		1	

Figure 9.4 Ranking of the Stakeholders' Requirements in Order of Importance to the Organization

	Measurement type	Requirements Weight Factor							
		Management	Investors	Customers	Suppliers	Employees	Special interest	Community	Total
Value-added per employee	F	27	30						57
Return on assets	F	27	20						47
Increased job security	N					24	15		39
Stock prices	F	18	20						38
Return on investment	F		30						30
Improved performance	N			19					19
Reduced cost	F			28.5					28.5
Safety of employees	N					10		18	28
Increased compensation	N					24			24
Improved growth potential	N					24			24
Increased return on investment (supplier)	F				21				21
Longer contracts	N				21				21
New or expanded capabilities	N			19					19
Improved responsiveness	N			19					19
Employment of people	N							18	18
Reduced operating expenses	F	18							18
Reduced pollution	N					5		12	17
Improved job satisfaction	N					16			16
Improved environment	N						15		15
Women in management	N						15		15
Longer cycle times	N				14				14
Improved communications/fewer interfaces	N				14				14
Increased tax base	F							12	12
Successful new products	N		10						10
Ease of use	N			9.5					9.5
Improved morale	N					8			8
Simplified requirements/fewer changes	N				7				7
Support of community activities	N							6	6

The sum of the weighting provides a set of numerical priorities for the strategic plan:

Strategic plan 1 =   70.5
Strategic plan 2 =   12
Strategic plan 3 = 624.5
Strategic plan 4 =   307
Total: 1,014

Figure 9.5 Strategic Action Plans Versus Stakeholders' Requirements

	Requirements weighting factor	Strategic action plan number				
		1	2	3	4	
Investor						
Return on investment	30	● 90	● 90	● 90	● 90	
Stock prices	30	▲ 30	○ 0	● 90	● 90	
Return on assets	20	● 90	● 90	▲ 20	▲ 20	
Market share	20	○ 0	○ 0	● 60	▲ 20	
Successful new products	10	N 0	○ 0	● 30	● 30	
		210	180	0 290	0 250	930
Employee						
Increased job security	24	N -72	N -72	● 72	○ 0	
Increased compensation	24	○ 0	○ 0	▲ 24	○ 0	
Improved growth potential	24	N -72	N -72	● 72	○ 0	
Improved job satisfaction	16	○ 0	○ 0	○ 0	○ 0	
Improved morale	8	N -24	N -24	● 24	○ 0	
		-168	-168	192	0	-144
Customer						
Reduced cost	28.5	▲ 28.5	○ 0.0	○ 0.0	○ 0.0	
New or expanded capabilities	19.0	○ 0.0	○ 0.0	● 57.0	● 57.0	
Improved performance	28.5	○ 0.0	○ 0.0	● 85.5	○	
Ease of use	9.5	○ 0.0	○ 0.0	○ 0.0	○ 0.0	
Improved responsiveness	19.0	○ 0.0	○ 0.0	○ 0.0	○ 0.0	
		28.5	0.0	142.5	57.0	228.0
Total		**70.5**	**12.0**	**624.5**	**307.0**	**1014.0**

●	= Very positive impact	= +3
▲	= Some positive impact	= +1
○	= No impact	= 0
N	= Negative impact	= −3

You will note that there is a negative overall value for employees of -144. This is a very poor condition because the strategic plan should bring some added value to all stakeholders. This is a good indication that you need to change the strategic plan to focus on meeting more of the employees' requirements.

> **"If you don't measure something, you can't tell if it was a success or not."**
> **—Rick Berquist**
> **CTO, Senior VP, PeopleSoft**

Now you must define what processes support the implementation of each strategic actions. Figure 9.6 lists sixteen typical major business processes. The **X** in figure 9.6 indicates that the related process will be involved in carrying out that specific strategic action. For example, the **X** after the order-processing process for the column labeled "Strategic Action Plan 1" indicates that the activity will involve the order-processing process. In real life this list of major processes would usually be between twenty to sixty major business processes (**O** = process is not involved, and **X** = process is involved).

Figure 9.6 List of Major Processes That Are Impacted by the Strategic Action Plan

Major processes	Strategic action plan number							Number of hits
	1	2	3	4	5	6	7	
Requirements identification	O	X	X	O	X	X	X	5
Product development	O	O	X	O	X	O	O	2
Customer acquisition	O	O	X	O	X	O	X	3
Order processing	X	O	X	X	O	O	X	4
Performance analysis	X	O	X	O	X	O	X	4
Reporting	X	X	X	X	X	X	X	7
Facilities setup	X	O	X	O	O	O	O	2
Post-sales service	O	O	X	O	O	O	O	1
Asset management	X	X	X	O	O	O	O	3
HR management	X	X	X	O	X	X	O	5
Project management	X	X	X	X	X	X	X	7
Resources allocation	X	X	X	O	X	X	X	6
Supplier approval	X	X	X	O	X	X	O	5
Financial controls	O	X	X	X	O	O	O	3
Financial planning	X	X	X	X	X	X	O	5
Acquisitions	X	X	O	X	O	O	O	2

Business Performance Scorecards

All organizations should have defined scorecards for auditing purposes. There are many ways to present them. For example, a project management (PM) scorecard is designed for anyone involved with projects and can be used as a visual display of a project's status, including the full range of PM performance characteristics needed for a more effective and efficient project effort. Easy to use, efficient for leading teams, and effective for status presentations to senior management, a scorecard unites all critically important categories of project success—including business case and project initiation, planning, execution, control, and closeout—into one integrated framework.

POOR-QUALITY COST

Poor quality costs your organization money. Good quality saves your organization money. It's as simple as that. James E. Olson, former president of AT&T, said, "A lot of people say quality costs you too much. It does not. It will cost you less." But many organizations today don't measure the cost of poor quality, and if you don't measure it, you can't control it. Why is it, then, that those in corporate management don't insist on the same good financial control over poor-quality cost (PQC) that they exercise over the purchase of materials, when often PQC exceeds the total materials budget?

The cost of not having quality—not quality cost—is what's important. It's often cheaper to provide high-quality products and services than to provide shabby ones. Quality isn't the cost of providing an output. It's the value the customer receives from the output. Ronald Reagan, wrote, "Consumers, by seeking quality and value, set the standards of acceptability for products and services by 'voting' with their marketplace dollars, rewarding efficient producers of better quality products and performance." Donald E. Peterson, past chairman of the board of Ford Motor Co., stated, "World-class quality means providing products and services that meet customer needs and expectations at a cost that represents value to the customer." Of course, it's not necessary to produce products or services that greatly exceed the customer's expectations, but it's always necessary to fully meet those expectations. It's almost as wasteful to produce paper cups that leak as it is to produce silver-plated drinking cups that will be thrown away after one use. You must have a system that will define the difference between luxury and fitness for use, between waste and optimum performance. Part of this system is a quantification of what your organization spends because all things, people, and materials are not perfect. To put it simply, the PQC reporting system is only one of the many tools needed in a comprehensive, organizationwide quality system, but it's an important tool in that it directs management attention and measures the success of the organization's efforts to improve. It also provides management with the necessary tools to ensure that suboptimization doesn't have a negative effect on the total system. The U.S. Department of Defense recognized the importance of PQC when it included a requirement for PQC systems in military standard MIL-Q-9858A, and by the world when it evolved into ISO 9004-1004 Implementation Guidelines and cost of quality (COQ).

Poor-quality cost is defined as all the cost incurred to help the employee do the job right every time (this includes process designs that include nonvalue-added activities) and the cost of determining if the output is acceptable, plus any cost the organization and the customer incurred because the output did not meet specifications and/or customer expectations. Figure 9.7 lists the elements of PQC.

Figure 9.7 Elements of Poor-Quality Cost

I. Direct poor-quality cost
  A. Controllable poor-quality cost
    1. Prevention cost
    2. Appraisal cost
    3. Nonvalue-added cost
  B. Resultant poor-quality cost
    1. Internal error cost
    2. External error cost
  C. Equipment poor-quality cost

II. Indirect poor-quality cost
  A. Customer-incurred cost
  B. Customer-dissatisfaction cost
  C. Loss-of-reputation cost
  D. Lost-opportunity cost

Where Is PQC Used?

During the 1960s and 1970s, PQC was used primarily to measure manufacturing and warranty costs, but in recent years management has realized that all departments (both blue-collar and white-collar) make errors. Numerous studies have shown that white-collar PQC accounts for 35 percent to 85 percent of the total effort expended by these departments without even considering indirect PQC. For example, when IBM started applying PQC to accounting, it was running at 62 percent of the accounting budget. In one European company, PQC in development engineering was running about 82 percent of its total budget. In organizations that add in indirect PQC, that cost often runs well over 100 percent of the organization's total budget. Most organizations accept as a way of life the cost of administrative errors and the resulting checks and balances. Applying PQC to the white-collar areas focuses management attention on this neglected waste.

It's also necessary to apply PQC systems to the impact that errors have on the customer. Frequently, the cost to the customer when an error occurs can far exceed the cost of repairing the defective item. Consider a ten-year-old boy who is delighted to find a new red and white bicycle beneath the Christmas tree. When he and his father try to assemble the bicycle, everything goes well until they attempt to put on the front wheel and find that a nut is missing. As a result, before the boy can ride the bicycle, the father must make a trip to the bicycle store, wait in line to get a new nut, and return home—a waste of one hour of valuable time and twenty-four miles of travel. The cost to the company is a $.05 nut; the cost to the customer is 300 times more.

Why Use PQC?

Poor-quality cost provides a very useful tool to change the way management and employees think about errors. PQC helps by:

- *Getting management's attention.* Talking to management in dollars provides information that it relates to. It takes quality out of the abstract and makes it a reality that can effectively compete with cost and schedule.

- *Changing the way employees think about errors.* When as a result of an employee's actions a defective gear is scrapped, the impact will be greater on his or her future performance if the employee knows it costs $100. In one case, what is thrown away is only a piece of metal; in the other case, it's a $100 bill. Employees must understand the cost of errors they make.

- *Providing better return on problem-solving efforts.* Poor-quality cost "dollarizes" problems so that you can direct corrective action at the solutions that will bring maximum return. James R. Houghton, former chairman of Corning Glass, has reported, "At Corning, cost of quality is being used to identify opportunities, to help prioritize those opportunities, and to set targets and measure progress. It's a tremendous tool, but we are taking great care to ensure that it is not used as a club."

- *Providing a means to measure the true impact of corrective action and changes made to improve the process.* By focusing on PQC of the total process, you can eliminate suboptimization.

- *Providing a simple, understandable method of measuring what effect poor quality has on the company and providing an effective way to measure the impact of the quality-improvement process.*

Armand V. Feigenbaum, while working at GE's Schenectady Works in 1943, developed a dollar-based reporting system called "cost of quality" (COQ). This system pulled together all the costs related to developing the quality system and inspecting products, as well as the cost incurred when the product failed to meet requirements. He then provided management with a report that got its attention—one that was based on dollars, the language of top management and the stockholder. The COQ system was adopted the next year by GE's Jet Engine Group in Massachusetts. By 1948, it was in use throughout GE USA.

Feigenbaum first published a brief view of COQ in the magazine of the American Institute of Electrical Engineers, and then again in 1951 in his book *Total Quality Control* (now in its fourth edition, McGraw-Hill, 1994). The first detailed publication appeared in a 1956 issue of *Harvard Business Review*. His 1943 concept divided cost of quality into the following four categories:

1. Prevention cost
2. Appraisal cost
3. Internal defect cost
4. External defect cost

In discussing quality cost, Feigenbaum stated, "Our original development of concept and quantification of quality costs has had the objective of equipping men and women throughout a company with the necessary practical tools and detailed economic know-how for identifying and managing their own costs of quality."

Through the years, Feigenbaum has refined and expanded his quality-cost concept to the point that today it provides an excellent management tool that can be used to direct quality-improvement activities and measure the effectiveness of the total quality system. He now calls quality costs the "cost of delivering customer satisfaction." In a conversation a few years ago, he stated, "We've added additional components to the concept that will be defined in the new edition of my *Total Quality Control* book."

REWARDS AND RECOGNITION

> "We're trying to get 'the ideal deal'—the combination of rewards and processes that create the utmost employee commitment and engagement."
> **—Daryl David**
> **Human Resources director, Xilinx**

Book III of this series discussed rewards and recognition in relation to change management. Because it's such a very important factor in individual and group performance, here are some other considerations regarding rewards and recognition.

It would be a big mistake to fail to point out the importance of a rewards-and-recognition system for excellence in discussing resource management because it's such an important human enabler.

Ingredients of a Company Recognition Process

> "What gets measured and rewarded, gets done."
> **—Gordon Bethune**
> **Chairman & CEO, Continental Airlines**

A good recognition process has six major objectives:

- To provide recognition to employees who make unusual contributions to the company to stimulate additional effort for further improvement
- To show the company's appreciation for superior performance
- To ensure maximum benefits from the recognition process by an effective communication system that highlights the individuals who were recognized
- To provide many ways to recognize employees for their efforts and stimulate management creativity in the recognition process. Management must understand that variation enhances the impact.

> "You need to go after and reward the short-term wins while maintaining a clear sense of direction."
> **—Joe W. Forehand**
> **CEO, Accenture**

- To improve morale through the proper use of recognition
- To reinforce behavioral patterns that management would like to see continued

Why does recognition matter? George Blomgren, president of Organizational Psychologists, puts it this way, "Recognition lets people see themselves in a winning identity role. There's a universal need for recognition, and most people are starved for it."

A National Science Foundation study made the same point. "The key to having workers who are both satisfied and productive is motivation, that is, arousing and maintaining the will to work effectively—having workers who are productive not because they are coerced but because they are committed."

The seven major types of recognition are:

- Financial compensation
- Monetary awards
- Personal public recognition
- Group public recognition
- Private recognition
- Peer recognition
- Organizational awards

Financial Compensation

A study by the Public Agenda Foundation revealed that:

- Employees are not rewarded for putting out extra effort.
- Almost two-thirds of the employees would like to see a better connection between performance and pay.
- More than 70 percent of employees think that the reason work effort has deteriorated is because there is no connection between pay and performance.

Bell Atlantic is trying a new pay for performance system. It is holding back pay from its 23,000 manager-level employees and will distribute this money to them at the end of the year, with more of it going to the high-performing managers.

Salaries are important, and the means for relating quality and productivity to salary and an effective performance appraisal system are important ingredients for motivation. But other types of financial compensation can also motivate improvements in productivity and quality. In addition to salaries, typical financial compensations are:

- Commissions
- Piecework pay
- Employee stock plans
- Cash bonuses
- Gain sharing

Commissions

Have you ever noticed how enthusiastic your Avon salesperson is when he or she knocks on your door? Did you see the same degree of enthusiasm in your company's order clerk the last time you placed an order for a gross of paper clips? The difference is that the clerk in the order department is working for a salary, while the door-to-door salesperson is working for a commission. The better the service to customers, the more return sales made and the more money earned. The successful salesperson is always turned on because he or she looks at the last sale as additional compensation that wasn't there before finding the client. But the clerk in the order department looks at the new order of paper clips as additional work that wasn't really needed and that has no impact upon personal financial status.

"If we have not made significant progress, I will expect to take a reduction in my personal compensation."
—Joe W. Forehand
CEO, Accenture

Customers in the service industry are being turned off today, not by price but by carelessness, discourtesy, and disinterest. Customers want a caring and friendly salesclerk, a cheerful "Good morning, may I help you?" They want to be treated as valuable individuals who are important to the clerk and to the company. If you show them this type of consideration, they will buy more and come back again and again. Commissions provide a means to motivate certain employees to do more and better work. Commissions work to improve the salesperson's productivity. This same principle can be applied to other white-collar activities. For example, a design engineer could receive a percentage of the profit from a product he or she designed.

Piecework Pay

Piecework was a popular method of increasing productivity in the first part of the twentieth century and still is widely practiced in some parts of the world. In essence, this system pays the employee a share of the value added to the item being processed, based upon the effort, skill, and time required to complete the task. Along with the sweatshop, piecework has slowly been phased out of the American scene because although it did increase raw productivity, it did not emphasize quality and it resulted in a great deal of suboptimization.

Employee Stock Plans

Employee stock plans are increasingly popular because they provide an effective means of focusing the employees' attention on the business aspects of the company by allowing them to share in the profits. They also help to break down the "we and they" feeling many employees have about the company because from their standpoint, the stockholders are the ones who make all the money from the employees' hard work.

In commenting about the stock purchase plan Hewlett-Packard (HP) uses, John Young, its former president, said, "The company contributes $1 for every $3 an employee puts in. More than three-fourths of our people participate in the plan. The result has been that since employees own part of the company, they feel ownership for some of the company's problems and successes."

More than 10 million U.S. workers already belong to employee stock plans, and within fifteen years more than 25 percent of all U.S. workers will join the parade. The number of new employee stock plans is growing at about 10 percent per year, spurred on by the 1984 U.S. tax incentive.

A recent study of 360 high-technology companies conducted by the National Center for Employee Ownership concluded that companies that share ownership with their employees grew two to four times faster than companies that did not have employee stock plans.

The object of an employee stock plan is literally to make capitalists out of all employees. Many plans have been developed and used to directly tie the employees' economic future into the success of the company. One of the more popular plans now in use is called the employee stock ownership plan. Lewis O. Kelso, a San Francisco lawyer, developed the theory behind this kind of plan.

Cash Bonuses and Gain Sharing

HRD Training Journal reports that more than 75 percent of manufacturing companies in the United States have an executive bonus plan. A study of 1,000 companies revealed that companies with executive bonus plans average better than 40 percent pretax profit.

Cash bonuses and gainsharing are not new—they can be traced back to Roman civilization. In modern times, they have been a proven, effective way for a company to share its profits with its employees. Suggestion awards should be separate from the bonus system and should be paid directly to the employee who makes the suggestion.

The bonus concept is used extensively in Japan, where many companies give bonuses twice a year, once just before summer vacation, and another during the first part of December. In very good years, the bonus has been known to almost equal the employee's salary. In bad years, the employees don't expect a bonus, and they are not disappointed when they don't get one.

John Young, former president of HP, explains that HP has "profit-sharing among all employees, where everyone gets the same percentage of base salary as a bonus. The amount people receive depends on our profitability, and that really helps get everyone in the organization pulling in the same direction." Companies that use gainsharing programs find their employees starting to think differently, starting to learn and use new vocabulary—words such as "profits," "gross sales," and "production costs" start to slip into their conversation because they see for the first time a direct correlation between their well-being and the well-being of the company.

At General Motors, managers tell employees about the plant's direct labor costs, scrap and rework costs, and profits compared to targets that the company has set for itself. This is information that only top management had in the 1970s. General Motors believes that providing employees with this kind of information helps to close the gap between management and labor. It has proven to be an effective way of aligning company and employee goals and developing a partnership between the two groups that until recently were in opposition to each other.

Most employees would be happy to have their salaries linked to higher productivity. To take advantage of this opportunity for employee involvement through the years, different kinds of bonus and gainsharing programs have been developed. Most of them focus on an equal division of a pool of money among the employees, tied to their base salaries. Of these programs, the best known are:

- Scanlon plan
- Rucker plan
- Improshare plan

Individual or Team Bonus Systems

Individual incentive or bonus programs are difficult (but not impossible) to administer in nonsales activities in large corporations. In small companies, individual incentive programs have very definite advantages. They require a lot of management attention and emphasis, but the resulting improvement is well worth the effort. Delta Business Systems, a $32 million company with headquarters in Orlando, Florida, applied thirteen different incentive programs to its more than 2,000 nonsales positions. For example:

- Warehouse workers divide up to $400 every two months for filling orders on schedule, processing paper so that the company receives the allowed cash discount, and keeping the operation working smoothly.
- For retaining their customer base, giving sales personnel leads, and getting maintenance agreements renewed, the field service technicians can increase their salaries by 3 percent to 25 percent.
- People in accounts payable were offered up to $200 a quarter to reduce outstanding unpaid bills. As a result, the long-term accounts payable were reduced by 50 percent.

Bryan King, president of the company, put it this way: "If we can see how fast someone's canoe moves in the water, we provide an incentive for him to improve."

Monetary Awards

Monetary awards are another class of recognition. The work "award" indicates it is a unique recognition of an individual or small group for unusual contributions to the company's goals. Monetary awards are one-time bonuses paid to the recipient immediately after an unusual or far-exceeds-expectations contribution. They may also be given to individuals for long-term, continuous, and high-level performance or unique leadership. The award should be specific, and management and fellow employees should perceive the person or people who receive the award as "special." The amount of the monetary award should vary based upon the magnitude of the contribution.

Typical Monetary Awards

The many types of monetary awards reflect differing degrees of contribution. These three are typical:

- Suggestions awards
- Patent awards
- Contribution awards

Suggestion awards. These tap into employees' creativity. Best practices result in each employee turning in two suggestions per month, with 80 percent of them being implemented. Examples of organizations that are performing at that level and how to accomplish it can be found in *The Idea Generator,* by Norman Bodek and Buniji Tozawa (PCS Press, 2001).

Patent Awards. This type of award may present a problem to management. In most cases, the people who are applying for patents are being paid to develop them. Nevertheless, you want to encourage the individual who is generating new creative ideas that are generating hundreds of jobs and large revenues for the company. Some companies use a plateau award system. In these systems, the employee accumulates points based on the number of patents received and the potential contribution that each patent makes to the company. As the employee moves up from one award level to the next level, the company gives more meaningful awards.

Contribution awards. An effective contribution award system must provide flexibility or recognition to management and equity to all employees. It must be based on actual contributions of the person and must be administered in all areas using the same ground rules. This discussion will use the following contribution award system.

As the contribution to the company increases, the value of the monetary reward increases, and it becomes increasingly difficult to obtain management approval to give the award (see figure 9.8). For example, a line manager should be able to give one of his employees a night out for two when the occasion warrants it. On the other hand, the outstanding contribution award should be supported with a very detailed written description of the contribution and its impact on the company. A company recognition review board should review it to ensure that the award system is being interpreted equitably in all areas of the company. The award should be presented at a formal meeting with the total function in attendance. In addition to the money, the employee should receive some special award jewelry (tie tack, ring, pin, etc.) and a framed certificate. The jewelry provides a continuous reminder to people that the program is viable and available to them.

Figure 9.8 Contribution Award System

Award	Dollar amount
Outstanding contribution award	1,000 to 50,000
Recognition award	500 to 1,000
Weekend on the town award	400
A night out for two award	85

Remember, the award system is designed to recognize people who have achieved something over and above what they are normally expected to accomplish. It's not given for a normal job well done. Only the truly outstanding people should receive contribution awards.

Personal Public Recognition

An almost endless list of types of recognition do not directly involve money. Here are some ideas that should stimulate your thinking and give you something to build on:

- Promotions
- Office layout, size, or possibly view
- Trips to customer locations
- Company recognition meetings
- Annual improvement conferences
- Jewelry
- Special parking spaces
- Articles in newsletter
- Public notice posted on the bulletin board (one plant in New York City has a huge billboard on top of the plant that flashes the names and accomplishments of special individuals)
- Employee's picture on a poster
- Verbal recognition at a department, division, or company meeting
- Special job assignments
- Plaque presented in front of fellow workers
- Plaque in the company entranceway with the employee's picture and name

Stacoswitch Corp. in Costa Mesa, California, provided all its supervisors with badges that read: "We do it right or we don't do it at all." Supervisors with the lowest reject rate had gold stars on their badges. When he was vice president of operations, Harry E. Williams wrote, "Supervisors soon took pride in being able to achieve the smallest number of rejects, and requests for refurbished tooling, drawing changes, and capital equipment increased notably."

National Car Rental uses commemorative plaques with individual employee names that hang in its business offices around the United States. A typical plaque would read: "Carrie Harrington deserves national attention for outstanding performance, second quarter, 1986."

Group Public Recognition

Recognition of the group makes the group think that it's a winner, and the members of the group get a sense of belonging that leads to increased company loyalty.

Again, management has an unlimited number of ways to recognize a group for contribution. Typical ways are:

- Articles about the group's improvement in the company's newsletter, accompanied by photographs of the group
- Department luncheons to recognize specific accomplishments
- Family recognition picnics
- Progress presentations to upper management
- Luncheons with upper management
- Group attendance at technical conferences
- Cake and coffee at a group meeting, paid for by the company
- Department improvement plaques
- Top management's attending group meetings to say thanks for a job well done
- Group mementos (pen sets, calculators, product models, etc.)

Private Recognition

Of all recognition categories, this is one of the most important because it directly relates to the interaction between management and the employee. The one-on-one interaction is very important in stimulating improvement and keeping morale high.

Many managers feel strange telling employees they are doing a good job, and frequently the employee has a hard time accepting compliments and reacts with comments such as: "Ah, knock off that bull!" or "Don't give me compliments, give me money!" But such comments don't mean they don't need the manager's appreciation. So don't let it prevent you from expressing your honest appreciation for a task well done. Employees need encouragement and must have management appreciation to reinforce their good acts. A sincere pat on the back at the right time is much better and more effective than a swift kick in the pants at any time.

Typical ways that management provides private recognition to an employee are:

- A simple, honest thank you for a job well done, given immediately after the task is completed
- A letter sent to the employee's house by his or her manager or upper manager, thanking him or her for a specific contribution
- Personal notes on letters or reports, complimenting the originator on content or layout
- Sending birthday cards and work anniversary cards to an employee's house, thanking the employee for the contributions that were made during the past year, not with general statements but with specific examples that let the employee know that management knows that the employee is there and what he or she is doing

The performance evaluation that takes place every three months is an ideal time to give private feedback to the employee about accomplishments. It shouldn't be the first time you will have expressed your appreciation, but you should use it to reinforce the favorable work patterns and summarize employee accomplishments. The most basic rule of performance evaluations is "no surprises."

Peer Recognition

One of the most significant rewards is the sincere appreciation of your peers for a job well done. Frequently, these types of rewards are associated with professional societies, where practicing professionals select the brightest and best in their profession to honor at an awards luncheon. The same concept has become a very positive motivating force within many organizations where award recipients are selected by the employees, not by management.

Often, management establishes the ground rules and financial constraints related to peer-recognition rewards. Employee representatives then define what types of behavior should be recognized and establish how they will be rewarded. Empowering employees to select the reward can provide management with very pleasant surprises about creative ways employees will apply a limited reward budget. Typically, when management prepares a rewards ceremony, it turns out to be a ceremony. When employees plan the same event, it often becomes a party, and the gifts that are presented come from the heart rather than the pocketbook.

Organizational Awards

The importance of building organizational trust and pride in employees' minds is a major objective of most improvement processes. Unfortunately, organizational pride has slipped in most Western organizations during the past forty years.

Organizations should start to rebuild the pride that employees have in their organizations, for when individuals are proud of their organizations, they will also take more pride in the things they do. One of the chief advantages that Japan has over Western countries is the pride and dedication that country's employees have for their organizations.

An effective way of building employees' pride is to have the organization recognized as outstanding by its peers. This is what the recent series of organizational improvement awards are accomplishing, as well as setting benchmarks for other organizations. Many award programs are implemented throughout the world to recognize excellence in individual organizations. Some of them are:

- Deming Prize—Japan
- Japan Quality Control Prize—Japan
- Malcolm Baldrige National Quality Award—United States
- Shingo Prize—United States
- NASA Award—United States
- President's Award—United States

- European Quality Award—Europe
- Australian Quality Award—Australia
- Best Hardware Laboratory—IBM worldwide
- International Asia Pacific Quality Award—Asia-Pacific

Implementing the Reward Process

To develop an effective reward process, you must take many factors into consideration. These steps will help you avoid most reward process problems:

- *Reward fund.* The organization should set aside a specific amount of money to use in the reward process. This amount will set the boundaries within which the reward process will operate.

> **"Don't go around saying the world owes you a living. The world owes you nothing; it was here first."**
> **—Mark Twain**

- *Reward task team (RTT).* This team will design and update the reward process.
- *Present reward process.* The RTT should pull together a list of all the formal and informal rewards that are now used within the organization.
- *Desired behaviors.* The RTT should prepare a list of the desired behaviors.
- *Present reward process analysis.* It should review the present reward process to identify the rewards that are not in keeping with the organization's present and projected future culture and visions.
- *Desired behavior analysis.* It now compares each desired behavior to the reward categories to see which category or categories should be used to reinforce the desired behavior. Each behavior should have at least two ways of rewarding people who practice the behavior.
- *Reward usage guide.* After defining the reward process, the RTT should prepare a reward usage guide. This guide should define the purpose of each of the reward categories and the procedures that will be used to formally process the reward. This guide will help management and employees understand the reward process and will help standardize the way rewards are used throughout the organization.
- *Management training.* Management should be trained (by the personnel department or a consultant) how to use the reward system, one of the most neglected parts of most management training processes. Most managers are far too conservative with their approach to rewards, while others misuse them.

In creating a reward process, consider the following:

- Always have it reinforce desired behaviors.
- Reward for exceptional customer service and performance.
- Publish why rewards are given.

- Create a point system that can be used to recognize teams and individuals for small and large contributions. The employee should be able to accumulate points through time to receive a higher level reward.
- Structure the reward process so that 50 percent of the employees will receive at least a first-level reward each year.
- Structure the reward process so that the managers can exercise their creativity and personal knowledge of the recipient in selecting the reward.
- Provide ways that anyone can recognize a person for his or her contributions.
- Provide an instant reward mechanism.

In her paper "Reinforcing Quality," Shelly Sweet, a Palo Alto, California, quality consultant, warns against these seven pitfalls:
- Cumbersome procedures that are costly to administer.
- Executives or middle managers who don't consistently support the program.
- Awards that are applied inconsistently.
- Unexpected behaviors result.
- Employees who perceive that the same employees are rewarded repeatedly.
- Enthusiasm wanes.
- Company cost-cutting curtails the program.

"I can live two months on a good compliment."
—Mark Twain

STAKEHOLDER MEASUREMENTS SUMMARY

Why do improvement efforts fail? One of the major reasons is a lack of hard, measurable results in all functions and areas of an organization. There's a real need to see the economic impact (for example, return on investment) for both the short term and the long term. The strategy, the objectives, and the associated measures are the keys to being a winner. When all employees understand the relationship between their performance and the organization's success, they will make the ultimate efforts to be winners and sustain their jobs and lifestyles.

The following shows how three types of organizations approach measurements.

- Attitude about measurement
  - ☐ Losers: It's not important.
  - ☐ Survivors: It's treated as an afterthought.
  - ☐ Winners: They set up the measurement process at the beginning of the process so that a baseline is defined and progress can be measured.

■ Targets
  ☐ Losers: Management sets targets.
  ☐ Survivors: Employees set targets for themselves.
  ☐ Winners: Management sets business targets. The employees set more stringent challenge targets for themselves. The target is less important than the trend.

■ Measurement communications
  ☐ Losers: Data are collected so that management can keep things under control.
  ☐ Survivors: Job-related measurements are shared with the employees.
  ☐ Winners: All the improvement measurements are posted for everyone to see and reviewed with the employees as a team at least four times a year.

■ How measurements are used
  ☐ Losers: To identify individuals who need to improve
  ☐ Survivors: To define problems and measure progress
  ☐ Winners: To help the individual understand his or her impact on the organization and align the individual goals to those of the organization

CHAPTER X

ORGANIZATIONAL STRUCTURE

"Don't fight the culture. Mold to it."
—HJH

ENTERPRISE STRUCTURE

Today's organizations face very different problems than ever before when determining how they should be organized. The participative environment has changed the way many organizations look at the organization chart. Organizations around the world have acted to flatten their structure, minimizing the number of handoff points between the CEO and the employees. The theorists thought that flattening the organization would result in more meaningful, challenging work for everyone. In truth, it has created an atmosphere in which management feels overburdened and underappreciated. Peter F. Drucker, the management guru, stated, "The cynicism out there is frightening. Middle management has become insecure and they feel unbelievably hurt. They feel like slaves on the auction block."

Middle and first-line managers are afraid to make decisions because if they do, they put themselves in jeopardy of becoming second-guessed later on. It's just safer to ask the boss what should be done than to stick your neck out. Of course, this type of attitude stifles creativity and initiative in any organization. The old Japanese saying describes the situation well: "The nail that sticks up the farthest is the first one to get knocked down." Even Japanese organizations don't trust middle management outside of Japan. A survey during the late 1990s of the major Japanese companies noted the following results:

- 67 percent were unwilling to let middle management take part in decisions on long-term funding.
- 66 percent did not involve middle managers in decisions on new plans.
- 42 percent would not let them take part in research and development.

Maybe it's wrong that management should think that the customer is king. Possibly the best way for the organization to survive and prosper is for management to believe that the employees are kings and queens and treat them as very special resources. If management focused on servicing its employees rather than the customers, it would allow its employees to provide the best possible service to the external customers, resulting in the organization's overall best performance.

Figure 10.1 Organization Charts (Old and New Look)

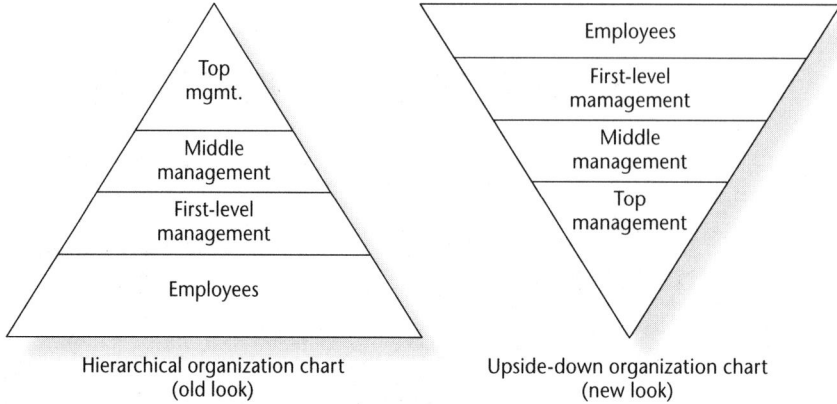

Hierarchical organization chart
(old look)

Upside-down organization chart
(new look)

Obviously, something must be done about organizational structure for survival in the twenty-first century. To accomplish this, many of the advanced organizations are talking about turning upside down the old pyramid with management on the top and the employee on the bottom. (See figure 10.1.)

Note that the upside-down pyramid rests on a single point, which is ridiculous. Anyone who would suggest this type of organization is looking at creating more problems for the organization. What could be more unstable than a pyramid resting on its point? Any little pressure on either side or off the centerline would cause the pyramid to topple. What's needed is a completely different model for organizational structure. (See figure 10.2.)

Note that in this model everyone is in touch with the resources to perform his or her assignment and is also in touch with the external customer's needs and requirements.

Figure 10.2 Preferred Organizational Model

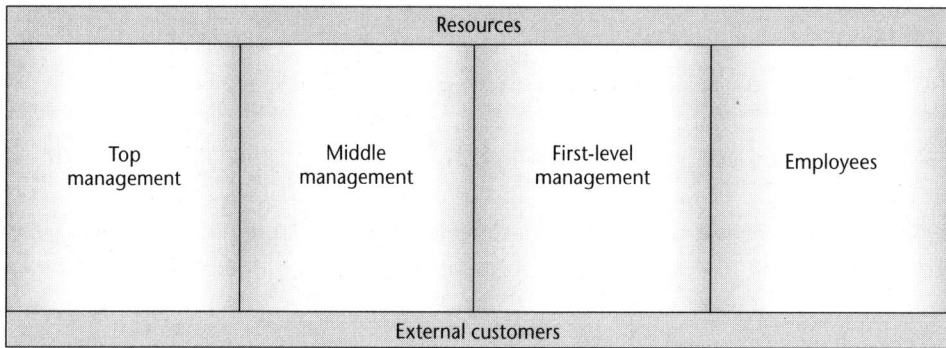

This model provides a rectangular structure that is stable, and it provides the basis for a truly knowledge-driven organization. It also lends itself to the concept that organizations should use processes that flow across boundaries to connect the organization's business. This way of looking at organizational structure indicates that all activities are important, that five-way communications exist, and that employees within the organization have an obligation to make the best use of the organization's resources for their efforts to service the internal and external customers.

> **"If you can streamline that (the organization structure) and focus just on the customer out there in the field and not try to build total organizations in every country, boy, you can be a lot more agile and focused and get a lot more sales time out of your organization while significantly reducing the number of people."**
> **—Robert J. Herbold**
> **Former COO, Microsoft**

The challenge facing all organizations is to continuously reinvent themselves in an environment that is driven by increased competition, shorter product life cycles, increased customer expectations, and with changes coming at them faster and faster. To develop an organization that is continuously reinventing itself, top management must consider developing a:

- Breakthrough risk-taking environment
- Exciting customer experience
- Flexible business model

> "An organization must continuously reinvent itself or it will continually slip backward."
>
> —HJH

IT'S TIME TO RESTRUCTURE YOUR ORGANIZATION

The methodology for organizational restructuring is based on five interdependent and distinct stages. (See figure 10.3.)

The first stage looks at the cultural aspects of the organization. In this stage, the level of the organization's readiness for the change program (culture assessment) is evaluated. The second stage, capability assessment, is the most comprehensive. Other stages include competency assessment (human resources issues) and competitiveness assessment (looking at deliverables in terms of expected benefits as well as approaches for deploying the strategic goals and monitoring the performance of the newly designed structure and work systems associated with it). The last stage, communication, is one that deals with project management, communication, information flow, and reporting aspects.

- Culture assessment
  - □ *Mission:* To gauge the level of readiness for the change program and to ensure that values are instilled in the right way, and the work climate is supportive of the restructuring initiative. To define the strengths and weakness of the present culture.

Figure 10.3 Customer-Centric Chain

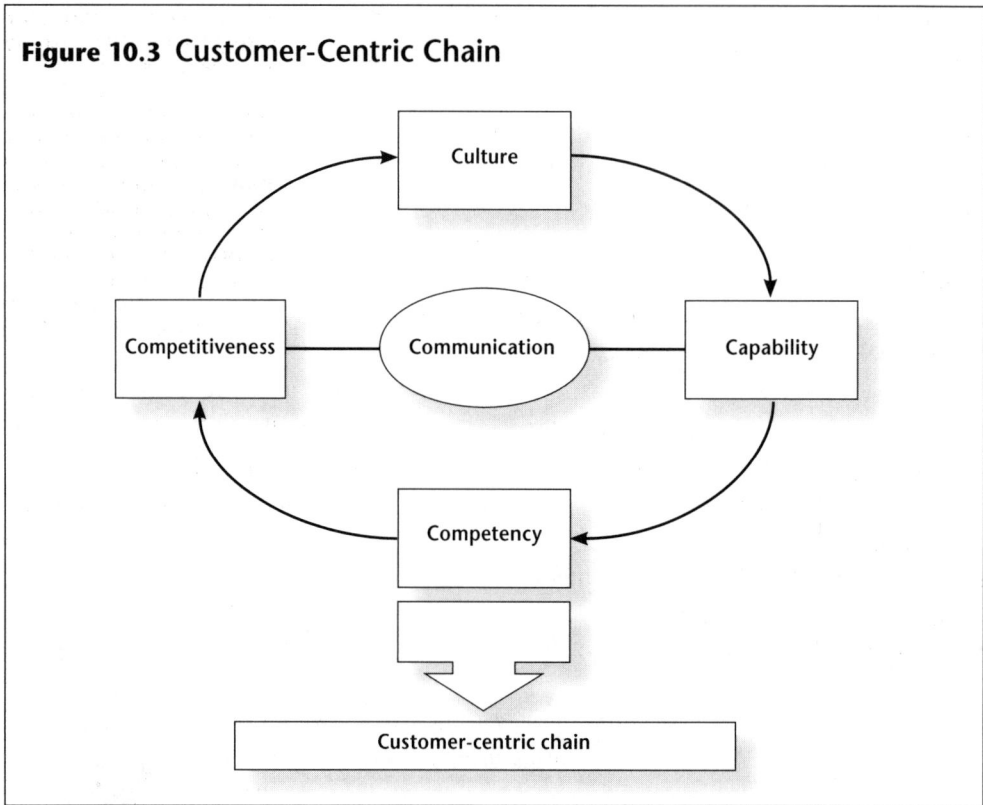

- Capability assessment
  - *Mission:* To analyze the status quo in terms of work organizational design and delivery. To conduct a comprehensive evaluation (gap analysis). To work on redesign options that are compatible with the organization's vision and strategy and that are viable in terms of helping deliver the sought after goals.

- Competency assessment
  - *Mission:* To evaluate the current human resources (HR) mix of skills and expertise level and to determine gaps in competency that are critical for implementing the new work systems needed to meet the strategy plan.

- Competitiveness Assessment
  - *Mission:* To ensure that the process by which the new structure is effected is in harmony with a systematic methodology for goal development and deployment, and to further ensure that performance evaluation and reporting can enable optimization of processes and results.

Figure 10.4 Five Phases of Organizational Alignment

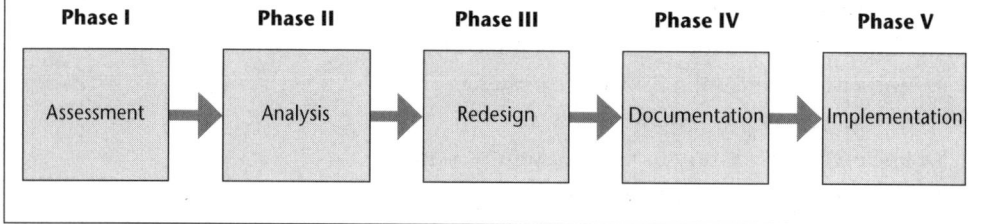

Phase I	Phase II	Phase III	Phase IV	Phase V
Assessment	Analysis	Redesign	Documentation	Implementation

- Communication assessment
  - *Mission:* To ensure that project planning, execution, and reporting are effective and to keep the right communication strategy at all levels. To align the information and knowledge flow with the needs of the strategy plan.

Aligning an Organization Chart With Its Strategy Plan

The following five-phase approach is used for realignment of the organization. (See figure 10. 4.)

1. *Assessment.* Analyze the organization's present structure to define its strengths and weaknesses.
2. *Analysis.* Review the organizational requirements.
3. *Redesign.* Redesign the organizational structure and processes.
4. *Documentation.* Document the redesign of the organizational structure and the flow of the major processes.
5. *Implementation.* Establish the interdepartmental and customer measurement and relationships.

Phase I—Assessment

During this phase you will need to conduct a comprehensive review and analysis of the present organizational design, governance, lines of business, operations, and services to identify strengths and weaknesses within the present processes. This analysis will focus on how work flows within, between, and out of the departments and different branches. Both workflow and knowledge-flow maps will aid in this analysis. Customers of all major processes will be interviewed to help define improvement opportunities.

Also during phase I you will measure the level of resistance to change so that you identify high- and medium-risk areas, and the organizational change management strategy will begin to take shape.

Another part of phase I will be to understand the measurement system and how effective it is. Then you should analyze which measurements are relevant to the new strategies and where the measurement system must be improved. Based upon the present workflow charts and the volume of work, you should then assess how well the human resources are aligned with the task at hand and the skills level required to perform the present assignments.

Phase I Major Activities

1. Review each organization's objectives/missions.
2. Define each organization's major processes.
3. Define each organization's workflow.
4. Define each area's ability to meet present workload.
5. Define shortcomings in the present system.
6. Develop knowledge maps.
7. Conduct customer interviews.
8. Conduct a culture assessment.
9. Develop a change management plan.
10. Prepare a communication plan.
11. Conduct an analysis of organizational resistance to change.
12. Analyze current measurement system.
13. Prepare and present reports.
14. Manage projects.
15. Prepare project plan.

Phase I Deliverables

1. Knowledge maps
2. Workflow maps
3. Report on risks and enablers of organizational change management
4. Present workload and skills analysis report
5. Lists of improvement opportunities
6. Status reports
7. Minutes of all key meetings

Phase II—Analysis

During this phase you should define the new requirements as they apply to each major process. These requirements will be based upon the organization's vision, mission, value, goals, and objectives, as well as any specific objectives that are individually set by individual sections and departments.

You will then compare these requirements to the current decentralized and outsourcing plan to define gaps and opportunities for improvement in overall performance. During this phase you will conduct a change management study to define the level of resistance to the new strategic plan and to define high- and medium-risk inhibitors that can cause the plan to fail or limit its effectiveness. This input will play an important role in the redesign process that occurs in phase III.

You will then analyze the functional capability and information flow for each department to define managerial, human-factor, equipment, and organizational constraints that will negatively affect the implementation of the strategic plan. You will also analyze the organization's change management plan and the level of skill that the organization's change agents have to define if additional skills are required.

Based upon the data collected in phase I and II, you should develop a set of design principles that address the eight "C" changes:

- Cultural change
- Capability change
- Communication change
- Consistency change
- Cooperational change
- Career-growth change
- Competency change
- Competitiveness change

These eight Cs are the driving force behind any organizational redesign and make up part of the "customer-centric change" process.

Phase II Major Activities

1. Implement the communication plan.
2. Implement the change management plan.
3. Obtain customer inputs related to the new strategies.
4. Analyze each major process to define how it needs to change.
5. Define gaps between today's process and the new processes.
6. Conduct a study to define the level of resistance to the new strategy.
7. Define high- and medium-risk inhibitors.
8. Compare the skills of present personnel to those required.
9. Conduct a benchmark study to define best practices for core processes.
10. Identify present processes that could be outsourced.
11. Develop a set of principles that will be used to redesign the organizational structure.
12. Define how the measurement system must be changed.
13. Define what measurement the new organizational structure would improve.
14. Prepare status meeting reports.
15. Manage project (coordination).

Phase II Deliverables

1. A gap analysis report between the current organization's capabilities and the required future-state capabilities
2. A set of principles to be used for realigning the organizational structure

3. A comprehensive list of design criteria that will be used to guide the redesign activities, including key performance indicators
4. A list of high- and medium-risk factors
5. A list of major obstacles to the required transformation
6. An analysis report of change agents' skills
7. Status reports
8. Minutes of all key meetings

Phase III—Redesign

By the time you start phase III, the improvement opportunities are well defined and, as a result, you must effectively implement the organizational change management plan. Organizational restructuring is one of the most stressful changes that any organization will undergo. You can't wait until the design is completed before you start to reduce the fear in every employee's mind about restructuring. As a result, you must start breaking down the managers' and employees' resistance to the organization's restructuring and start to build a resilient organization. This is a time when concepts such as cascading sponsorship and pain management become very important. It's a time when you need to identify the key informal leaders and incorporate them into the activities of the design concept team.

At the beginning of phase III, you should define a set of key measurable, functional parameters that will guide the redesign team and will be used to show improvements over the present structure of the organization. *The organizational restructuring should never be carried out unless there is a significant measurable improvement in the organization's performance as a result of the restructuring.* Although these measurements are important, the organization's culture must also play an important consideration in selecting the final design.

It's often a good idea to apply two very different approaches to organizational restructuring of an organization's operations. They are:

- Approach I—Design the organization around the processes that service the external customers. The support processes are then added as necessary to support the key delivery processes.
- Approach II—Design the organization around the core capabilities and competencies of the organization.

Although these two approaches are very process oriented, you should fully understand the advantages and disadvantages of the functional and matrix organizational structures (i.e., approaches I and II, respectively). You must remember that cultural and change management considerations always play a very key part in the final organizational design, and you must take them into consideration.

Of course, you should consider all of the enablers when you are analyzing the redesign process. Enablers such as technology, people, processes, and change are all key to optimizing total organizational performance. You will apply all these considerations to the process design after you streamline the processes and define the outsourcing opportunities. This leads directly to defining the organizational structure and the individual units' roles, responsibilities, and reporting structure.

Once this is defined, you should develop knowledge (communication) maps that link the individual units. When you implement the final organizational design, you should use methodologies such as area activity analysis to develop interunit performance specifications and goals for each natural work team. My book *Area Activity Analysis* (McGraw-Hill, 1998) provides a detailed explanation of how this is accomplished.

Once the design is complete, you should develop detailed descriptions of each function's responsibilities and functional flowcharts. Also, you should complete an analysis of present skills and required skills. The alignment team then should work with key staff to develop estimates of how the new organizational structure will affect the key performance measurements and establish a timeline for improved performance objectives. These analyses will be key in establishing redesign alternatives. This will lead directly to the preparation of a value proposition for the redesign.

In addition, you should conduct a risk analysis for both redesign alternatives, keeping in mind the personalities of the key leaders, the organization's culture, the resistance to change, the level of present workload, the skill of organization's change agents, and the aggressiveness of the change process within the organization that will be going on in parallel with the restructuring activities and emotional stress.

Phase III Major Activities
1. Implement the change management plan.
2. Implement the communication plan.
3. Define the improvement goals for the new processes.
4. Define the culture enablers and inhibitors.
5. Redesign the organization around the major customer-related processes.
6. Redesign the organization around the core capabilities.
7. Review the results of the previous two activities to define a better combination.
8. Develop knowledge-flow maps.
9. Refine designs.
10. Develop functional-level flowcharts.
11. Conduct a competency analysis to define skill gaps.
12. Develop improvement estimates and compare to goals.
13. Conduct a risk analysis on each process design.
14. Develop functional responsibilities for each design.
15. Prepare advantages/disadvantages lists for each design.
16. Prepare status meeting reports.
17. Manage project (coordination).

Phase III—Deliverables

1. A minimum of two organizational restructuring solutions along with the advantages and disadvantages of each compared to the current organizational structure
2. A presentation of the redesign impact (short- and long-range positive and negative) as reflected in the key performance measurement
3. A detailed description of each function's responsibilities for each option
4. An organization chart for each sector for each option
5. Status reports
6. Minutes of all key meetings

Phase IV—Documentation

Once the preferred process is selected, the team should prepare detailed assignment-description responsibilities and mission statements for the functions. Organization charts should be prepared for each sector, department, section, and unit. These organization charts will define the formal reporting structure. They will be included in a revised organizational structure manual.

Phase IV Major Activities

1. Implement the communication plan.
2. Implement the change management plan.
3. Prepare detailed assignment descriptions of responsibilities and mission statements for all functions.
4. Prepare organizational charts for all sectors, departments, sections, and units.
5. Revise the organizational structure manual.
6. Prepare a list of recommendations to help make the transformation go smoothly.
7. Prepare status reports.
8. Prepare final report.
9. Manage project (coordination).

Phase IV—Deliverables

1. Detailed descriptions for each function's responsibilities
2. Organization charts for each sector's department, section, and unit
3. Revised organizational structuring manual
4. List of implementation recommendations
5. Status reports
6. Final report
7. Minutes of all key meetings

Phase V—Implementation

Now the real challenge is to carry out the organizational redesign, adjusting as you do so to any unforeseen situation. All too often people follow the plan blindly without taking into consideration new information that was not available to the people doing the planning.

GOOD GOVERNANCE

> "The lack of sound corporate governance in the public and private sectors has enabled bribery, capitalism, and corruption to flourish throughout the world, suppressing sound and sustainable economic decisions."
>
> —HJH

Speaking to the Stern Graduate School of Business in 2002, Alan Greenspan, then chairman of the Federal Reserve Bank, stated:

> "Generally speaking, the resulting structure of business incentives, reporting, and accountability has served us well. We could not have achieved our current level of national productivity if corporate governance had been deeply flawed.
>
> "Thus, it has increasingly fallen to corporate officers, especially the chief executive officer, to guide the business, hopefully in what he or she perceives to be in the best interests of shareholders. Indeed, the boards of directors appointed by shareholders are in the overwhelming majority of cases chosen from the slate proposed by the CEO [chief executive officer]. The CEO sets the organization's business strategy and strongly influences the choice of the accounting practices that measure the ongoing degree of success or failure of that strategy. Outside auditors are generally chosen by the CEO or by an audit committee of CEO-chosen directors. Shareholders usually perfunctorily affirm such choices.
>
> "To be sure, a CEO can maintain control over corporate governance only so long as companies are not demonstrably in difficulty. When companies do run into trouble, the carte blanche granted CEOs by shareholders is withdrawn. Existing shareholders, or successful hostile bidders for the corporation, usually then displace the board of directors and the CEO. Such changes in corporate leadership have been relatively rare but, more often than not, have contributed to a more-effective allocation of corporate capital."

To get this section of this chapter on corporate governance started, here's a definition of *corporate governance*.

Corporate governance is a structural system of institutional policies, rules for implementing these policies, and best practices for business controls that establish a framework under which corporations are managed and operate. This framework governs all actions of corporations, from initial founding through their period of entrepreneurship and growth, through their development into a mature structure for their administration and governance, and to the point of their exit from the market as an independent identity (by merger, dissolution, or insolvency).

This definition raises the question: Who governs (participates in making decisions and with what degree of authority) and to what extent is their power exercised in management of the capital that the financial market has invested in the corporation?

In 2002 the Cone Corporate Citizenship Survey asked what consumers do when they hear reports of bad corporate citizenship.

- 91 percent consider switching to another company's products or services.
- 85 percent speak out against that company among family and friends.
- 83 percent refuse to invest in that company's stock.
- 80 percent refuse to work at that company.
- 76 percent boycott that company's products or services.

Good corporate governance characteristics include:

- Transparency
- Accountability
- Probability
- Protection of minority shareholders

The International Academy for Quality white paper, "The Impact of Corporate Governance on the Quality of Management" (June 2005), pointed out:

> "Governance is based on three cornerstone principles: ownership, stewardship, and accountability:
>
> - *Principle of ownership.* Ownership is a principle that describes the way an individual cares for a resource. Owners will establish a system of business control for preservation of capital and risk management methodologies for defining and operating with their personal comfort zone for potential loss of capital (or any owned asset) in order to achieve their desired level of return.
> - *Principle of stewardship.* Stewardship is a principle that directs a person to take responsibility for the management of resources that have been entrusted into his or her care by an owner. Corporate stewardship

implies that the value of capital investments is preserved and enhanced by the actions of management. Stewardship affects all business issues (e.g., social, health, and environmental ramifications of the production methodologies as well as the use and eventual disposal of products). The primary roles in ensuring stewardship in the life cycle of a product typically involve manufacturers, retailers, service providers, consumers, and government. Stewardship acts on behalf of these participating communities to preserve value and exercise due diligence in the management of the organization's resources to achieve its purposeful ends.

- *Principle of accountability.* Delegation of authority and resources from an owner to a designated steward brings accountability for how the authority is used and how the resources are deployed or consumed."

"In a corporate governance structure, owners are the shareholders while the CEO is the steward," noted to the white paper. "The board of directors provides the mechanism by which owners delegate authority to the steward. How are these three principles integrated into a draft definition of 'good governance' that can be used in a corporate context for quality management?"

The board of directors is a very valuable resource, but too often its members turn into puppets and lose their value-added properties. The value of an independent board that is capable and assertive enough to challenge management has been vividly demonstrated by organizations such as Enron. The results of the board of directors' poor management has focused the world's attention on corporate governance. It also was one of the factors that caused the world's stock markets to drop so drastically in 2002, costing the average U.S. family approximately $60,000 per year.

Everyone has the capacity for good and evil. Genetics accounts for about 50 percent of behavioral tendencies, such as personality and moral behaviors. The remaining 50 percent is defined by culture and environment. Dr. Michael Shermer, author of *The Science of Good and Evil* (Times Books, 2004), stated, "As adults we are particularly influenced to do good or evil by the immediate social context and community. When you're surrounded by co-workers all hyped about a get-rich-quick pyramid scheme, it is truly hard to resist."

> **"Good corporate governance requires management in both the public and private sectors to obey not only the letter, but all the intent and spirit of the law, using sound ethics and moral judgment to ensure long-term organizational sustainability as opposed to short-term personal gains."**
> **—Unknown author**

This means that even the best organizations must have adequate checks and balances placed upon the executive team, important as it is to the organization. This is the job of the board of directors. Too often boards don't have the courage to stand up to the executive team. They take the easy way out and just rubber-stamp the executive team's recommendations. Even more often, many boards of directors are made up mostly of members of the executive team or people the executive team can easily control.

Sanjay Kumar, CEO of Computer Associates, said, "In the post-Enron days governance has become critical." This statement, although correct, is an understatement. The truth is that good corporate governance has always been critical to the success of any organization. All organizations must have boards of directors that are watchdogs, and too many boards are lapdogs.

Today's board members must have a high degree of personal ethics and values. They must understand the business and the validity of the data they are using to approve the organization's operations. They must be as ethical as Babe Didrikson Zaharias, the late golf champion. She once disqualified herself from a tournament because she hit a wrong ball out of the rough. When a friend asked, "Why did you do it? No one would know," Babe simply answered, "I would have known."

Because organizations around the world have done such a poor job of corporate governance, governments are beginning to pass more stringent laws. In the United States, Congress passed, and President George W. Bush signed, the Public Company Accounting Reform and Investor Protection Act. The act requires that CEOs, CFOs, and the board members personally certify all financial statements. This act, called the Sarbanes-Oxley Act of 2003, calls for:

- An increased degree of transparency in corporate accounting and reporting
- The personal responsibility of top executives and board members for the accuracy of financial statements their companies release
- A greater emphasis on, and a new structural framework around, efforts to prevent, detect, investigate, and remediate fraud and misconduct

> "The teams at Goodyear are now telling the boss how to run things. And I must say, I'm not doing a half-bad job because of it."
> —Stanley Gault
> Chairman, Goodyear

The legality of this act has been challenged by Richard Srusky, the former CEO of HealthSouth, who is charged with masterminding a $2.7 billion swindle. The challenge is based on the grounds that it is unconstitutional to hold officers of an organization accountable for signing something that they did not prepare. I believe as Dwight Eisenhower did when he said, "The buck stops here."

In light of the new laws and loss of public confidence, it has become a requirement that board members become educated about the increased risk associated with being a board member. Board members must understand their fiduciary, ethical, and legal oversight responsibilities. The basic job description for board members has been rewritten, and it includes much higher expectations and penalties. Board members are now under increased pressure and intense public scrutiny. They are required to improve organizational value and performance as well as acting in the best interests of the organization's shareholders.

All board members are faced with greater legal liability for the organization's financial reporting accuracy and its performance. The board members must become valuable contributors to the organization's growth.

Fortune magazine in 2003 evaluated the Fortune 500 firms to assess the quality of the corporate governance structure. The stocks of organizations that had the best boards of directors outperformed the worst organizations by two to one. The retained earnings of the best corporate governance organizations were 51.7 percent, while the worst organization was 12.9 percent. Here's a list of organizations that were classified as having the best boards of directors:

- 3M
- Apria Healthcare
- Colgate-Palmolive
- GE
- The Home Depot
- Intel
- Johnson & Johnson
- Medtronic
- Pfizer
- Texas Instruments

The following is a list of boards of directors that needed to improve:

- Apple
- Conseco
- Dillard's
- Gap
- Kmart
- Qwest
- Tyson Foods
- Xerox
- AT&T
- Ford
- HP

What principles guide good corporate governance? The Organization for Economic Cooperation and Development's OECD Principles of Corporate Governance provide some good guidelines for evaluating corporate governance structure. It consists of five major headings.

- *The right of the shareholders.* The corporate governance framework should protect shareholders' rights.

- *The equitable treatment of shareholders.* The corporate governance framework should ensure the equitable treatment of all shareholders, including minority and foreign shareholders. All shareholders should have the opportunity to obtain effective redress for violation of their rights.

- *The role of stakeholders in corporate governance.* The corporate governance framework should recognize the rights of stakeholders, as established by law, and encourage active cooperation between corporations and stakeholders in creating wealth, jobs, and the sustainability of financially sound enterprises.

- *Disclosure and transparency.* The corporate governance framework should ensure that timely and accurate disclosure is made of all material matters regarding the corporation, including financial situation, performance, ownership, and governance of the company.

- *The responsibilities of the board.* The corporate governance framework should ensure the strategic guidance of the organization, the effective monitoring of management by the board, and the board's accountability to the organization and the shareholders.

Although all five principles are important to good corporate governance, I will discuss only the fifth principle, the responsibilities of the board, as the board is a primary resource that is extremely important to organizational excellence.

The board of directors is primarily responsible for monitoring managerial performance and achieving an adequate return for the stockholders while also preventing conflict of interests and balancing competing demands on the organization. The directors are also responsible for ensuring that the organization's systems and processes are designed so that the organization will be in compliance with applicable laws, including tax, compensation, labor, environmental, equal opportunity, health, and safety laws. To live up to these responsibilities, the members of the board of directors must be substantially independent from the organization's management team. It's easy to see that the board members must be working members. The common view of a board made up of fat cats that come in two to four times a year to smoke cigars and have a good meal is a misconception. For the board to function satisfactorily, it requires its members to do a great deal of preparation before the meetings and to have an extensive background in the organization's operations and the related legal and financial requirements.

> **"And our experience shows that effective corporate governance is a key foundation for providing the all-important business operating results of: empowering a companywide culture of superior performance, and providing and emphasizing customer value leadership throughout all the company's products and services."**
> **—Armand V. Feigenbaum**
> **"The Impact of Corporate Governance on the Quality of Management,"** *Annual Quality Congress Proceedings,* **May 2004**

To have good corporate governance, the board of directors:

- Acts on a fully informed basis with good faith and due diligence and care and in the best interest of the organization and its shareholders

- Must consider the needs and wants of all stakeholders and treat them fairly
- Must ensure that the organization is in compliance with all applicable legislation, taking into consideration the interests of the shareholders
- Should approve corporate strategies, major plans of action, annual budgets, and business plans, which includes major capital expenditures, acquisitions, and diversifications
- Should set performance objectives, monitor implementation of the planning process, and measure corporate performance
- Monitors the performance of key executives and determine what relative compensation should be awarded to these key individuals. If necessary, it must take action to replace those who are not performing at an acceptable level. It is also responsible for ensuring that an effective succession plan is in place and that the successors are being developed as necessary.
- Develops a formal and transparent board nomination process, reviewing the performance of all board members to ensure that they are living up to their responsibilities
- Ensures that corporate assets are not being misused
- Manages potential conflicts of interest between management, board members, and shareholders
- Validates the integrity of the corporate and financial reporting system, including the independent audits
- Ensures that the disclosure and communication process is working effectively

The makeup of the board should be such that it can exercise objective, independent analysis related to corporate affairs without undue influence by the management team. It should have an appropriate balance of power, ensuring accountability and its capability for independent decision making. The board should be made up of between five and fifteen people. H. Carl McCall, former chairman of the compensation committee at the New York Stock Exchange, pointed out that the exchange's board is too unwieldy with its twenty-seven directors. He suggested that a board of ten to twelve members would be more efficient.

Only nonexecutive board members should be assigned to board subcommittees that cover areas of potential conflict of interest (for example, financial, nominating, and executive and board remuneration).

Board members must receive accurate, relative, and timely information related to the organization's activities. This is necessary if they are to fulfill their responsibilities and ensure they make knowledgeable decisions.

Here are some useful guidelines that will help the organization maintain a good corporate governance board of directors' structure.

- Independence

- ☐ No more than two company executives should be on the board or no more than 20 percent of the board, whichever is less.
- ☐ None of the members of the board should be doing business with the organization (for example, providing consulting or legal services).
- ☐ The audit, compensation, and nominating committees should include no company executives.
- ☐ The chief executive officer or chief operating officer should not serve as chairman of the board.

■ Stock ownership
- ☐ Each director should have a minimum equity stake of US$150,000; an exception would be a new board member who would build up the equity stake within two years.
- ☐ Board members should be restricted from selling stock until they are off the board.

■ Quality of the directors
- ☐ One independent director should have experience in the organization's core business.
- ☐ One should be a CEO of an equivalent-size company.
- ☐ One should be a performance improvement expert.
- ☐ None of the directors should be on more than four boards.
- ☐ Retired directors should be on no more than seven boards.
- ☐ All directors should attend a minimum of 75 percent of the meetings.
- ☐ The board should evaluate each member's performance each year and provide formal feedback to each board member.
- ☐ New board appointees should undergo a training program to ensure that they are abreast of the relevant laws, regulations, business environment, changing commercial risks, organizational structure, and the organization's products and services.

■ Board activities
- ☐ The board should meet without management's presence at least once a year.
- ☐ The audit committee should meet at least four times per year.
- ☐ The board should be frugal with executive pay.
- ☐ The board should develop a very robust CEO and COO succession plan.
- ☐ The board should be quick to react to troubles.

Donald Peterson, retired CEO of Ford Motor Co., stated, "The place that the longest amount of continuity is achieved among leadership in any organization is at its board of directors, and it is essential that they have an ingrained appreciation for the benefits of quality and value proposition that it offers to the organization for the long term."

Good board members are getting hard to find, particularly for small and start-up organizations. Today board members are required to practice more stringent overseeing, which can mean putting in up to 200 hours annually. For example, The Home Depot expects all of its board members to visit and report on twelve of the company's stores outside of their home states each year. Shareholder lawsuits are increasing, and the members of the board of directors can be personally liable and financially responsible for the judgments and court costs. These risks must be offset by outstanding stock options that act as a lure, and the board members must be motivated by the intellectual challenge of being part of a growing organization.

> **"Money should not be a prime motivator for board service; if it is, then you have the wrong person."**
> **—Bruce E. Beebe**
> **Editor of *Directorship* newsletter**

Ram Charan and Julie Schlosser have devised ten questions that board members should ask (*Fortune,* November 10, 2003). They present a simple, but good, starting point. They are:

1. How does the company make money?
2. Are your customers paying up?
3. What could really hurt—or kill—the company in the next few years?
4. How are we doing relative to our competitors?
5. If the CEO were hit by a bus tomorrow, who could run the company?
6. How are we going to grow?
7. Are we living within our means?
8. How much does the CEO get paid?
9. How does bad news get to the top?
10. Do I understand the answers to 1 through 9?

When I first read this article, I thought the questions were so basic that I would be embarrassed to ask them, but I agreed to try them at the next board meeting I attended. The results were very gratifying. The meeting took on new dimensions. I was asking simple questions that the management team had a hard time answering. It was obvious the CEO was uncomfortable trying to answer some of them. It wasn't just what he was saying but what he wasn't saying and how he was trying to avoid some of the important issues. I had thought I understood the CEO's and COO's total compensation packages. I knew what their salaries were but grossly underestimated their performance-related bonuses. Remember the shock wave that went through the stock market when Dick Grasso, director of the New York Stock Exchange, was granted $139.5 million in a compensation package? All too often board members don't really know what the key executives' compensation packages are really worth.

A number of the other questions also hit home, such as succession planning and risk management. Although these questions are not intended to be a comprehensive list of things that board members should understand, they do provide a starting point that can stimulate additional questions. And to get the most from all your questions, remember to ask "why" five times.

How Good Is Your Board of Directors?

In the June 2005 white paper prepared for the International Academy for Quality (IAQ), "The Impact of Corporate Governance in the Quality of Management," Marcos E. J. Bertin, partner with Voyer International, and Hugo Strachan, director with EDDE, suggested an excellent approach to measuring the quality of your corporate governance process. They suggest the board of directors be evaluated based upon seven criteria categories (see figure 10.5). They are:

- Mission and principles
- Board structure
- Board operating procedures
- Board and management
- Board and shareholders
- Board and community
- Board contributions

Mission and Principles

This is a key area of corporate governance in which the values and the mission of the company are established, aligned through it, and enforced. The basic board mission should be to ensure the strategic guidance of the company and the effective monitoring of management. In this sense it covers the following areas:

- Legal framework—liabilities
- Code of corporate governance best practices

Board Structure

The composition of the board varies depending on the needs of the company. It's not possible to formulate or design a model board that would represent the best solution for even a small proportion of companies. In this sense it covers the following areas:

- Board size
- Chairman (separation of chairman and CEO—lead director)
- Mix of inside and external independent directors
- Board committees

Board Operating Procedures

Regarding the BOD's internal operating structure, the following areas are covered:

- How to select new members
- Definition of independence
- Description of directors' function
- Training and orienting directors
- Meetings, agendas, minutes, and follow-up
- Election term/term limits/ mandatory retirement
- Board compensation review
- Participation of senior managers and other nondirectors in meetings
- Assessment of board and directors
- Self-assessment (The board should have an effective process for assessing its own performance.)

Board and Management

A clear distinction between the board and management functions is mandatory. Typical activities related to this are:

- Formal evaluation of CEO
- Senior management's compensation
- Board access to senior management
- CEO succession planning
- Company information
- Risk assessment and risk management
- Clear definitions of the board's and top management's roles

Board and Shareholders

The board responsibilities regarding its accountability to shareholders are presented through areas such as:

- Content and character of disclosure
- Compliance with basic shareholders' rights

Board and Community

Disclosure to government and community should comply with the law, its regulations, and its spirit. Covered in this area are:

- Disclosure to government and the community
- Company communications to institutional investors, customers, and to the press
- Company actions related to community issues

Board Contributions

In the end all board activities should proactively contribute to company results. In this sense, covered are areas such as:

- Company results
- Company competitive access to capital
- Generation of value
- Stakeholders' perception of board contributions

Figure 10.5 Weighting Factor Table

	Weighting Factor
1. Mission and principles	20
2. Board structure	7
3. Board operating procedures	7
4. Board and management	10
5. Board and shareholders	10
6. Board and community	6
7. Board contributions	40
Total	100

Bertin and Strachan also weighted each of these seven criteria categories based upon their importance:

Evaluation of the board should be based upon the present state of the art. They suggest performing your evaluation using the OECD Principles of Corporate Governance 2004 (*www.oecd.org*) as the target model. They divided the evaluation into four levels for each of the seven categories. These levels and related points are listed in figure 10.6.

Here's an excerpt from the paper:

"The evaluation matrix is composed of seven columns, the criteria categories, and four levels.... The levels considered in each category can be used as a way to build a continuum, which helps the company progress toward excellence in the board of directors. In order to work with actionable results a certain score must be assigned to each level as well as a factor for each category, for a total maximum score of, say, 1,000.

"Once a certain score is developed for a company, country or region, a matrix similar to that of [figure 10.7] is obtained, which contains a certain range of values for each level and a factor for each category.

"The system should be dynamic, dependent on time and geography, and the scores and factors in the system must be updated on a timely basis according to the company, country, or region process.

"A model of the matrix is shown, with a selection of scores and factors as an example:"

The same IAQ white paper describes in detail each of the four levels of the seven criteria categories. Here is the detailed breakdown for just the last category, board contributions.

Figure 10.6 Board Evaluation (Four Levels)

Level	Related points
1. Understanding the need to improve corporate governance	0–1
2. First concrete steps toward establishing best practices	>1–3
3. Implementation of best practices	>3–7
4. Leadership	>7–10

Board Contributions

Level One

■ Company financial results aren't aligned with shareholders'/owners' expectations/needs.

■ The board is not contributing to the company's competitive access to capital.

■ The board is not helping the company to improve its performance indicators.

■ The board is not a factor in generating either brand value or an excellent company image.

■ Intangible capital is not a board concern.

■ Stakeholders' evaluation/perception of the board is poor.

■ The board is not a key factor in generating critical/needed strategies.

■ Company contribution to the community is neither evaluated nor perceived as good enough.

Figure 10.7 Board Evaluation Matrix

Level	Score	Mission and principles	Structure	Board operation procedures	Board and management	Board and shareholders	Board and community	Board contribution	Total evaluation
1	0–1								
2	>1–3		3						
3	>3–7	6		5		4		6	
4	>7–10				8		7		
Score		6	3	5	8	4	7	6	
Factor		20	7	7	10	10	6	40	
Total		120	21	35	80	40	42	240	578

Level Two

- The board is proactively aligning needed financial results with shareholders'/owners' expectations/needs; results are still below industry standards, but the trend is positive.
- The board is not aware of its role in helping the company to obtain competitive access to capital.
- The board is helping the company to improve its performance indicators, which are not in the desired state yet.
- The board is proactively working on improving brand value and company image.
- Goals haven't been met.
- The board is active in generating/preserving the value of the company's intellectual capital.
- The first signs of improvement are present.
- Stakeholders' evaluation/perception of the board is improving, but not at an industry standard level.
- Evaluation/perception of the company's contribution to the community is starting to improve.

Level Three

- Financial results are consistent with industry expectations. The board is recognized as a key factor in obtaining such results.
- The company is obtaining competitive access to capital. The board is very helpful in this regard.
- The company's performance indicators are within accepted industry parameters.
- The company's brand value is aligned with industry standards. Company image is very good. The board has been instrumental to this situation.
- The board is active in generating/preserving the value of the company's intellectual capital, with very good results.
- Stakeholders' evaluation of the board is very good.
- Community evaluation/perception of the company as a whole is very good.

Level Four

- Financial results are better than those of leading companies in the industry, and the board is recognized as a key factor in obtaining such results.
- Company access to capital is within the best in the industry. Board activity is critical in this regard.
- The company's performance indicators are among the best in the industry.
- The company's brand value is better than industry standards. Company image is excellent. The board has been instrumental to this situation.
- The board is recognized as a key factor in generating/preserving the value of the company's intellectual capital. Results are excellent.

- Stakeholders' evaluation of the board is excellent.
- Community evaluation/perception of the company as a whole is excellent.
- There are training/development plans for management, which contributes to the excellent results of the company."

For detailed information about the other six categories, read the IAQ white paper, available from the American Society for Quality (*www.asq.org*).

ORGANIZATIONAL STRUCTURE SUMMARY

The organization's structure is key to the way all the other resources are used. It has a major impact on the organization's culture and its stakeholders. Many different organizational structures are used. The most popular ones are:

- Vertical
- Bureaucratic
- Decentralized
- Networked:
  - ☐ Case management
  - ☐ Horizontal process management
- Matrix

"In a further endeavor to align boards of directors with shareholders, rather than with management, considerable attention has been placed on filling board seats with so-called independent directors. However, in my experience, few directors in modern times have seen their interests as separate from those of the CEO, who effectively appointed them and, presumably, could remove them from future slates of directors submitted to shareholders. I do not deny that laws could be passed to force selection of slates of directors who are patently independent of CEO influence and thereby significantly diminish the role of the CEO. I suspect, however, that such an initiative, while ensuring independent directors, would create competing power centers within a corporation, and thus dilute coherent control and impair effective governance."
—**Alan Greenspan**
Former chairman of the Federal Reserve Bank

"A major restructuring change in any organization should be undertaken only when it will produce a very significant improvement in performance, and then it must be accompanied with an effective organizational change management plan."

—HJH

Motorola is a good example of an organization that is moving toward a network organization, but even Motorola has not adopted the full network concept and it probably won't. To provide the best total service to all its stakeholders, an organization must use and modify a combination of organizational structures to meet the unique needs of its situation.

To achieve the exponential results from reorganization needed to survive in today's rapidly changing environment, organizations must consider new structures. Tomorrow's successful organizations will be those making standard decisions based on processes, customers, and teams rather than on the old models based on the specialization of labor and command hierarchies. Used properly, these alternatives offer a tremendous potential for success.

However, even the network model of organizational structure may not reign for long. New paradigms of structure will be necessary as unimagined technology becomes commonplace and work-force demographics shift dramatically. The organizational structures of tomorrow will be very different from those now in use. Perhaps belonging to an organization may simply mean having an access code to its computer network. Now what are the structural implications of that?

> "As much as I would like to tell you that everyone should evolve to a matrix organization, I cannot. My experience indicates that all five organizational structures and even a combination of them must be considered depending on the organization's environment."
>
> —HJH

Once you have made the decision to change your organization's structure, the next question usually is, "What is the best organizational fit for my strategy and competitive environment, and what makes best use of my distinct core competencies?" The answer comes not from a single diagnostic tool but rather from a technique of "informed dialogue," which is a combination of analysis and dialogue conducted in an iterative way.

"What is the best way to decide on the 'right' structure and fit for my organization?"

The first step in this process is to look at the organization from three perspectives: strategic, operational, and tactical.

The strategic perspective looks at the organization from the top down and determines the overall shape of the organization. It's a process of moving the big boxes around to determine the right fit.

The operational perspective deals with strategic business units. In this case you look at the organization from two directions. You review the strategic fit looking from the top down. You ensure the appropriate mix of operational, managerial, and support processes through a bottom-up review.

Finally, the tactical perspective takes a bottom-up approach and determines the work teams and job designs.

The strategic, operational, and tactical views comprise what is called organizational structure. The combination of strategic, operational, and tactical decisions will be the basis for determining the "right" organization structure.

Then you look at the questions that you can ask at each of the levels.

CHAPTER XI

RESOURCE MANAGEMENT SUMMARY

Of the five organizational excellence pillars, resource management is probably the most important because it's the starting point for all the others. Processes, projects, change, and knowledge within the organization depend upon having the correct level of trained, competent, and experienced resources available when you need them. Resource management cannot be an afterthought. It must be the basis for all executive decisions. It requires a lot of planning, coordination, reporting, and continuous refining to do an excellent job at resource management. Too many successful organizations manage their operations by throwing more resources into the pot. They may be very successful with this approach as long as they have very little competition, but even the giants fall if they don't do an outstanding job of resource management. Just look at what happened to Big Blue (IBM in the 1980s). Poor resource management transformed IBM from the most admired organization in the world to the one that set the world's record for losing the most money in one year in the early part of the 1990s, only to be outdone in bad performance the next year by General Motors.

> "Leadership used to be structured and hierarchical. Today, it requires quick wits, quick decisions, judgment calls, guts, and passion. This market won't wait for those who fall behind or who miss a turn."
>
> —Joe W. Forehand
> CEO, Accenture

HARLEY-DAVIDSON—AN AMERICAN SUCCESS STORY

In the 1970s Harley-Davidson was the world's leader in motorcycle production with 70 percent of the market share. By 1983 its market share had dropped to only 23 percent. The company was about to file for Chapter 11 bankruptcy when a last-minute buyout by the executive management team saved it. The future was clear—the organization had to change drastically or go out of business. It was "do or die." Even the very loyal customer base was beginning to talk about the poor quality of the new bikes. Fortunately, CEO Richard Teerlink stepped in and took a firm position—quality would not be sacrificed. He stated, " We created a vision that was simple: survival."

Teerlink led a whole cultural change, one that was based upon five core values:

- Tell the truth.
- Keep your promises.
- Be fair.
- Respect the individual.
- Encourage intellectual curiosity.

These values, plus Teerlink's commitment to total quality and continuous improvement, brought about a change in the total employee population. Managers not only asked employees questions, but they also required employees to ask questions, make suggestions, and challenge things that looked wrong to them or that could be improved. Everyone was trained in team dynamics, problem solving, and other quality tools.

Teerlink also took another drastic measure; he unloaded many business units that were not in direct alignment with manufacturing motorcycles. This allowed the total organization to focus on building the best possible bikes. The organization began to focus its attention on its most important asset, its client base. It established a number of ways to get direct feedback from the customers. A typical example of this proactive way of obtaining the "voice of the customer" were the Harley rallies, which were put on as a way of getting input from the customers. Even Teerlink rode up to these rallies wearing leather and riding a big, well-used Harley. (He believed that if he and his team did not use the products they manufactured, why would anyone else want to buy them?) These rallies also served to increase customer loyalty as the customers felt they were part of the Harley-Davidson family. The organization believed it sold more than just a bike; it sold freedom and a break from the daily routine and work schedule.

> **"Capital is more than the allocation of line-item resources to a venture or outside funding in the form of cash and/or debt for equity. Building a strategy around capital means considering all sources of capital."**
>
> **—Joey Tamer**
> **Strategic consultant and author, "Successful Strategies for New Venture Development,"** *Handbook of Business Strategy* **2005**

Simultaneously Harley-Davidson began to push the slogan "We sell excitement, a way of life." Its customers began to relate to each other, forming a customer community that had its own identity and an ever-growing degree of customer loyalty.

At first Harley-Davidson focused on its products and responded to what it learned from its customers. Next it moved to bring a focus on process to the organization. It retained John Fitzpatrick, who at the time was working with me in process redesign consulting, to provide support to the fledgling process initiative. As Harley-Davidson began planning to open a new plant in Kansas City, it tapped Fitzpatrick to lead the nonmanufacturing process work. He understood that quality had to be built into the product and that processes are what usually limit the quality of output. He also believed that empowered teams produced the best results at the lowest cost and had the biggest positive impact on customer satisfaction. His efforts at Kansas City demonstrated that processes should be designed to align with the organization's culture.

In parallel with the new customer trust, or more probably as a result of that trust, the organization itself changed internally. People took on more responsibility. Everyone throughout the organization experienced an increased feeling of ownership and personal commitment to excellence. This led to more open communications, participation, high productivity, and an empowered workforce that would not tolerate poor quality. The span of control increased and the layers of management collapsed. The transformation was reflected in the way that they talked about themselves. "We are in the business of motor-cycles by the people and for the people."

What really saved Harley? It:

- Had a purpose to save the organization
- Had an identity that it wanted to uphold
- Had a loyal customer set that worked with it
- Developed a set of values that the total team related to
- Was empowered to succeed, which built pride throughout the organization

What did all this change accomplish? Today Harley-Davidson produces the best possible motorcycles in the world. Even Japanese cyclists place Harley-Davidson as the number one choice. Sales and production have tripled, and it has experienced seventeen years of record sales and growth in profits.

The Harley-Davidson story is one of a true transformation that was brought about by a leader who infused a new vision, beliefs, heart, and spirit into the organization. But it isn't a story about one man; it's a story about how an organization can come together to bring about positive changes. It proves that when an organization is prepared for a change and when the people who are affected by that change are involved in making the change happen, the seemingly impossible feat becomes commonplace. There is just no way to stop this type of organization from being successful.

Now, ask yourself if your organization is a Harley-Davidson type of organization or is it still uncommitted to being the best that it can be? If the latter is the case, what can you do to help make the needed changes? At a very minimum, you can decide to make a personal commitment right now to bring about the needed changes within your organization, and that's at least a start.

> "Be better today than you were yesterday, and better tomorrow
> than you are today—this is a requirement, not a nicety."
>
> —HJH

CHAPTER XII

ORGANIZATIONAL EXCELLENCE SUMMARY

"Fifty percent of organizations are below average. You must excel in your core competencies to keep from being below average and in all areas of your business to be in the upper 10 percent."

—HJH

THE FALLACY OF UNIVERSAL BEST PRACTICES

Winners of the Malcolm Baldrige National Quality Award, the Deming Prize, and the European Quality Award are held up as models of how organizations should be managed. Unfortunately, what may be good for them can be disastrous for your organization. During the 1990s, Ernst & Young and the American Society for Quality (ASQ) conducted a study that developed one of the world's largest databases on international management practices and provides statistically sound conclusions that can change the way you think about best practices, benchmarking, and the way you are managing your organization's improvement effort.

Background

In 1987, I completed a study of sixty organizations that I believe set the standards for management practices. It included organizations such as Hewlett-Packard, IBM, 3M, Daimler-Benz, and Sony. As a result, I wrote *The Improvement Process* (McGraw-Hill, 1987). I then focused my efforts on organizations that were following the example of these leaders, and I was surprised that they didn't obtain the same excellent results when they applied the same improvement tools. In the early 1990s, prestigious magazines published a series of articles documenting how individual organizations had failed in their total quality management (TQM) efforts. Authors were estimating that between 15 percent and 50 percent of all the TQM efforts undertaken within the United States failed.

It became obvious that the quality practices being recommended by the quality professionals had been accepted based on gut feelings and individual success stories. Detailed research revealed that there was not a statistically sound database available that would verify which, if any, of the individual or combination of improvement tools would improve an organization's performance. In fact, it became obvious that the quality practitioners had not related the TQM or Six Sigma process to organizational performance. They had mistakenly assumed that improved customer satisfaction equaled improved organizational performance. In fact, the top 10 percent of the organizations listed as *Fortune* magazine's most admired companies turned out to be better role models for business than the organizations that won the Malcolm Baldrige National Quality Award. Organizations such as Rubbermaid, Johnson & Johnson, Microsoft, Coca-Cola, Merck, Intel, and Hewlett-Packard should be the role models, not IBM and General Motors.

Conceptual definition: For an organization's performance to improve, it must experience a positive improvement in one or more of the following three business measurements without a negative impact on any one of the other two measurements.

- Return on investment (ROI)
- Value added per employee (VAE)
- Customer satisfaction (CS)

These three measurements evaluate the critical three performance dimensions for most organizations: profitability, productivity, and quality.

The ASQ formed a nonprofit research organization called the American Quality Foundation, and Robert C. Stempel (former chairman of the board for General Motors) agreed to serve as its chairman. One of the projects the foundation undertook was to develop an international database of management practices large enough to allow statistically sound conclusions to be generated based on its data. Ernst & Young agreed to fund this multimillion dollar project and provide the labor to collect and analyze the data. The project was called the International Quality Study (IQS).

The Database

As soon as the Ernst & Young statisticians began to design the experiment, it became evident that it would be too costly and time-consuming to develop a statistically sound international database on all industries. So the scope of the project was limited to four countries and four industries. Japan was selected as the best-performing country in Asia, Germany for Europe, and the United States and Canada for the Americas. It was also determined that the project would use two manufacturing and two service industries. The manufacturing industries were the automotive and computer equipment industries, and the service industries were acute-care hospitals and commercial banks.

The Collapse of Prevailing Wisdom

There's a big difference between wisdom and knowledge. *Wisdom* can be defined as intuitive beliefs and understanding. Wisdom is based on experiences, education, and culture. *Knowledge,* on the other hand, is information that is backed up by statistically sound research. Often, as we gain knowledge, the wisdom of the past is proven wrong. Simply put, wisdom reflects our beliefs, and knowledge is based on facts. At long last, as a result of the IQS, we can manage our improvement processes based on facts rather than beliefs.

As the results of the statistical analysis began to come in, the idea of a universally beneficial set of best practices proved to be unsound. Many of the practices that had been considered to be basic principles of TQM and the quality movement proved to be ineffective or even detrimental under some conditions. For example:

- Eliminating quality control inspection
- The use of natural work teams
- Empowerment of the workforce
- Benchmarking
- Not inspecting quality into the product/service

The truth is that these aren't principles, they are conceptual beliefs.

Only Five Real Best Practices

After studying the data for many months, the statisticians could identify only five practices as being universal best practices and, even then, there is a 5 percent chance that these approaches may not improve your organization's performance. They are:

- Cycle-time analysis
- Process value analysis
- Process simplification
- Strategic planning
- Formal supplier certification programs

Of all the practices we studied, this group of improvement practices showed a beneficial impact on performance, no matter how the organization was performing at the time.

Process Improvement Methods

Organizations that made frequent use of such practices as process value analysis, process simplification, and process cycle-time analysis tended to have higher performance than the other organizations. Although the impact was significant on all three performance dimensions—profitability, productivity, and quality—it was strongest for the productivity measure.

Increasing the use of the process improvement practices can be a means to competitive advantage. These techniques are underused: Organizations are not applying them with nearly the frequency that the IQS shows to be beneficial. Most organizations say they "occasionally" use these techniques, whereas the best performers say they use them "always or almost always." The benefits of these techniques are becoming more well known, and competitors are adopting them in significant numbers.

Deploying the Strategic Plan

Widespread understanding of the strategic plan by people inside and outside the organization has a broad beneficial impact. The two groups whose understanding showed the strongest impact on performance are middle management (or the medical staff among the hospitals in the study) and customers. Suppliers' understanding of the plan was also generally beneficial.

Most organizations said that their middle management partially understands the strategic plan; increasing that understanding from partial to full is a strategy to gain competitive advantage—with positive impacts on profit, quality, and productivity. Organizations generally said that customers had little understanding and that suppliers had no understanding of their strategic plan. Increasing customers' knowledge to full understanding and suppliers' knowledge to at least a partial understanding also showed widespread benefits.

Supplier Certification Programs

Formal programs for certifying suppliers showed an across-the-board beneficial impact on performance—especially in quality and productivity.

Among the IQS participants, certifying vendors is already a standard practice for a large majority (79 percent) of the manufacturers. It's a rare practice in banks and hospitals (33 percent of banks and 10 percent of hospitals). The IQS data show such broad benefits of vendor certification programs that organizations without such programs should reevaluate whether one may be appropriate for even a part of their business. ISO 9001 provides an excellent starting point for a supplier certification program.

The Awakening

Imagine our disappointment after spending millions of dollars and writing many books on improvement tools to find that only five of the many improvement tools now in use are universal best practices. Well, we saved the day when we stratified the data into three groupings.

The analysis team decided to divide the data into three relative performance categories called high, medium, and low performers.

Statistical analysis of the data related to each of the stratified groups revealed that there were a number of positive and negative practices that had previously been falsely considered universal best practices. This analysis also proved that it takes a very different set of activities and beliefs to move a low-performing organization up to the medium-performance level than it does to move a medium-performing organization up to the high-performance level. The analysis also showed that when an organization moves from the medium-performance level to the high-performance level, the organization will need to adopt a very different set of activities and beliefs to maintain its high level of performance. Organizations that continue to do the same things that they did to move from the medium- to the high-performance level soon slip back and become medium performers again.

It always amazes me that so many things are obvious once they are called to my attention. It should be obvious that you have to manage an organization very differently if it is on the verge of bankruptcy than you would if it were setting the standards for its industry. Therefore, it's obvious that the organization's approach to improvement should differ based on its current performance. This conclusion is exactly what the data collected during the study statistically revealed to the study team.

The Good, the Bad, and the Ugly

Based on our statistical analysis of the stratified database, we found that a single practice can have three impacts on an organization depending on which performance level the organization finds itself in:

- *The good.* The practice has a statistically proven positive impact on the organization's performance.
- *The bad.* The practice has no statistically proven impact on the organization's performance. There are probably better ways the organization should be investing its money.
- *The ugly.* The practice has a statistically proven negative impact on the organization's performance.

Figure 12.1 provides an overview of how some of the different management practices affect the future of the organization's performance based on the current level of performance.

Figure 12.1 How Different Practices Affect Performance

Practice	Performance level		
	Low	Medium	High
Statistical process control	Bad	Bad	Bad
Department-level teams	Good	Bad	Ugly
Quality-related meetings	Bad	Good	Bad
Assessing top management on quality	Ugly	Bad	Good
Assessing mid-management on quality	Bad	Good	Good
Process benchmarking	Ugly	Good	Good
Increased training	Good	Good	Ugly
Get customers' input on new product	Good	Good	Ugly
Evaluating technology	Bad	Good	Ugly
Measuring improvement efforts	Bad	Good	Bad

☺ = Good   😐 = Bad   ☹ = Ugly

When a Best Practice Can Get You Into Trouble

Depending on the organization's level of development, you must concentrate on very different things. Using the three relative performance categories, let's see which management practices could cause trouble.

Here's a list of management practices that could get you into trouble if you are a low-performing organization.

- Emphasizing quality when assessing your senior managers
- Encouraging widespread participation in quality meetings
- Using world-class benchmarking
- Emphasizing technological forecasting or competitor activities to identify new products
- Emphasizing technology considerations for selecting vendors
- Relying on surveys to obtain feedback from customers
- Regularly using business partners as a source of process technology
- Emphasizing empowerment
- Opening planning on a widespread basis throughout the organization
- Developing process technology internally
- Using geographical expansion as the strategy for future growth
- Removing quality control inspection
- Benchmarking marketing and sales processes

Here's a list of management practices that could get you into trouble if you are a medium-performing organization.

- Emphasizing quality and team performance in assessing senior management
- Increasing hours of training in general knowledge topics
- Selecting suppliers based on their general reputation
- Using cross-functional teams or teams with customers on them to create design specifications
- Shifting primary responsibilities for compliance with quality standards away from the quality assurance (QA) function
- Downsizing the business by offering fewer services
- Focusing on cost reduction to make decisions about acquiring technologies

Here's a list of management practices that could get you into trouble if you are a high-performing organization.

- Increasing participation in department-level improvement teams
- Increasing hours of training in general knowledge topics
- Making education and championing a primary role for the QA function
- Focusing your technology on production processes
- Relying on customer surveys as a primary input for improvement
- Using cross-functional teams with customers on them to create design specifications

Summary

This research should make all organizations cautious about the role model they are using to be sure it's right for them based upon their performance level. All organizations have different needs depending on their key executives' personalities, their customers, their competition, their organization's culture, and their products. The truth is that there's no one right answer. So don't just follow the "flavor of the month." Step back and design your improvement process as carefully as you would design that new product that would be your showcase for the coming years, for your improvement process could be even more important to the organization.

THE ORGANIZATION'S STAKEHOLDERS: RESOURCE OR OBLIGATION?

I'm often asked, "Of all the stakeholders, which one is the most important? Which one is the most valuable resource that the organization must be sure is satisfied?" Let's look at who the stakeholders are.

- Investors
- Management
- Employees
- Customers
- Suppliers
- Employees' families
- Community/humankind
- Special interest groups

> **"If you want to be the greatest company, you have to start acting like one today."**
> **—Tom Watson Sr.**
> **Former CEO, IBM**

Investors

Investors are the first people whom the organization promised to provide with an income that is better than they could get from any other place. As a result, they invested their hard-earned money in the organization. Often this money is from retirement funds that support the aging. When IBM cut its dividends by 75 percent, it caused major hardships on many of its retired employees. This occurred more than ten years ago. During the same period no other classification of stockholders got a cut in income from IBM. In fact, they all got big increases.

The organization has an ongoing obligation to provide its investors with an equitable return on investment based on the risks they are taking. Between 2000 and 2003, investors lost 35 percent of the money they invested to U.S. corporations. However, few managers and employees got their base pay cut; in fact, most of them received increases.

Management

Management is the next group of people that an organization promises to provide with a good income if they can develop the organization and make it profitable. They often work long hours (fifty to sixty hours a week on average). They give up a lot of their family life for the organization. Often when the organization is starting up, they work for little or no pay. Certainly the organization has an obligation to its managers to provide them financial security and give them meaningful work assignments.

Employees

Employees are the next people to come on board to produce and sell the products and services that will be delivered to the external customers. Essentially the employees are selling a big part of their lives to the organization to receive a fair day's pay for a fair day's work.

Customers

Customers are fourth in line because they provide the money that allows the organization to meet its obligations to the first three stakeholders. The organization must have satisfied customers to meet its other obligations.

Suppliers

Suppliers are important because very few organizations can exist without good suppliers. I can't think of any organization that can exist without suppliers that provide it with needed input to its processes. Organizations must work with their suppliers to help them improve and pay them a fair price for their products and services so they can meet their obligations.

Employees' Families

Employees' families are important because the organization uses more than 60 percent of the family breadwinners' waking hours even if they put in no overtime. The organization has an obligation to provide its employees with enough time to meet their obligations to their families—time to take care of the business of running a home and time to spend with their spouses and children.

Community and Humankind

The community is important because it's a supplier that organizations need to build roads, provide electricity, police protection, and so on. Without the community, they would not be able to survive. As a result, organizations have an obligation to their communities to keep the environment clean, to participate in school activities, to pay taxes, and to support community activities.

Special Interest Groups

Special interest groups provide a special service to humanity. Some of their services are very worthy while others are not, depending on your point of view. But in either case they can cause the organization a lot of trouble if the organization doesn't work with the special interest groups that are in keeping with the best interests of the nation.

Which Stakeholder Is Most Important?

When you look at all of the stakeholders, which one is most important? I believe that it boils down to two: the *customer* and the *investor*. Selecting the business model is to take a very unpopular position on this subject. In a for-profit organization, investors are the most important stakeholder because the organization is formed using their money with a promise to give them a fair return on their investment. The best way to do that is to have very satisfied customers. However, if you can't take good care of your investors, then you are either selling the wrong product/service or you are approaching the wrong customers, and you must act to correct this problem. Remember, all customers are not equal. Some customers cost so much to service that you don't make a fair profit. You want these to go to your competitor. The first obligation that management and the employees have is to provide their investors with a fair return on their investment. Management and the employees often lose sight of this most important stakeholder as they give out regular increases to themselves but don't increase the dividends they pay. The investors must come first.

The employees' primary customer is management because management pays the employees to do their jobs. Management's primary customer is the board of directors because the board gives management its assignments. The board of directors' primary customers are the investors because they provide the money to develop the organization and as such, they are the true owners of the organization. That's why Ford sold me my Mustang convertible for $25,000 (in 1995) and would not take a penny less. As a customer, I would have been extremely happy if I could have negotiated the price down to $2,500 instead. In fact, I probably would have bought another car for my son. Making a fair return on the investor's money is the first obligation that an organization has. That means that profits are what the game is all about.

An excellent organization is one that is profitable and pays high dividends. It provides output that is higher in quality, less costly, and provides more value than the customers can get from any other source. It pays well enough and provides enough benefits that the employees can live comfortably on one paycheck, and one of the spouses can stay home and take care of the children if he or she wishes. It recognizes that it has an obligation to its suppliers to provide them with orders far enough in advance that they can do proper planning and make good use of their limited resources, and it's willing to pay them a fair price for their output, allowing the supplier to make a fair profit. The excellent organization also realizes that it has an obligation to the community/humankind. It adopts standards such as ISO 14001, not because it's forced to but because it realizes that it's good for the fragile environment that we all live in. It encourages its employees to participate in community and professional activities by subsidizing any additional costs that the employees may incur as a result. It even has sabbatical programs that allow the employees to take on a special community service full-time without adversely affecting their salaries.

Yes, excellent organizations care about all of the stakeholders and develop measurement systems that highlight to management and the stakeholders how well they are doing in meeting all of the stakeholders' needs.

How do excellent organizations accomplish all this? They do it by managing all five of the organization's excellence pillars at the same time and shifting priorities and emphasis based upon the external and internal environments. To excel, all organizations have to learn how to simultaneously manage all five systems to optimize total value to all stakeholders.

You must manage five elements to achieve excellence, but a number of things run across all of them. For example:

- Communication
- Teamwork
- Empowerment
- Respect for one another
- Honesty
- Leadership
- Quality
- Fairness
- Technology

"If I had a brick for every time I've repeated the phrase 'Quality, Service, Cleanliness, and Value,' I think I'd probably be able to bridge the Atlantic Ocean with them."
—Ray Kroc
Founder, McDonald's

All these key factors are built into the word *manage*. These are the things that turn an employee into an individual who owns his or her job, thereby bringing satisfaction and dignity to the person when the job is well done.

In today's worldwide marketplace, customers don't have to settle for second best. Overnight mail brings the best to everyone's doorstep. The Internet lets your customers shop internationally, so it's easy for them to get the best quality, reliability, and price, no matter which organization offers it. Customers are concerned about the products they buy, but they are equally or more concerned about dealing with organizations that care, that are quick to respond, and that will listen and react to their unique needs. This demands that, to succeed in the twenty-first century, organizations must excel in all parts of their business. You must have an organization that excels at what it is doing but that also is recognized for its excellence to win today's savvy customers.

EXCEL INC.

Organizations that excel set high standards for themselves and their employees. The following are some best practices guidelines for a hypothetical company called Excel Inc.

The following was developed by Abdul Rahman Awl, senior vice president of the Harrington Institute, based on the book *Energy Meter,* by the Danish professor Claus Muller.

Mission Statement

■ Excel Inc. has a well-defined mission statement, a clear business plan, and a long-term strategy for existing.

■ The mission statement is known by everyone.

■ Excel Inc. deploys resources only in areas that naturally fit its mission statement.

> **"Excellence is the gradual result of always striving to do better."**
> **—Pat Reilly**
> **Basketball coach**

Vision

■ Excel Inc. has a vision: a major, valuable, ambitious goal clearly described as a *desirable state* achieved at a particular moment.

■ Management inspires commitment to a clear vision and definite objectives.

■ The mission is communicated to everyone in such a way that all know it and understand it.

■ The vision is sufficiently ambitious and meaningful to enable everyone to contribute to its implementation.

■ The vision penetrates the life of the organization, mobilizes energy, and creates a passion for success.

(President John F. Kennedy gave a good example of a convincing and challenging vision when he declared that the United States would send a man to the moon and bring him back safely before the end of the 1960s.)

Organization

■ Excel Inc. has an organization chart that is unambiguous and shows who is responsible for what and who reports to whom.

■ All functions and departments have clear goals and key areas (main categories of tasks on which to concentrate to achieve results).

■ It has a relatively flat organization with few layers within its hierarchy.

■ Although it has a clear organization chart, it is extremely flexible. Excel Inc. compiles project groups and teams from all levels and departments within the organization.

■ Although it respects the formal line of authority, it doesn't allow bureaucratic procedures to stifle initiative or compromise effective communication.

Management System

- In Excel Inc. all functions, departments, managers, and staff have clear, coordinated goals and key areas of responsibility.
- Responsibilities for functions and tasks are delegated to all parts and individuals of the organization without any personal bias.
- Managers pay attention to the details of people management—employees' performance, their career progress and advancement, their morale, and so on.
- Managers coach staff and help them carry out delegated tasks well.
- In Excel Inc., delegation is a process, which implies responsibility for both the person who delegates and the person to whom tasks are delegated.
- Decisions are made quickly by the people who work specifically with the problems and who have the necessary knowledge and skills.
- It uses the principles of "time-based management"; in other words, it's flexible, it sees time as a decisive strategic factor, it adapts quickly when facing new demands, and every person respect every other's time.

"We" Culture

- Excel Inc. has a "we" culture, as opposed to a "we/they" culture: Employees experience a community spirit on all levels—on a work group level, team level, departmental level, and on an organizational level.
- People treat one another with mutual respect and trust—regardless of profession, rank, grade, gender, nationality, language, and other traditional boundaries.
- At Excel Inc. "we" means staff, which includes employees, part-time employees, managers, executives, and the board of directors.
- Excel Inc. evaluates and rewards groups and individuals, both on the basis of their own results and their contributions to the overall results of the organization. It rewards people for their efforts, activities, and knowledge.
- In Excel Inc., teams are not placed in competitive situations in which one team wins at the expense of another. Teams and work groups are inspired to coordinate resources to achieve the best overall results.

Management Style

- Excel Inc. discourages poor management styles, which are characterized by commands, detailed orders, sanctions, monologues, and patronization.
- Managers communicate visions and goals clearly, set priorities for tasks, and give clear assignments to staff. The staff is involved in discussions about how to achieve the goals.
- At Excel Inc., dialogue is the managers' most important means of motivating and involving everyone. People talk *with* each other, not to or about each other.

- Managers make a determined effort to create an environment where all employees get an opportunity to demonstrate what they can do.
- Managers encourage creativity and innovation. Good ideas are welcomed and rewarded.
- Excel Inc.'s staff is empowered and motivated to take responsibility.
- Managers gain confidence and respect from others through their competence. They don't take their positions too solemnly and do not need status symbols to demonstrate who or what they are.

Personnel Policies

- At Excel Inc. the personnel policies describe both frameworks: rules and regulations for the hard areas and frameworks and guidelines for the soft areas.
- Excel Inc. believes that its people are the most important resource.
- It believes that the development of the organization depends on the development of the individual employee.
- Its personnel policies are based on the conviction that the relationship between the organization and the employees is based on a balance between input and output.
- The organization is obligated toward every employee who displays responsibility, loyalty, and initiative. The organization does everything in its power to fulfill this obligation.
- Excel Inc. has a culture that contributes to bringing out the best in people. This culture is characterized by openness, honesty, trust, mutual respect, commitment, and a genuine interest in helping each other.
- The organization is not bureaucratic.
- Excel Inc. encourages innovation. All ideas are welcomed and good ideas are rewarded.
- The organization is multifunctional. Employees can do more than one job; they can perform more than one function, and they can work throughout the organization and beyond professional boundaries.
- Excel Inc. is a multicultural organization. Its strength lies in its diversity.

The Employment Contract

- At Excel Inc. the employment contract contains two parts: the hard and the soft contract.
- The contract contains the organization's expectations from the employee in the hard areas (the concrete contents of the employment) and in the soft areas (commitment, responsibility, loyalty, initiative, flexibility, quality awareness, etc.)
- The contract contains the employee's expectations from the organization in both hard and soft areas (recognition, openness toward new ideas, contributory influence, development opportunities, working environment, etc.)
- The contract—especially the soft part—is "negotiated" and is adjusted either during informal talks or more formal appraisal interviews.

- Its managers use a partnership model of performance management—a relationship in which two partners (manager and employee) agree on a performance agreement.
- At Excel Inc. performance appraisal is a continuous process—occurring on a daily or a weekly basis with quarterly reviews.
- Line managers own the performance appraisal process and use it as a tool to help employees succeed rather than relying on human resources or senior management to drive the process as a bureaucratic exercise.
- In the performance appraisal system, managers and employees agree on whether objective measures were met or not rather than relying on subjective evaluation from the supervisor.

Remuneration and Recognition

- At Excel Inc. the employees are paid a salary and benefits that are at least equivalent to those of comparable organizations.
- The organization recognizes everyone's contribution and rewards exceptional performance and results. The procedure for recognizing achievement and rewarding performance is clearly understood and administered with objectivity and transparency.
- Excel Inc. rewards both team performance and individual performance.

Career Development

- Excel Inc. makes a goal-directed effort to attract and keep competent staff members—in other words, people who can and will perform.
- It offers those employees who can and will more responsibility, freedom of action, and new challenges.
- It fills open management positions through competitive, internal recruitment as much as possible.
- In Excel Inc., high-performing employees can advance to higher professional grades without filling managerial positions.
- It motivates, supports, and faces with demands those employees who can, but will not.
- It educates, tests, and supports those employees who will, but cannot.
- It releases employees who neither can nor will and those employees whom it cannot help or motivate to be able and willing.
- Excel Inc. encourages and contributes to the professional and personal development of all its employees.

Learning Organizations

- Excel Inc. is a learning organization. People use each other's skills and knowledge and learn from each other all the time.
- It organizes training courses for people from all functions, departments, and professions. It invests in its people.

■ It encourages new employees to contribute their knowledge and first-hand impressions. It encourages them to question the organization's routines and habits.

■ Everyone—regardless of age, seniority, position, and qualifications—learns from others. Everyone teaches others something.

■ When an employee attends a course, seminar, or conference, others in the organization will benefit from the newfound knowledge. Excel Inc. reserves time for the participant to tell others about what he or she has learned. People discuss how the new knowledge can be applied.

■ Excel Inc. encourages everyone to take an interest in other people's work and to pass on information about his or her own work.

■ It gives the employees an opportunity to use their knowledge and encourages them to take the initiative to keep acquiring new skills.

■ Excel desires, expects, and appreciates ideas and creative suggestions for improvement from the employees.

■ It encourages all employees to develop their personal competence on professional and personal levels. It rewards initiatives for personal development—visibly and noticeably.

■ Employees don't just learn enough to survive. They acquire knowledge, both inside and in external dealings with stakeholders and partners, to transform the organization into a center of excellence in knowledge management.

Information Systems

■ Excel Inc.'s information system contains both hard and soft information.

■ It frequently surveys stakeholder satisfaction (clients, donors, partners, etc.). It knows how much support it has and why.

■ It frequently researches employee satisfaction. When an employee gives notice, it investigates why it lost him or her.

■ It makes regular image surveys.

■ It regularly evaluates the organization's culture, systems, and policies.

■ Its annual report, newsletter, and other outreach publications cover the people in the organization, their energies, and their commitment to the development of the organization.

■ It keeps informed about the productivity, relations, and quality of people and departments.

Communication

■ At Excel Inc. the tone is relaxed, friendly, and humorous.

■ The management gives open and honest information to all employees.

■ People make only promises that can be kept.

■ Everybody in the organization is listened to. Communication is based on dialogues.

- The switchboard functions as an effective communication center that always knows when people are available. People use voice-mail services to receive and leave messages.
- In Excel Inc. everyone contributes to effective, internal communication. Whenever people leave their desks, they leave a message as to when they will be available again. They keep the promise.
- Meetings are effective and well organized. People show respect for each other's time—meetings start and finish on time, and all participants are active.
- Staff movements, such as missions, leaves, transfers, promotions, and recruitments, are publicly announced.
- Everyone knows the organization's development goals, strategies, and policies.
- All employees know their own and their colleagues' key areas of responsibility and authority. The lines of communication are clear.
- The in-house newsletter appears regularly and carries information about staff movements, job openings, press releases, and other announcements.
- The flow of information is free and sufficient between managers and employees.
- Excel Inc. has established who is responsible for the organization's contacts with outside target groups. It has clear guidelines for external communication.
- It has a standardized databank, which is regularly updated to enable it to quickly supply stakeholders with relevant information.

Ten Things the Best Coaches Do

In Excel Inc., managers use the following tools of effective coaching:

- They take time to listen to their employees.
- They see their employees as people, not just overhead.
- They care about their employees personally, helping if they have personal problems.
- They set a good example for their employees.
- They let their employees know they can accomplish more than they thought they could.
- They encourage their people.
- They never pull rank.
- They don't keep their employees in the dark, letting them know what is going on in a given situation.
- They praise their employees for a job well done.
- They let their people know in a straightforward manner when they don't do their jobs well.

"Excelling is a state of mind, not just the bottom line."
—HJH

A CLOSING THOUGHT FROM ROBERT FULGHUM

"Most of what I really need to know about how to live and what to do and how to be I learned in kindergarten. . . . These are the things that I learned:

- Share everything.
- Play fair.
- Don't hit people.
- Put things back where you found them.
- Clean up your own mess.
- Don't take things that aren't yours.
- Say you're sorry when you hurt somebody.
- Flush.
- Warm cookies and cold milk are good for you.
- Live a balanced life—learn some and think some and draw and paint and sing and dance and play and work every day some.
- Take a nap every afternoon.
- When you go out into the world, watch out for traffic, hold hands, and stick together.
- Be aware of wonder."

—Robert Fulghum
All I Really Need To Know I Learned in Kindergarten (Villard Books, 1988)

Robert Fulghum sums it all up. You just need to get back to good basic management principles, beliefs, and honesty to excel.

APPENDIX A

DEFINITIONS

- **Acquisition**—The process by which a corporation's stock or assets are transferred to a buyer either through a purchase of stock or assets.
- **Activities**—Elements of a process usually performed by a single department or individual.
- **Activity definition**—Identifying and documenting specific activities that must be performed to produce the deliverables and sub-deliverables identified in the work breakdown structure.
- **Activity duration**—The best estimate of the time (e.g., hours, days, weeks, or months) necessary to accomplish the work involved in an activity, considering the nature of the work and resources needed.
- **Activity-on-arrow (AOA)**—A method of depicting a network plan that indicates work is performed on the lines between nodes (i.e., events).
- **Activity-on-node (AON)**—A method of depicting a network plan that indicates work is performed on the nodes; lines connect the nodes to show the network's logic.
- **Actual cost of work performed (ACWP)**—Total costs incurred (direct and indirect) in accomplishing work during a given time period.
- **Adjusted (recast) earnings**—Earnings that result from the adjustment of historical financial statements reflecting items that are unrelated to the ongoing business.
- **Affinity diagram**—A technique for organizing a variety of subjective data (such as options) into categories based on the intuitive relationships among individual pieces of information. The diagram is often used to find common points among concerns and ideas.
- **Agent (agent technology)**—A software program that transparently executes procedures to support fathering, delivering, categorizing, profiling information, or notifying the knowledge-seeker about the existence of, or changes to, an area of interest.
- **Agreement**—A step in contract negotiation in which the final agreement is documented.
- **Alliance**—An agreement between two or more parties to achieve common goals and secure common interests.
- **Alliance partnership**—A strategic partnership between two or more parties. Frequently, one corporation provides the engineering, manufacturing, or product development services, and a smaller organization provides the creative solution. The result is the creation of a specialized new product. Typically, the larger firm supplies capital and the necessary

product development, marketing, manufacturing, and distribution characteristics while the smaller firm supplies specialized technical or creative experience.

- **Alternatives identification**—Using various methods to determine which risk events might affect a project and documenting their characteristics.

- **Analogous estimating**—Using the actual duration of a previous, similar activity as the basis for estimating the duration of a future activity; a form of expert judgment.

- **Architecture**—A cohesive and consistent solution framework for achieving business objectives. Every solution architecture is composed of business process, data, technology infrastructure, application, and organizational architectures.

- **Arrow diagram**—A way to define the most effective sequence of events and control the activity to meet a specific objective in a minimum amount of time. The diagram is an adaptation of the program evaluation and review technique (PERT) or critical path method (CPM).

- **Artificial intelligence**—Using human models for cognition and perception to create computer systems to solve human-like problems.

- **Asset-based approach**—A method of determining the value of an organization's assets and/or equity interest using one or more methods based directly on the market value of the assets or the business, less liabilities.

- **Asset management**—The process of acquiring, building, maintaining, and disposing of assets.

- **Assets**—The entire property of a person, association, corporation, or estate. Any tangible piece of equipment, hardware, or software that's purchased, leased, used, maintained, and tracked by a project team.

- **Assumption analysis**—A technique used to explore the accuracy, consistency, or completeness of an assumption.

- **Assumptions**—Factors that will be considered true, real, or certain for planning purposes.

- **Autonomous work team (self-managed work team)**—A team approach that's used when a natural work team and the measurement system have developed to the point that employees can manage themselves. These teams select the improvement opportunities they will work on.

- **Balanced matrix**—An organizational structure in which some staff is involved in project work as coordinators or expeditors while other staff is involved full-time (e.g., the project manager).

- **Balanced scorecard**—A concept for measuring a company's activities in terms of its vision and strategy. It balances a financial perspective with customer, internal processes, and learning and growth perspectives. The concept was developed by Robert S. Kaplan and David Norton.

- **Benchmark**—A point or a measurement against which other things are compared. It was originally used as a reference point for surveying. Today it's often used to compare performance, projects, products, or processes between organizations.

- **Benchmarking (BMKG)**—A systematic way to identify, understand, and creatively evolve superior processes, products, services, design, equipment, and practices to improve an organization's real performance. This is done by gaining a detailed understanding of an organization's activities and then adapting them to similar activities within another organization.

- **Benefit-cost ratio**—Comparative analysis of benefits versus costs that can be used to determine potential returns from a project. If the ratio is greater than one, benefits exceed costs; if it's less than one, it's not profitable because costs exceed benefits; if it equals one, benefits equal costs.

- **Benefit-measurement method**—A method of project selection that includes items such as cost benefit analysis, present value, payback period, return on investment, and internal rate of return.

- **Book assets**—Tangible assets plus financial assets.

- **Book value**—(1) With respect to assets, the capitalized cost of an asset less accumulated depreciation, depletion, or amortization as it appears on an organization's books. (2) With respect to a business enterprise, the difference between an enterprise's total assets (net of depreciation, depletion, and amortization) and total liabilities as they appear on the balance sheet. It's synonymous with net book value, net worth, and shareholder's equity.

- **Bottom-up estimate**—an approach that estimates cost starting at the lower levels of the work breakdown structure (WBS) and then summing up to successively higher WBS levels.

- **Brainstorming**—A technique used by a group to quickly generate large lists of ideas, problems, or issues. The emphasis is on quantity of ideas, not quality.

- **Browser**—A program that allows users to access documents on the World Wide Web, typically using the HTTP protocol. Browsers can be either text or graphic. They read HTML and interpret the code into what we see as Web pages. Browsers are often used as the primary front-end interface for knowledge management systems that rely on intranet technology.

- **Budget at completion (BAC)**—The estimated total cost of a project when done.

- **Budgeted cost of work performed (BCWP)**—The sum of the approved cost estimates (including any overhead allocation) for activities, or portions of activities, completed during a given period (usually project to date).

- **Budgeted cost of work scheduled (BCWS)**—The sum of the approved cost estimates (including any overhead allocation) for activities, or portions of activities, scheduled to be performed during a given period (usually project to date).

- **Bureaucracy elimination method**—An approach to identify and eliminate checks and balances activities that aren't cost-justified.

- **Business enterprise**—A commercial, industrial, or service organization pursuing an economic activity. A business enterprise can be seen as the sum of all operating assets of the business, including normal working capital, operating fixed assets, and all intangible assets related to the production of the income and cash-flow stream being valued.

- **Business objectives**—These goals define what an organization wants to accomplish during the next five to ten years. They provide a big-picture focus that's usually not quantified.

- **Business operating system (BOS)**—An environment that represents an organization's vast warehouses of knowledge; the way a business is run, the way people and information come together to add value to a business process. A BOS is a repository comprising a common operating environment, a business process library, and enterprise workflow. The BOS is expressed through a consistent standardized desktop metaphor.

- **Business risk**—The inherent chances for both profit and loss associated with a particular endeavor.

- **Business system analyst (BSA)**—A project team member who serves as the primary point of contact with an information technology organization and is accountable for business integration.

- **Business valuation**—The act or process of arriving at an opinion or determination of the economic value of a business or enterprise or an interest therein. A business valuation can be conducted for a variety of purposes including, but not limited to a merger or acquisition; gift estate, or inheritance tax planning; ESOPs and other employee benefit plans; going public; buy/sell agreements; marital partnership; and corporate dissolution and bankruptcy reorganizations.

- **Call center**—A centralized office used for receiving and transmitting a large volume of requests by telephone. Companies use call centers to administer incoming product support and information inquiries from customers. They can also handle outgoing calls for telemarketing, debt collection, and follow-up. Often a call center collectively handles letters, faxes, and e-mails at one location called a "contact center."

- **Capability maturity model (CMM)**—This model defines five levels of process development in a software environment. Software Engineering Institute (SEI) developed the model during the mid-1980s as a family of process models that followed the evolution of a software development organization. The CMM is used to assess an organization against a scale of five process maturity levels.

- **Capital turnover**—A financial measurement that's calculated by dividing the capital employed into sales. This is a measure of the relationship between sales and core financing.

- **Capital turnover performance**—A financial measurement used to evaluate management's effectiveness with sales in relationship to assets deployed. It's calculated by dividing capital employed into net sales.

- **Career planning**—A subset of career management that applies the concepts of strategic planning and marketing to taking charge of one's professional future. The individual must be in charge of his or her career plan, but the individual's manager can be of great assistance.

■ **Cash flow**—The excess of sources of cash over uses of cash. Cash flow is used in performing the discounted cash-flow analysis.

■ **Cause-and-effect diagram**—A visual presentation of possible causes of a specific problem or condition. The effect is listed on the right-hand side, and the causes are listed at right angles to it. The diagram is sometimes called a "fishbone" or "Ishikawa" diagram.

■ **Certification**—A designed experiment applied to a single activity or piece of equipment. The item is considered certified when the evaluating team is confident that the individual activity, individual, or piece of equipment, when following the related procedures, will provide output that meets the next activity requirement.

■ **Change control**—The project management function of monitoring and dealing with changes to a project's scope or its objectives.

■ **Change control board (CCB)**—A formally constituted group of stakeholders responsible for approving or rejecting changes to the project baselines.

■ **Checksheet**—A simple form on which data are recorded in a uniform manner. The forms are used to minimize the risk of errors and facilitate the organized collection and analysis of data.

■ **Chief knowledge officer (CKO) or chief learning officer**—An individual who oversees efforts to use technology for knowledge capture and distribution. CKOs have three critical responsibilities: creating a knowledge management infrastructure, building a knowledge culture, and making it all pay off. The CKO is responsible for enterprisewide coordination of all knowledge leadership and is typically chartered by the CEO. The CKO's focus is the practice of knowledge leadership, usually a solo performer role with no immediate job responsibility. Before a culture of knowledge sharing, incentives, and the basic precepts of knowledge leadership have been acknowledged by the enterprise, the CKO is powerless.

■ **Closure**—A step in contract negotiation in which positions are summarized and final concessions are made.

■ **Cognition**—The ability to synthesize diverse sources of information when making a decision. Cognition is the aspect of knowledge management solutions used to facilitate decision making. As part of a knowledge map, cognition is the application of knowledge that's been exchanged through intermediation, externalization, and internalization.

■ **Communications management plan**—A document that provides a collection and filing structure that details what methods will be used to gather and store various types of information; a distribution structure that details to whom information will flow and methods to be used.

■ **Communication processes**—The information technology and cultural processes that enable people to share information in an efficient and effective manner. Process, in this case, doesn't describe just the technical process underlying message delivery but the whole act of communicating. To describe it as a purely technical process doesn't take into consideration knowledge management, where the human/cultural side is as important as the technological side.

- **Community of practice (CoP)**—Groups of virtual or local members with similar specializations. Such a community forms where people assume roles based on their abilities and skills instead of their titles and hierarchical structure. It's sometimes called a "community of interest."

- **Competency management**—The ability to use KM to consistently facilitate the formation of new ideas, products, and services that support the core competency of the organization.

- **Competency modeling**—an activity that identifies peak performers and creates profiles and models that specify employees' skill sets, personalities, values, and other attributes. Competency modeling is closely related to leveraging intellectual assets, but it's more forward-looking, and it focuses on the people aspect.

- **Computer-supported collaborative work (CSCW)**—The shared development of knowledge artifacts. CSCW is also called "groupware" or "artifact-based" collaboration.

- **Concept-based search**—A form of content-based indexing, search, and retrieval in which the search engine possesses a level of intelligence regarding semantics and lexicons. In such a system, internalization and externalization can be achieved at a conceptual level, providing results far beyond that of word-based queries.

- **Concept mapping**—An educational technique for improving understanding and retention. As an aid to writing, a concept map is a picture of the ideas or topics contained in the information and the ways these relate to each other. It's a visual summary that shows the structure of the material the writer will describe.

- **Confidentiality agreement**—Signed by potential buyers, this agreement requires them to keep the information contained in the confidential business review and ensuing discussions confidential.

- **Configuration management**—Any documented procedure used to apply technical and administrative direction and surveillance to identify and document the functional and physical characteristics of an item or system; control any changes to such characteristics; record and report the change and its implementation status; and audit the items and system to verify conformance to requirements.

- **Constraint**—Factors that limit the project management team's options for planning purposes.

- **Content directors**—Executive management levels that design, set, and execute strategies on issues for which they provide focus regarding the process of knowledge sharing.

- **Content mapping**—The process of identifying and organizing a high-level description of the meaning contained in a collection of electronic documents. Content maps are usually rendered as hierarchical "outlines," but many kinds of more suggestive displays are available through graphical visualization techniques. Content maps are used to facilitate the comprehension of the knowledge base.

- **Context sensitivity**—The ability of a knowledge management system to provide insight that takes into consideration the contextual nature of a user's request based on history, associations, and subject-matter experience.
- **Contingency allowance**—Provision to mitigate cost and/or schedule risk.
- **Contingency plans**—Predefined actions to take if an identified risk occurs. An active risk acceptance response. Identifying alternative strategies to be used if the risk occurs.
- **Continuous risk management**—An approach to software risk management developed by the Software Engineering Institute with processes, methods, and tools for managing risks in a project. It provides a disciplined environment for proactive decision making to continuously assess what could go wrong (i.e., risks), determine which risks are critical enough to warrant taking action, and implement strategies to deal with them.
- **Contract**—A mutually binding agreement that obligates the seller to provide the specified product and obligates the buyer to pay for it. A legal relationship subject to remedy in the courts.
- **Contract work breakdown structure (CWBS)**—This describes the total product and work to be done to satisfy a specific contract.
- **Contribution monitoring and valuation**—A method for analyzing the relative value of an individual's knowledge-supporting activities in a knowledge management system, utilizing a variety of metrics. These could include approaches such as numbers of contributions to knowledge forums, numbers of successful problem resolutions associated with an individual's contributions, and amount of message traffic targeted to take advantage of an individual's expertise. Contribution valuation must be grounded in agreed-upon knowledge-management metrics.
- **Control chart**—A graphical chart that provides a picture of the way a process is performing. It includes control limits and plotted values. The values are a statistical measure for a series of samples or subgroups of the process output. A solid line shows the mean (i.e., average) of the output.
- **Core competency**—An organization's overriding value statement. Core competency differs from product and market competency in that an organization's core competency outlives (by a significant margin) product life cycles and market swings. AT&T's core competency, for example, is connecting people, not telecommunications.
- **Corporate governance**—A structural system of institutional policies, implementing rules, and business controls that establishes a framework under which corporations or organizations are managed and operated. This framework governs all actions of corporations, from initial funding through their period of entrepreneurialship and growth, through their development into a mature structure, and to the point of their exit from the market as an independent entity.
- **Corporate memory (institutional memory)**—The coherent integration of know-how of (geographically) dispersed groups of people in an organization. This know-how may relate to problem-solving expertise in functional disciplines (e.g., design, testing, and

production), project management issues (e.g., social and organizational aspects related to the project team), innovation and design technical issues (e.g., design rationales and concurrent engineering techniques), and lessons learned. Corporate memory is an unquestioned tacit or explicit understanding of an organization's people, process, or products, and many experts feel that it's one of the keys to continued innovation.

- **Cost benefit analysis**—Comparative analysis of cost versus benefits that can be used to determine a project's net returns.

- **Cost performance index (CPI)**—The ratio of budgeted costs to actual costs (BCWP/ACWP). CPI is often used to predict the magnitude of a possible cost overrun using the following formula: original cost estimate/CPI = projected cost at completion.

- **Cost risk**—(1) Failure to complete tasks within the estimated budget allowances. (2) The degree of uncertainty associated with system acquisition life cycle budgets and outlays that could negatively affect a project.

- **Cost variance (CV)**—(1) Any difference between the estimated cost of an activity and its actual costs. (2) In earned value, the numerical difference between budgeted cost of work performed (BCWP) less actual costs (ACWP).

- **Creativity**—A mental process involving the generation of new ideas or concepts or new association between existing ideas and concepts. Creativity is the act of making something new. Although intuitively this is a simple phenomenon, it is in fact quite complex. Unlike most phenomena in science, there is no single authoritative perspective or definition of creativity. Unlike many phenomena in psychology, there is no standardized measurement technique.

- **Critical path**—In a project network diagram, the series of activities that determine the earliest completion of the project. It's the path with the greatest duration.

- **Capital turnover**—A financial measurement that's calculated by dividing the capital employed into sales. This is a measure of the relationship between sales and core financing.

- **Capital turnover performance**—A financial measurement used to evaluate management's effectiveness with sales in relationship to assets deployed. It's calculated by dividing capital employed into net sales.

- **Critical success factors**—These are specific items that must be accomplished to meet the strategic plan.

- **Current state assessment**—An evaluation of how a process, activity, or organization is functioning at the present time. The assessment can include flowcharting, collecting measurement data, and interviews with key personnel.

- **Customer capital**—Customer capital's value is based on how well the organization understands its customers' needs and expectations.

- **Customer-centric chain**—This is a five-stage approach that looks at an organization's culture aspects. It includes cultural, capabilities, competencies, and competitiveness assessments as well as communications. Often this is referred to as the "five Cs."

- **Data**—Raw transactional representations and outputs without inherent meaning.
- **Data mining**—A technique to analyze data in very large databases with the goal of revealing trends and patterns, and converting them into information.
- **Data warehouse**—A large storage area for highly structured content. It's a resource of unquestionable value when you need to mine factual data. A data warehouse contains clean, structured, and organized data.
- **Debt to working capital**—A financial term that measures the dependency of working capital on receivables. It's calculated by dividing current assets, minus current liabilities, into debtors.
- **Delphi narrowing technique**—A technique in which team members' priorities are used to reduce a list of alternatives to a few of the most important alternatives.
- **Design of experiments (DOE)**—Structured evaluations designed to yield a maximum amount of information at a defined confidence level for the least expense.
- **Digital nervous system**—The computing infrastructure (e.g., desktops, servers, networks, and software) used to inform and support an organization's decision-making processes. Knowledge management may be part of a digital nervous system.
- **Discontinuity of knowledge**—A phenomenon that occurs when experienced knowledge workers move from one position to another (inside or outside an organization), without having adequate time or knowledge management facilities to transfer their knowledge to co-workers.
- **Distance learning**—The technology to simultaneously instruct students at remote locations.
- **Distributed and open hypertext systems**—Used for generating and leveraging organizational knowledge.
- **Document control**—A process designed to remove obsolete documents from the operational area and ensure that only the correct level document is available to employees.
- **Document management**—A system that controls the change level of the documents within the system and includes the ability to develop a database of documents and classify them automatically. Document management standards, such as Web DAV and DMA, allow document management solutions to be tightly integrated within a knowledge management system.
- **Due diligence**—The assessment of the benefits and liabilities of a proposed acquisition by inquiring into all relevant aspects of the past, present, and predictable future of the business to be purchased. Due diligence occurs subsequent to the letter of intent.
- **Duration**—The number of work periods (not including holidays or other nonworking periods) required to complete an activity or other project element.
- **Earned value analysis (EVA)**—A method for measuring project performance. It compares the amount of work that was planned with what was actually accomplished to determine if cost and schedule performance is functioning as planned.

- **Earning per share**—A financial measure that's calculated by dividing the number of shares issued into the profit attributable to shareholders.

- **Economic life**—The period over which tangible (e.g., real estate or equipment) and intangible (e.g., goodwill or research and development) property may be profitably used.

- **Electronic yellow page**—An online, searchable listing of personnel, their competencies, and their contact information. Similar to skill lists, with more content added to them by past users. It's used as a pointer to the person who actually contributed the knowledge and to facilitate knowledge flow.

- **Employee stock ownership plan (ESOP)**—A type of defined contribution plan under which employees may purchase or acquire securities issued by their employer. ESOPs are a valuable vehicle for corporate financing, including raising new capital, or for financing a leveraged buyout.

- **Empowerment**—Refers loosely to processes for giving subordinates (or workers generally) greater discretion and resources; distributing control to better serve both customers and the interests of employing organizations. (This use of the word appears somewhat at odds with other usage, which most often assumes the empowerment of groups and of individuals to better serve their own interests.) The people doing the work have the authority and responsibility to carry it out and are able to make decisions concerning it.

- **Error-proofing**—Designing a product and processes so that it's difficult for errors to occur.

- **Estimate**—To make a judgment as to the likely or appropriate cost, quality, or duration; to evaluate a rough calculation, a preliminary calculation of cost of work to be undertaken, or an opinion.

- **Estimate at completion (EAC)**—The expected total cost of an activity, group of activities, or a project when the defined scope of work has been completed. A forecast of total project costs based on project performance.

- **Estimated cost to complete (ECC)**—An estimate of what the cost is expected to be at project completion.

- **Estimate to complete (ETC)**—The expected additional cost needed to complete an activity, a group of activities, or the total project. Most techniques for forecasting ETC include some adjustment to the original estimate based on project performance to date.

- **Excellence**—The point at which the output from an individual or an organization exceeds the best possible output from its competitors as viewed by the output's users. It's the point of highest quality and splendor, or exceptionally good for its kind of output.

- **Exception report**—A report indicating conditions outside the expected normal range.

- **Expected monetary value**—The product of an event's probability of occurrence and the gain or loss that will result.

- **Explicit (hard) knowledge**—Knowledge that's stored in a semi-structured content, such as documents, e-mail, voicemail, or video media. It can be articulated in formal language and readily transmitted to other people; it's conveyed from one person to another in a systematic way.

■ **Exposure**—The susceptibility to loss, perception of a risk, or a threat to an asset or asset-producing process, usually quantified in dollars. An exposure is the total dollars at risk without regard to the probability of a negative event; a measure of importance.

■ **External awareness**—The fourth component of the knowledge chain, which represents an organization's ability to understand the market's perceived value of its products and services as well as the changing directions and requirements of its markets. When coupled with internal awareness, external awareness can lead to the discovery of successful new markets.

■ **External customer**—An individual or organization that's not within the supplier's organization but receives a product, service, or information from the supplier.

■ **Externalization**—The transfer of knowledge from the minds of its holders to an external repository in the most efficient way possible. Externalization tools help build knowledge maps. They capture and organize incoming bodies of explicit knowledge and create clusters of knowledge bodies. It's one of the four key knowledge-management functions.

■ **External responsiveness**—The third component of the knowledge chain, which emphasizes the perpetual ability to meet the market on its own terms even when the market can't articulate them. It's a level of responsiveness to environmental conditions that's significantly faster and based on better connections between resources and markets.

■ **External risks**—Risks that are beyond the control or influence of the project team; these are addressed in risk identification.

■ **Failure mode and effects analysis (FMEA)**—Identifies potential failures or causes of failures that might occur as a result of process-design weaknesses.

■ **Fifty-fifty approach**—In earned value analysis, the fifty-fifty rule or approach is used to estimate the amount of each task that's been completed. As soon as a task has started, it's assumed that half the effort is completed, and half the budgeted cost of work-scheduled (BCWS) value associated with the task is entered into the project accounts book. Only after the task is completed is the remaining half of the BCWS value entered into the accounts.

■ **Financial capital**—Any liquid media or mechanism that represents wealth or other styles of capital. A contract regarding any combination of capital assets is called a "financial instrument" and may serve as a media of exchange, standard of deferred payment, unit of accounts, or store of value.

■ **Finish-to-finish relationship**—This relationship restricts the finish of the work activity until some specified duration following the finish of another work activity.

■ **Finish-to-start relationship**—The relationship where work activity can start just as soon as another work activity is finished.

- **5S**—A system designed to bring organization to the workplace. A translation of the original "5S" terms from Japanese to English is:
  - ☐ *Seiri*—organization
  - ☐ *Seiton*—orderliness
  - ☐ *Seiso*—cleanliness
  - ☐ *Seiketsu*—standardized cleanup
  - ☐ *Shitsuke*—discipline
- **5W + 2H**—A rigid, structured approach to problem solving that probes into and defines a problem by asking a specific set of questions related to a previously defined opportunity or problem statement. The 5W+2H stand for:
  - ☐ W1—What?
  - ☐ W2—Why?
  - ☐ W3—Where?
  - ☐ W4—Who?
  - ☐ W5—When?
  - ☐ H1—How did it happen?
  - ☐ H2—How much did it cost?
- **Five-way communication**—Frequently referred to as "star-type communication." It points out that communication must go in five directions: up, down, sideways, to the customer, and to the supplier.
- **Flowchart**—A method of graphically describing a process (existing or proposed) by using simple symbols, lines, and words to display the sequence of activities in the process.
- **Force field analysis**—A visual aid for pinpointing and analyzing elements that resist change (i.e., restraining forces) or push for change (i.e., driving forces). This technique helps drive improvement by developing plans to overcome the restraining forces and make maximum use of the driving forces.
- **Forecasting**—The process of estimating an unknown situation. It's similar to predictions and is commonly used in discussions concerning time-series-data. For example, sales may forecast the number of units to be sold during the next three months.
- **Forward-looking view**—A principle of continuous risk management that requires thinking toward tomorrow, identifying uncertainties, anticipating potential outcomes, and managing project resources and activities while anticipating uncertainties.
- **Function diagrams**—A systematic way of graphically displaying detailed tasks related to broader objectives or detailed issues related to broader issues.
- **Gatekeepers**—People who control the flow of information that's communicated to a specific part of the organization.
- **Geographic information systems (GIS)**—A technology that involves a digitized map, powerful computer, and software that permits the superimposition and manipulation of various kinds of demographic and corporate data on the map.

■ **Goals**—The end toward which effort is directed; the terminal point of a race. These are always specified in time and magnitude so they're easy to measure.

■ **Goodwill or intangible value**—The amount by which the consideration paid exceeds the fair market value of the company's operating assets after step-up in basis.

■ **Graphs**—Visual displays of quantitative data that summarize a set of numbers or statistics.

■ **Gross profit to net sales**—A financial measurement used to assess the productivity of sales. It's calculated by dividing net sales into gross profit.

■ **Guess**—To predict or assume (an event or fact) without enough information to be sure; to suppose; to judge.

■ **Heuristic software**—A software solution that learns about its users and the knowledge they possess by monitoring the user's interaction with the system. Thus, over time, its ability to provide users with relevant knowledge should improve.

■ **Histogram**—A visual representation of the spread or distribution using a series of rectangles (or bars) of equal class sizes or widths. The heights of the bars indicate the relative number of data points in each class.

■ **Hubs**—People who collect and share data.

■ **Human capital**—The collective value of an organization's know-how. Human capital refers to the value, usually not reflected in accounting systems, which results from the investment an organization must make to re-create the knowledge in its employees. This is a way of defining and categorizing peoples' skills and abilities as used when employed and as they otherwise contribute to the economy. It's one of three forms of intellectual capital; the other two are structural and customer capital.

■ **Hypertext**—A semantic network with (substantial) content at the nodes, although the content itself (i.e., the traditional document model) seems to be the driving organizational force, not the network of links. In most hypertext documents, the links aren't semantically typed, although they're typed at times according to the medium of the object displayed by traversing the link.

■ **ISO 9000 series**—A set of standards released by the International Organization for Standardization that defines the fundamental building blocks for a quality management system and the associated accreditation and registration of quality management systems.

■ **Impact**—The loss or effect on a project if a risk occurs.

■ **Independent cost estimate**—An estimate of project costs conducted by individuals external to the normal project management structure.

■ **Indirect costs**—Part of the overall cost of doing business in the organization that's shared by all projects underway. Examples include receptionists, security guards, insurance, and taxes.

■ **Information**—Data endowed with relevance and purpose (i.e., analyzed data).

■ **Information economics**—The study of the tangible value to business enterprises of information holdings.

- **Information mining (or knowledge mining)**—The use of technology to extract additional value from intellectual assets. It begins with finding and managing the right data sources.

- **Information modeling**—An approach that's used to transform precise specification into relevant text, and to make relationships of meaning explicit; often used for rapid and accurate development of new software applications for business requirements. It provides detail about what type of information should be included in a particular information product.

- **Information technology manager (ITM)**—An individual who serves as primary manager of the information technology organization's participants and is accountable for coordinating and oversight of IT effort across the project. Provides subproject(s) status to project manager by rolling up project statuses provided by IT team leaders.

- **Information warehouse**—A storage area for the results of data analysis.

- **Initial public offering (IPO)**—The first sale of stock by a private company to the public. IPOs are often smaller, younger companies seeking capital to expand their business.

- **Innovation**—"Changes that create a new dimension of performance." (Peter Drucker) This term may refer to both radical and incremental changes to products, processes, or services. The goal of innovation often is to solve a problem. Although innovation typically adds value, it may also have a negative effect as new developments change old organizational forms and practices.

- **Intangible (hidden) assets**—The assets of a business that have value but are nonphysical and not shown on the balance sheet, such as patents, software, heavily depreciated fixed assets, strong contractual relationships, and an experienced workforce.

- **Integrated knowledge environment**—Information technology that supports the flow of knowledge throughout the enterprise.

- **Intellectual assets and intellectual capital**—An organization's recorded information and human talent itself. Often some of it is documented in patents. The terms reflect the understanding that information is a growing part of every company's assets, and that such information and knowledge is typically either inefficiently warehoused or simply lost, especially in large, physically dispersed organizations. Intellectual capital is intangible assets that can't be measured but are used by the company to its advantage. It usually represents a major organizational investment. (Also known as "intangible" and "invisible" assets.)

- **Intermediation**—The brokerage function that brings together knowledge-seekers (with questions) with knowledge-providers (with answers). Intermediation technologies facilitate the connections between people and the communication of knowledge between seeker and provider.

- **Internal customer**—A person, process, or department within an organization that receives output from another person and/or process within the same organization.

- **Internal rate of return (IRR)**—The measure of a project's expected profitability or the average rate of return for the project. The interest rate that makes the present value of costs equal to the present value of benefits. The higher the IRR, the better the project.
- **Internal risks**—Risks under the control or influence of the project team; addressed in risk identification.
- **Interrelationship diagram**—A way to graphically map out the cause-and-effect links among related items.
- **Interviewing techniques**—a structured discussion with one or more people for the purpose of collecting information related to a specific subject.
- **Intranets**—Intra-corporation networks that use the Internet's protocol standard. They not only permit sharing of information but also allow viewing of the organization's information (including structured resources such as relational databases as well as unstructured text) through Web browsers.
- **Inventory management**—A process of minimizing the stock of items on hand at a particular location or business. The objective is to maximize the number of turns of inventory per year. The just-in-time concept is part of inventory management. It also includes the one-minute process changeover, SNED, *kanban*, TPN, lean, cell manufacturing, *poka-yoke*, *kaizan* blast, just-in-time production flow, single unit built, and build to order.
- **Job description**—A list of activities, duties, tasks, and responsibilities that an individual is required to perform within a specific job classification or process area.
- **Just-in-time**—A major strategy that allows an organization to produce only what's needed, when it's needed, to satisfy immediate customer requirements, thus minimizing storage costs and improving quality. Implemented effectively, the just-in-time concept will almost eliminate in-process stock.
- *Kaizen*—the Japanese word meaning "continuous improvement."
- *Kanban*—A Japanese term for just-in-time systems. It's a card containing a set of manufacturing specifications and requirements used to regulate the supply of components. The concept was originated by Toyota Motor Corp.
- **Key process areas (KPA)**—Each key process area identifies a cluster of related activities that, when performed collectively, achieves a set of goals considered important for establishing process capability at that maturity level. The capability maturity model integration (CMMI) contains twenty-five key process areas indicating the aspects of product development that are to be covered by a company's software processes. Both the stages representation and the continuous representation contain all twenty-five key process areas.
- **Kickoff meeting**—A meeting conducted to acquaint participants with a project and each other; the project kickoff meeting presumes the presence of the customer, facilitates an initial review of project scope and activities, and usually is conducted after contract award.

- **Knowledge**—A mixture of experience, practices, traditions, values, contextual information, expert insight, and sound intuition that provides an environment and framework for evaluation and incorporating new experiences and information. It's divided into two major categories: explicit and tacit.

- **Knowledge acquisition**—The process of developing and creating insight, skills, and relationships. Knowledge acquisition is the primary job function of a knowledge engineer; traditionally, it consists of reducing a large body of information to a precise set of facts and rules and is associated with expert systems. Recently, these functions have been applied to broad organizational objectives.

- **Knowledge analyst**—An individual who collects, organizes, and disseminates knowledge, usually on demand. A knowledge analyst provides knowledge leadership by becoming a "walking repository" of best practices, a library of how knowledge is shared across an organization.

- **Knowledge artifact**—A defined piece of recorded knowledge that exists in a format that can be retrieved and used by others. A process drawn on a napkin at lunch can become a knowledge artifact if it can be recorded for someone else to use. Typically, artifacts are something more tangible—e.g., a document, picture or graphic, video, audio, project plan, presentation, or template.

- **Knowledge asset**—The source of an organization's core and sustainable competitive advantage. Knowledge is the most important asset. Also known as intellectual capital.

- **Knowledge base (knowledge warehouse)**—Data and "rules of thumb" produced by the knowledge-acquisition and compilation phases of creating an expert system application. It has broadened to include every imaginable corporate intellectual asset. The knowledge base is the absolute collection of all expertise, experience, and knowledge of those within any organization. It's typically used to describe any collection of information that also includes contextual or experiential references to other metadata.

- **Knowledge capital**—The intellectual material, knowledge, information, property, and experience that can be put to use to create wealth. It's collective brainpower. Knowledge capital is also the present value of all future knowledge earnings, discounted at an appropriate rate.

- **Knowledge chain**—Corporate instinct, stemming from the flow of knowledge through four definitive stages: internal awareness, internal responsiveness, external awareness, and external responsiveness.

- **Knowledge deficit**—A metric that captures the inefficiency and cost associated with intellectual rework, substandard performance, and employee inability to find knowledge resources.

- **Knowledge earnings**—The portion of normalized earnings over and above expected earnings attributable to book assets.

- **Knowledge engineers**—Individuals who reduce a large body of knowledge to a precise set of facts and rules, or a new breed of middle managers who remake reality according to the company's vision. Knowledge engineers convert explicit knowledge to instructions, program systems, and codified applications.

- **Knowledge half-life**—The point at which the acquisition of new knowledge is more cost-effective and offers greater returns than maintaining existing knowledge.

- **Knowledge harvesting**—Work performed by the knowledge engineer. It's the act of selecting, through analysis, information that's new or actionable and should be added to the knowledge warehouse.

- **Knowledge librarian**—An individual who performs custom searches on the knowledge warehouse for individuals within the organization.

- **Knowledge management (KM)**—A strategy that turns an organization's intellectual assets, both recorded information and the talents of its members, into greater productivity, new value, and increased competitiveness.

- **Knowledge management audit (KMA)**—The premier methodology for conducting a knowledge audit. KMA exposes and defines an organization's propensity for KM, the value of knowledge, its ability and speed in traversing the knowledge cycle, and the current sources of knowledge. KMA also uncovers pockets of deviance from the organizational norm, thereby identifying key opportunities that can be leveraged within the organization, and key obstacles that must be overcome.

- **Knowledge management experts (strategists)**—Individuals who develop high-level KM strategies.

- **Knowledge management system (KMS)**—A proactive, systematic process by which value is generated from intellectual- or knowledge-based assets and disseminated to stakeholders.

- **Knowledge maps (knowledge mapping, information maps)**—Finding where information is in an organization. The term also describes concerns with how to structure knowledge. Maps can range from simple directories of names, titles, and department affiliation, to elaborate online search engines with hypertext links to databases of human expertise, research material, and abstracts of published information. Knowledge mapping is also called "knowledge taxonomy." It's the process that provides an organization with a picture of the specific knowledge it requires to support its business processes.

- **Knowledge query and manipulation language (KQML)**—A language and protocol for exchanging information and knowledge; a message-format and message-handling protocol to support run-time knowledge sharing among agents. KQML can be used as a language through which an application program interacts with an intelligent system or through which two or more intelligent systems share knowledge in support of cooperative problem solving.

- **Knowledge representation**—Explicit specification of knowledge objects and the relationships among them. It takes many forms, with variations in emphasis and formality. Knowledge representation allows computers to reconfigure and reuse information that they store in ways not narrowly specified in advance. Concept mapping, semantic networks, hypertext, information modeling, and conceptual indexing all exemplify knowledge representation in somewhat different ways.

- **Knowledge segment**—Everything an organization's professionals and systems know about a specific domain.

- **Knowledge sharing (information sharing, decision coordination)**—Knowledge sharing and information sharing are the precision of expression and access needed to meet an objective of rapid product development. Information sharing and decision coordination are central problems for large-scale product development.

- **Knowledge spiral**—The growth of knowledge based upon the knowledge already present within the organization.

- **Knowledge steward**—An individual who provides minimal, ongoing support to knowledge users in the form of expertise in the tools, practices, and methods of knowledge leadership.

- **Knowledge topology**—A framework that segments knowledge management into its four key categories.

- **Knowledge transfer experts (practitioners)**—People who extract knowledge from those who have it, reorder it into a form anyone can use, and periodically update and edit the knowledge warehouse.

- **Knowledge worker**—An individual who works primarily with information or develops and uses knowledge in the workplace. The term was created by Peter Drucker in 1959.

- **Known/unknown risks**—Risks that are identified, assessed, and qualified and for which plans can be made.

- **K-spots**—Represent the knowledge niches on which a company must focus its knowledge management efforts. Based on how the audit process populates the strategic capability framework, it's possible to identify promising processes that stand to gain the most through KM.

- **Late-finish date (LF)**—In the critical path method, the latest possible point in time that an activity can be completed without delaying a specified milestone (usually the project finish date).

- **Late-start date (LS)**—In the critical path method, the latest possible point in time that an activity can begin without delaying a specified milestone (usually the project finish date).

- **Law of diminishing returns**—As more is put into something, less is received from it proportionately; a concept that indicates that after a possible initial increase in marginal returns, the marginal physical product of an input will fall as the total amount of the input rises (holding all other inputs constant). As the total investment increases, the total return on investment as a proportion of the total investment decreases. For example, for $1 million invested, the yearly return on investment (ROI) is 15 percent; if you invest $2 million in the same process, the ROI drops to 12 percent.

- **Learning organization (knowledge-creating organization)**—Organizational strategies for creating new knowledge as a competitive advantage; the collective, group, and interpersonal communication, shared visions, uncovering of hidden assumptions that hinder learning, and "new sensibilities" all figure prominently in these approaches.

■ **Leveling**—The practice of constraining resource use to practical limits and applying these constraints to the project schedule after completing the building of the unconstrained schedule.

■ **Long-term liability to capital**—A financial term that's calculated by dividing the current assets, minus the current liabilities, into long-term liabilities.

■ **Loyalty**—Faithfulness or dedication to a person, cause, or organization.

■ **Major risk**—A risk that has a high or medium likelihood of occurring with a significant adverse impact on the affected item(s).

■ **Mandatory dependencies**—Hard logic; they involve the physical or technological limitations of the work to be done.

■ **Matrix diagram**—A systematic way of selecting from large lists of alternatives. The diagram is used to choose between problems, root causes, or solutions. Also known as a "decision matrix."

■ **Merger**—The combination of one corporation with another.

■ **Metadata**—Information added to a document or a smaller unit of information that makes it easier to access and reuse that content. Metadata come in many different forms, including key words in a software help system and the document profile information attached to documents in a document management system. They're data that provide context to existing information to make it more valuable as part of a knowledge management system. It's most often used to connect information in relevant ways to people, processes, or products.

■ **Metaskills**—The basic tools of generative learning. These are aimed at ensuring three things: skills-adaptability, autonomous decision making, and an emotional aptitude for change.

■ **Milestone**—(1) A significant event during a project, usually completion of a major deliverable. (2) A clearly identifiable point in a project or set of activities that commonly denotes a reporting requirement or completion of a large or important set of activities. (3) A task with a duration of zero that's used to measure a project's progress or signify completion of a major deliverable.

■ **Milestone chart**—A scheduling technique that depicts the start and completion of tasks through the use of events (or milestones) on a time-scale chart.

■ **Milestone graph**—A graph that shows the goals or target to be achieved by depicting the projected schedule of a process. This graph's primary purpose is to help organize projects and coordinate activities.

■ **Mind map**—An unstructured cause-and-effect diagram. Also called a "mind-flow" or "brain web."

■ **Minor risk**—A risk that doesn't cause significant problems and represents a relatively small financial amount.

- **Mission statement**—This defines the type of business an organization is in. Some organizations call it a "purpose statement" or the "central reason why we're in business."

- **Mitigation**—In project risk management, taking steps to lessen risk by lowering the probability of a risk event's occurrence or reducing its effect should it occur. Mitigation deals with a risk by developing strategies and actions for reducing or eliminating its impact, probability, or both to an acceptable level. It might also involve shifting the time frame when action must be taken.

- **Mitigation plan**—An action plan for mitigating risks. It documents strategies, actions, goals, schedule dates, tracking requirements, and all other supporting information needed to carry out the mitigation strategy.

- **Monitoring**—Capturing, analyzing, and reporting project performance, usually as compared to planned performance.

- **Most likely time**—In program evaluation and review technique (PERT), a term used for the modal value of the distribution of the value that's most likely to occur more often than any other.

- **Monte Carlo analysis**—A type of simulation in which a distribution of probable results is defined for each activity and is used to calculate a distribution of probable results for the total project.

- **Net assets**—Total assets less total liabilities.

- **Net cash flow**—Cash available for distribution after taxes and after the effects of financing. Calculated as net income, plus depreciation, less expenditures required for working capital, capital items, and debt repayment.

- **Net profits to fixed assets**—A financial measurement of how effectively an organization is investing its fixed assets. It's calculated by dividing net fixed assets into net sales.

- **Net sales to working capital**—A financial measurement that measures the demands placed on working capital to support sales. It's calculated by dividing working capital into net sales.

- **No-layoff policy**—A document stating that no individual will be laid off because of improvements made as a result of an improvement process activity or because his or her suggestions successfully reduced his or her work effort. Under this policy individuals, whose jobs are eliminated, are retrained for an equivalent or more responsible job.

- **Nominal group technique**—A technique useful for situations where individual judgments must be tapped and combined to arrive at decisions.

- **Objectives**—Something toward which efforts are directed; an aim or end action.

- **Ontologies (computer-based)**—Formal, structured representations of a domain of knowledge. They're commonly associated with artificial intelligence technology, where they served as the raw material for computer reasoning and computer-based agents. An ontology is a set of definitions of content-specific knowledge representation primitives, e.g., classes, relations, functions, and object constants.

- **Opportunities**—The things that an organization could take advantage of to make it stronger and improve its performance.
- **Opportunity cost**—The cost of choosing one alternative over another.
- **Order of magnitude estimate (-25 percent, +75 percent)**—An approximate estimate made without detailed data, usually produced from a cost-capacity curve, scale-up or scale-down factors that are appropriately escalated, and approximate cost capacity ratios. This estimate is used during the formative stages of an expenditure program for initial project evaluation.
- **Organizational change management (OCM)**—A methodology that analyzes an organization's environment, defines the risks related to change, and defines how to overcome these risks. It's designed to lessen the stress and resistance of employees and management to individual critical changes. OCM manages the process of change.
- **Organizational vision statement**—A statement developed to describe how the organization wants to position itself ten to fifteen years in the future. It should be a short statement, no more than three sentences, prepared by the executive team.
- **Outsourcing**—The delegation of an organization's nonessential internal operations to an external organization that specializes in managing and operating these activities. The decision to outsource is often made in the interests of lowering an organization's cost, redirecting or converting energy directed at the competencies of a particular business, or to ensure more effective use of its worldwide labor, capital, technology, and resources. Outsourcing allows an organization to focus on its core competencies, although it's still responsible for the outsourced output. It's a form of subcontracting.
- **Payback period**—Defined as the period required to recover the cost of an investment.
- **Percent complete (PC)**—An estimate, expressed as a percent, of the amount of work that's been completed on an activity or group of activities, typically based on resource use. It's used in calculating earned value.
- **Performance evaluation**—A periodic review of an individual's accomplishments as it relates to his or her assigned tasks. It's frequently called an "appraisal."
- **Performance goals**—These are key elements that specifically state the targets for improvement and the time interval in which the improvements will be accomplished. Usually they're short-range in nature, one to five years.
- **Performance plans**—These provide a more detailed description of the contribution that an individual is expected to make to complete the tasks that the department has agreed to accomplish during the coming years. It serves as the basis for the individual's performance evaluation.
- **Performance reviews**—Meetings held to assess project progress.
- **Performance risk**—The degree of uncertainty in the development and deployment process that might keep a system from meeting its technical specifications or that might result in the system being unsuitable for its intended use.

- **Performance standard**—A standard that defines the expected level of efficiency and effectiveness that the average trained person should be operating at when performing a specific assignment.
- **Persistence**—The ability to pursue an objective until it's accomplished.
- **Personalization**—Retrieving and structuring knowledge to best meet the preferences and skill sets of the knowledge-seeker.
- **Phase gates**—See tollgates.
- **Plan**—A proposed or intended method of getting from one set of circumstances to another. A plan is often used to move from the present situation toward the achievement of one or more objectives or goals.
- **Poor quality cost**—A modification of the quality cost methodology to include the effect upon the external customer. It includes two major categories: direct poor quality costs that consist of prevention costs, appraisal costs, internal error cost, and external error cost; and indirect poor quality costs that include customer-incurred cost, customer dissatisfaction cost, loss of reputation cost, and lost opportunity cost.
- **Predict**—To state, tell about, or make known in advance; foretell.
- **Present value**—Translates future flows of money to the current value to evaluate a project against today's currency value rather than a future value. The present value of a future payment or stream of payments discounted at a risk-adjustment rate of return. Consider a project for possible selection if the sum of its net present values of all estimated cash flows is positive. Also known as "discounted cash flow."
- **Process**—A series of interconnected activities that takes input, adds value to it, and produces output. It's how organizations perform their day-to-day routines. An organization's processes define how it operates.
- **Process adaptability**—The flexibility of a process to handle future, changing customer expectations and today's individual, special customer requests. It's managing the process to meet today's special needs and future requirements. Adaptability is an area largely ignored but critical for gaining a competitive edge in the marketplace.
- **Process-based knowledge mapping (PKM)**—A diagram that visually displays knowledge within the context of a business process. It shows how knowledge should be used within the process and the sources of knowledge.
- **Process benchmarking**—A systematic way to identify superior processes and practices that are adapted for a process to reduce cost, decrease cycle time, cut inventory, and provide greater satisfaction for internal and external customers.
- **Process capability studies**—A statistical comparison of a measurement pattern or distribution against specification limits to determine if a process can consistently deliver products within those limits.
- **Process decision program chart**—A method that maps out the events and contingencies that might occur when moving from an identified problem to one or more possible solutions.

- **Process effectiveness**—The extent to which outputs of a process or subprocess meet the needs and expectations of its customers. Similar to quality but more inclusive. Effectiveness is having the right output at the right place, at the right time, and at the right price.

- **Process efficiency**—The extent to which resources are minimized and waste is eliminated in the pursuit of effectiveness. Productivity is a measure of efficiency.

- **Process owner (PO)**—A project team member who serves as primary point of contact to the business, develops service-level agreements (SLA), and ensures that authorizations, funding, and engagement personnel are in place. The project manager coordinates with the PO when providing status to the project sponsor.

- **Profiling**—The creation of chronicles that track a user's interest levels and areas of expertise. In an automated approach, profiles are created by monitoring each user's work submitted, work reviewed, and query habits. Profiling is used to feed agent technology, user-sensitivity systems, and document management systems.

- **Program**—A group of projects managed in a coordinated way to obtain benefits not available from managing them individually. Many programs also include elements of ongoing operations.

- **Program evaluation and review technique (PERT)**—An event-oriented and probability-based network analysis technique used to estimate project duration when a high degree of uncertainty exists with the individual activity duration estimates. PERT applies the critical-path method to a weighted average duration estimate.

- **Project**—A temporary endeavor undertaken to create a unique product or service.

- **Project audit**—A review of a project to provide an objective appraisal and identify potential problems or positive practices for use on other projects.

- **Project charter**—A document that formally recognizes a project's existence by senior management and provides a project manager with the authority to apply organizational resources to project activities.

- **Project closeout**—A process that involves completing various project records, making the final revisions on documentation to reflect the as-built condition, and issuing and retaining essential project documentation. The project sponsor also accepts the project during closeout.

- **Project control**—Systems and methods that assist a project manager and team in managing a project.

- **Project cost management**—A subset of project management that includes the processes required to ensure a project is completed within the approved budget. It consists of resource planning, cost estimating, cost budgeting, and cost control.

- **Project human resource management**—A subset of project management that includes the processes required to effectively use the people involved with a project. It consists of organizational planning, staff acquisition, and team development.

- **Project life cycle**—A collection of generally sequential project phases whose names and numbers are determined by the control needs of the organization(s) involved in the project. It defines the project's beginning and end. Each phase is marked by the completion of a deliverable.
- **Project management**—The application of knowledge, skills, tools, and techniques to project activities to meet or exceed stakeholders' needs and expectations from a project.
- **Project Management Body of Knowledge (PMBOK)**—An inclusive term that describes the sum of knowledge within the profession of project management. As with other professions, the body of knowledge rests with the practitioners and academics who apply and advance it. PMBOK includes proven, traditional practices that are widely applied as well as innovative and advanced ones that have been used on a limited basis.
- **Project management information system**—Provides information on projects to support decision making. It involves tools and techniques to gather, integrate, and distribute information from other project management processes. It can be automated or manual.
- **Project management processes**—Processes concerned with describing and organizing the work of a project.
- **Project manager**—The individual responsible for managing the overall project and its deliverables. Acts as the customer's single point of contact for services delivered within the project's scope. Controls scope planning, resources, and executing of activities to meet established cost, time, and quality goals.
- **Project network diagram**—Any schematic display of the logical relationships of project activities. It's always drawn from left to right to reflect project chronology.
- **Project plan**—A formal, approved document used to guide both project execution and control. The plan's primary uses are to document planning assumptions and decisions; facilitate communication among stakeholders; and document approved scope, cost, and schedule baselines. A project plan can be a summary or detailed report.
- **Project portfolio**—A centralized grouping of two or more projects that are being conducted within an organization.
- **Project procurement management**—A subset of project management that includes the processes required to acquire goods and services from outside the performing organization. It consists of procurement planning, solicitation planning, solicitation, source selection, contract administration, and contract closeout.
- **Project quality management**—A subset of project management that includes the processes required to ensure the project will satisfy the needs for which it was undertaken. It consists of quality planning, assurance, and control. It includes all the activities of the overall management function that determine the quality policy, objectives, and responsibilities, and implements them through quality planning, control, assurance, and improvement within the quality system.
- **Project review**—The periodic monitoring of project activities and tasks; a tool used to monitor and control projects. It can be either periodic or topical.

- **Project risk**—The cumulative effect of the chances of uncertain occurrences that will adversely affect project objectives. It's the degree of exposure to negative events and their probable consequences. Project risk is characterized by three factors: risk event, risk probability, and the amount at stake.
- **Project risk management**—A subset of project management that includes the processes concerned with identifying, analyzing, and responding to project risk. It consists of risk identification, quantification, response development, and response control.
- **Project schedule**—The planned dates for performing activities and meeting milestones.
- **Project scope management**—A subset of project management consisting of processes to ensure a project includes all the work required, and only the work required, for successful completion. It consists of initiation, scope planning, definition, verification, and change control.
- **Project selection method**—A process that places weighted scores against project deliverables so the project selected is aligned with an organization's strategic plans.
- **Project sponsor**—An individual whose support and approval is required for a project to continue. He or she initiates project requests, approves business deliverables, and provides active sponsorship.
- **Project stakeholder**—Individuals and organizations that are actively involved in a project or whose interests might be positively or negatively affected as a result of project execution or successful project completion.
- **Project team**—The group of people who share responsibility for accomplishing project goals and who report either part-time or full-time to the project manager.
- **Project time management**—A subset of project management that includes the processes required to ensure a project's timely completion. It consists of activity definition, sequencing, duration estimating, and schedule development and control.
- **Proposal**—A plan of action submitted by sellers in response to a solicitation or as a result of a need perceived by the seller.
- **Pulse takers**—People who build relationships that keep them informed about what's going on in an organization.
- **Qualification**—A designed experiment that involves evaluating a complex process consisting of many individual certified activities to determine whether the process can perform at an appropriate level when the activities are linked together. To be qualified, the process must demonstrate it can repeatedly deliver products and/or services on time, at the appropriate cost, and meet customer expectations on an ongoing basis.
- **Quality control circles**—Teams made up mostly of volunteers, who hold short meetings over a definite period of time and work on either departmental or organizational problems that they select. As Kaoru Ishikawa, the founder of the quality circle, stated, "Quality control circles are to motivate employees, not to reduce costs."
- **Quality costs**—A system of converting quality measurements into dollars so they can be summarized in a manner that's easily understood by management. It consists of

four parts: prevention, appraisal, internal failure, and external failure. This concept was originated by Armand V. Feigenbaum during the 1950s when he was working with General Electric.

- **Quality function deployment**—A structured process for taking the "voice of the customer," translating it into measurable customer requirements, translating the customer requirements into measurable counterpart characteristics, and deploying those requirements into every level of the product and manufacturing process design and all customer service processes.
- **Quality management plan**—A plan that describes how a project management team will implement its quality policy. It provides input to the overall project plan and must address the project's quality control, assurance, and improvement.
- **Rapid application development (RAD)**—A term used to describe parallel efforts associated with developing information systems. The coding process takes project requirements and translates them into specific language constructs. The step prior to coding is usually completing a detailed design document, where requirements are broken down into modules of impacted code.
- **Ranking**—The process of establishing the order or priority.
- **Rate of return (ROR)**—An amount of income (or loss) and/or change in value realized or anticipated on an investment expressed as a percentage of that investment.
- **Request for proposal (RFP)**—A formal document used to request a proposal from a seller, usually for complex or nonstandard items of higher monetary value.
- **Request for quotations (RFQ)**—A formal document used to request a proposal from a seller for low monetary purchases, usually for commodity items.
- **Residual risks**—Risks that remain after a response action has been taken. Also includes minor risks that have been accepted and addressed by, for example, adding contingency amounts to the cost or time allowed.
- **Resource leveling**—Any form of network analysis in which scheduling decisions (e.g., start and finish dates) are driven by resource management concerns (e.g., limited resource availability or difficult-to-mange changes in resource levels). It offers approaches for evening out the peaks and valleys of resource requirements so that a fixed amount of resources can be used over time.
- **Resource planning**—Determining the physical resources and quantities of each required to perform project activities.
- **Resources**—A source of supply or support and available means.
- **Responsibility assignment matrix (RAM)**—A structure that relates the project organization structure to the work breakdown structure to help ensure that each element of the project's work scope is assigned to a responsible individual. Assigns roles and responsibilities for specific activities to particular individuals.
- **Return-on-capital**—A financial measurement that's calculated by dividing capital employed into the return rate.

- **Return-on-capital employment (ROCE)**—A financial term that measures the earnings of a significant return on investment in assets to ensure perpetuation of the investment, profit, or investment cycle. A ratio that indicates the efficiency and profitability of a company's capital investments. ROCE should always be higher than the rate at which the company borrows; otherwise, any increase in borrowing will reduce shareholders' earnings. It's calculated by measuring capital employed into net profits before taxes.

- **Return on equity (ROE)**—A measure of how well a company used reinvested earnings to generate additional earnings equal to a fiscal year's after-tax income divided by book value and expressed as a percentage.

- **Return on investment (ROI)**—The rate of return at which the sum of the discounted future cash flows for the five pro-forma years plus the discounted residual value equals the initial cash outlay. It's a comparison of the money earned (or lost) on an investment to the amount of money invested.

- **Return on sales**—A financial measurement of the profit per item sold. It's the best measure of overall organizational effectiveness. It's calculated by dividing net sales into profit before taxes.

- **Risk**—A concept that denotes a potential negative effect to an asset or some characteristic of value that may arise from a present process or future event. It's synonymous with the probability of a loss or a threat.

- **Risk assessment**—The act of performing a qualitative analysis of risks and conditions to prioritize their effects on project objectives. The analysis of the probability of a negative event occurring, including the effect that event would have.

- **Risk baseline**—A snapshot of all currently-known risks to a project, used to begin the process of implementing continuous risk management of a project.

- **Risk categories**—Sources of possible risk that could affect the project for better or worse, typically organized in terms of technical, quality, or performance risks; project-management risks; organization risks; and external risks.

- **Risk event**—A discrete occurrence that might affect a project for better or worse.

- **Risk identification**—The act of determining which risk events might affect a project and documenting their characteristics.

- **Risk management plan**—A plan that documents the procedures to be used to manage risk throughout a project. It covers who's responsible for managing various areas of risk, how the initial identification and quantification outputs will be maintained, how contingency plans will be implemented, and how reserves will be allocated. It's a subsidiary element of the project plan.

- **Risk metric**—A standard way of measuring an attribute of the risk management process.

- **Risk monitoring and control**—The process of monitoring risks, identifying residual risks, executing risk reduction plans, and evaluating their effectiveness in a project life cycle.

- **Risk probability**—The act of determining how likely a risk event is to occur.

- **Risk response planning**—The act of developing procedures and techniques to enhance opportunities and reduce risks to a project's objectives.
- **Risk symptom**—A trigger or indirect manifestation of a risk event.
- **Risk threshold**—The level of risk acceptable to an organization.
- **Root-cause analysis**—The process of identifying the various causes affecting a particular problem, process, or issue and determining the real reasons that caused the condition.
- **Run charts**—A graphic display of data used to assess the stability of a process over time or over a sequence of events (such as the number of batches produced). The run chart is the simplest form of control chart.
- **Scatter diagrams**—A graphic tool used to study the relationship between two variables. It's used to test for possible cause-and-effect relationships. It doesn't prove that one variable causes the other, but it does show whether a relationship exists and, if so, reveals the character of that relationship.
- **Schedule baseline**—The approved project schedule to provide the basis for measuring and reporting schedule performance.
- **Schedule change control system**—A process that defines the procedures by which a schedule can be changed. It includes the paperwork, tracking systems, and approval levels necessary for authorizing changes.
- **Schedule management plan**—A plan that defines how changes to a schedule will be managed. It's a subsidiary element of the project plan.
- **Schedule performance index (SPI)**—The ratio of work performed to work scheduled (BCWP/BCWS). SPI < 1 indicates a project is behind schedule.
- **Schedule variance (SV)**—(1) Any difference between the scheduled completion of an activity and its actual completion. (2) In earned value analysis, it's the BCWP less BCWS. SV < 0 indicates that a project is behind schedule.
- **Scope change**—Any modification to the agreed-upon scope as defined by the work breakdown schedule.
- **Scope change control**—Controlling changes to project scope; influencing the factors that create scope changes to ensure that changes are beneficial; determining that a scope change has occurred; and managing the actual changes when and if they occur.
- **Scope creep**—Occurs when a project's scope increases gradually so that the project management team or customer doesn't notice it. This occurs because the customer adds additional requirements, but when several minor changes are added together, they can collectively result in a significant change in cost and budget over-runs.
- **Scope definition**—Subdividing the major project deliverables as identified in the scope statement into smaller, more manageable components.
- **Scope management plan**—A document that describes how project scope will be managed and how scope changes will be integrated into the project. It should also include a clear description of how scope changes will be identified and classified.

- **Secondary risks**—Risks that arise as a direct result of implementing a risk response.
- **Semantic networks**—A technique for representing knowledge. As with other networks, these consist of nodes with links between them. The nodes in a semantic network represent concepts.
- **Shareholder value**—Business enterprise value less the debt retained in the business and assumed by the new owners.
- **Shewhart cycle**—A structured approach for improving services, products, and/or processes, developed by Walter Shewhart. Also known as the "plan-do-check-act cycle."
- **Simulation modeling**—A computer program that generates imitations of an actual product or process. It generally simulates something representing key characteristics or behaviors of a selected physical or abstract system. Simulation modeling includes modeling of natural or human systems to gain insight into their functions. It's often used in process redesign or reengineering to predict how future-state solutions will perform over a long period of time.
- **Situation analysis**—A general assessment of a company's past, present, and future. A situation analysis oftentimes provides a benchmark to the business's future growth potential.
- **Six Sigma program**—A methodology designed to reduce error rates to a maximum of 3.44 errors per million units, developed by Motorola during the late 1980s.
- **Smart networks**—A combination of hard and soft networks that results in effective linking of smart business strategies to every employee throughout the company. Smart organizations are entirely process- and team-based, and use knowledge as their primary asset. Also know as "intelligent networks."
- **Smoothing**—A conflict-resolution approach that de-emphasizes or avoids areas of differences and emphasizes areas of agreement.
- **Soft knowledge**—See tacit knowledge.
- **Sponsor**—Individual or group in the performing organization that provides the financial resources, in cash or kind, for the project or a program.
- **Stages**—A set of prescribed and concurrent activities that should incorporate best practices. Also known as "phases."
- **Stage gates**—See tollgates.
- **Stakeholder**—Any individual or group that's interested or affected by an organization's operation. It includes, but isn't limited to, management, investors, customers, suppliers, employees, employee's family, the community, and special interest groups.
- **Start-to-finish relationship**—This relationship restricts the finish of work activity until some duration following the start of another work activity.
- **Start-to-start relationship**—This relationship restricts the start of work activity until some specified duration following the start of the preceding work activity.
- **Statement of requirements (SOR)**—Variation on the statement of work used for a procurement item that's presented as a problem to solve.

- **Statement of risk**—A description of the risk typically defined in terms of condition-consequence format to show the conditions causing concern for a potential loss to the project, followed by a description of these conditions' potential consequences.
- **Statement of work (SOW)**—A narrative description of products or services to be supplied under contract.
- **Statistical process control (SPC)**—A mathematical approach to understanding and managing activities, using data for controlling processes, or making outputs of products or services predictable. It includes three statistical quality tools: design of experiments, control charts, and process characterization.
- **Status reviews**—A meeting held to determine where a project stands compared to its schedule.
- **Strategic knowledge management**—This links the building of a company's knowledge to a business strategy using a quality function deployment (QFD) approach. These links are created through knowledge maps.
- **Strategic planning**—A multiyear plan that identifies an organization's strategic direction and action steps. A good strategic plan is divided into three major parts: setting direction, establishing expectations, and defining actions. Setting direction includes the mission statement, value statement, organization's vision statements, strategic focus, risks analysis, and critical success factors. Establishing expectations includes objectives and goals. Defining action includes strategies, tactics, budgets, and performance plans for the individual.
- **Strategic focus**—This identifies four or five areas of focus characterized by the following:
  - ☐ Technology or function that the organization has that defines its specific areas of excellence
  - ☐ Activities that are most valuable to the customer
  - ☐ Areas that the organization is especially good at
  - ☐ Areas that will distinguish the organization from its competition
- **Strategies**—Objectives that define the approach that will be used to meet performance goals.
- **Strengths**—The things that an organization is good at and/or sets the organization apart from other organizations.
- **Strength-weakness-opportunity-threat analysis (SWOT)**—A risk-identification tool and technique used to examine a project in terms of its strengths, weaknesses, opportunities, and threats to increase the breadth of risks examined and considered.
- **Structural capital**—The speed at which an organization can convert customer and intellectual capital into a product or service. The shorter the cycle time, the greater the value of structural capital.
- **Succession planning**—Identifying individuals and preparing them to take on more responsible assignments when the person presently doing the assignment moves to another assignment.

- **Suggestion system**—A system that asks employees to document their ideas and hand them into their managers, who assign them to someone for investigation and implementation if acceptable. Usually the employee(s) who turned in the idea shares the money the organization gets from implementing the idea. The suggestion approach was started by National Cash Register in 1896.

- **Suggestive software**—Capable of deducing a user's knowledge needs and suggesting knowledge associations the user can't make.

- **Supplier qualification**—Evaluating a supplier to determine if it has an adequate management system to ensure there's a high probability that it will provide an output that meets requirements.

- **Supplier rating**—A method of evaluating a supplier's performance level based on the combination of quality, cost, and delivery. Each of the three items is weighted based upon its importance to the receiving organization.

- **Supply chain**—Aligning the capabilities of suppliers, manufacturers, channel partners, and customers to control the physical flow of products from source to the point of use. It provides customers with improved service and decreased cost by blending activities of all participants to increase productivity and reduce costs for all involved.

- **System**—Groups of related processes that might or might not be connected.

- **Tacit (soft) knowledge**—Knowledge that's formed around intangible factors embedded in an individual's experience. It often takes the form of beliefs, values, principles, and morals. It guides an individual's actions. It's embedded in the individual's ideas, insights, values, and judgment. It's only accessible through the direct corroboration and communication with the individual who has the knowledge.

- **Tactics**—The art or skill of employing available means to accomplish an end. Tactics are actions that are scheduled to be taken to implement strategies.

- **Tangible assets**—Assets that have physical existence such as cash, real estate, and machinery.

- **Tasks**—Steps that are required to perform a specific activity; a well-defined piece of project work that appears at the lowest level of a project's work breakdown structure. Each task accomplishes a discrete work item. An activity that's composed of input and output, has an owner, and is performed within a specified duration.

- **Task forces**—Teams used when a major improvement opportunity that must be reacted to immediately is identified by management.

- **Task teams**—Teams used when management identifies an improvement opportunity and assigns employees to solve it.

- **Team**—Individuals working together on common goals. Effective teams are an integral part of meeting common goals and sustaining results. Industry has seen increasing efforts through training and cross-training to help people to work together more effectively and accomplish shared goals.

- **Team charter**—Serves as a mission statement for the project team and describes the roles and responsibilities of team members. It also describes the team's operational ground rules.
- **Teamwork**—A condition where people work to complement each other, not to compete with each other. A culture of teamwork usually starts with building teams that eventually become less important than the relationships that are developed within the team.
- **Technology**—A broad term dealing with the use of knowledge or experience. It usually takes the form of software; a proven way to do something or a product.
- **Threats**—Things that could happen which would have a negative effect on an organization and/or its strategic plan; a potentially negative outcome as a result of risk.
- **Time frame**—The period when action is required to mitigate a risk; an attribute of a risk.
- **Tollgate**—A template, or road map, for driving projects from idea to launch or install and beyond; a decision point that allows for sponsor review. Also called "phase gates" or "stage gates."
- **Top-down estimate**—An approach to cost estimating that starts at the top level of the work breakdown schedule and then works down to successively lower levels.
- **Total float (TF)**—The amount of time in work units that an activity might be delayed from its early start without delaying the project finish date. Total float is equal to an activity's late start minus its early start.
- **Touch points**—The priority areas for the application of knowledge management; typically interactions with customers, suppliers, and employees. Each touch point represents an area of potential process or quality improvement and competitive advantage. Touch points represent areas where human interaction is often most intense.
- **Training**—The process by which an individual acquires the ability to do something that's job related and which he or she was unable to do before. It can be formal or informal, structured or unstructured, self-directed or facilitated.
- **Tree diagram**—A systematic approach that helps the user to think about each phase or aspect of solving a problem, reaching a target, or achieving a goal.
- **Trigger**—Thresholds for indicators that specify when an action, such as implementing a contingency plan, might need to be taken. Triggers generally are used to provide warning of an impending critical event, indicate the need to implement a contingency plan to preempt a problem, and request immediate attention for a risk.
- **Trust**—The willing acceptance of someone's power when it affects another person.
- **Unacceptable risk**—Exposure to risks that can jeopardize an organization's strategy and/or present dangers to human lives and/or represent a significant financial exposure.
- **Unknown risk**—Risks that aren't yet identified or are impossible to predict.
- **Urgency**—A feeling that something must be done in the immediate future.
- **Value-added analysis**—A procedure for analyzing every activity within a process, classifying it as value-adding or nonvalue-adding, and then taking positive action to eliminate, or at least minimize, the nonvalue-adding activities or tasks.

- **Value analysis**—Identifying the required functions for a product, establishing values for the required functions, and suggesting an approach to provide the required functions at the lowest overall cost without performance loss to optimize cost performance.

- **Value statements**—A set of statements that provide the operating and management rules that serve as the foundation for an organization's morale and cultural operations. It's like a bill of rights for employees. These statements are also called "operating principles," "guiding principles," "basic beliefs" and "operating rules."

- **Variance analysis**—Comparing actual project results to planned or expected results.

- **Variables management style**—A theory where management should vary its interface to each employee based upon his or her particular attributes and the assignment he or she is given. It divides employees into four attributes groups: planners, networkers, doers, and leaders.

- **Virtual team**—A project team that's not located in the same physical location but works across organizational boundaries, relying primarily on technology for communications. Team members can be distributed across buildings, states, and countries.

- **WBS**—See work breakdown structure.

- **Weaknesses**—The things that other organizations do better; the things that an organization isn't prepared to handle.

- **Workaround**—A response to a negative risk event. Distinguished from a contingency plan in that a workaround isn't planned in advance of the risk event's occurrence.

- **Work breakdown structure (WBS)**—A deliverable-oriented grouping of project elements that organizes and defines a project's total scope. Each descending level represents an increasingly detailed definition of a project component, which might be a product or service.

- **Workflow**—One of the tools used for creating process assets. A proactive toolset for analyzing, compressing, and automating business activities.

- **Working capital**—The excess of current assets over current liabilities.

- **World class**—The ability to favorably compete with the best products and services provided any place in the world.

- **Wrappers**—Scripts and connection modules that allow personal computers and modern networks to access legacy data. Knowledge query and manipulation language (KQML), tool command language, and traditional knowledge are often used to write these wrappers.

Note: Some of these definitions are excerpts from an extensive list of project management terms and definitions created by Ginger Levin.

APPENDIX B

NONMANUFACTURING MEASUREMENTS

Nonmanufacturing measurements, which are sometimes difficult to establish, might include the following:

Accounting
- Percent of late reports
- Computer input incorrect
- Errors in specific reports as audited
- Percentage of significant errors in reports; total number of reports
- Percentage of late reports; total number of reports. Average reduction in time spans associated with important reports
- Pinpointing high-cost manufacturing elements for correction
- Pinpointing jobs yielding low or no profit for correction
- Providing various departments with the specific cost tools they need to manage their operations for lowest cost

Administrative
- Success in maximizing discount opportunities through consolidated ordering
- Success in eliminating security violations
- Success in affecting pricing actions so as to preclude subsequent upward revisions
- Success in estimating inventory requirements
- Success in responses to customer inquiries to maximize customer satisfaction

Clerical
- Accurate typing, spelling, hyphenation
- Decimal points correctly placed
- Correct calculations in bills, purchase orders, journal entries, payrolls, and bills of lading
- Time spent in locating filed material
- Percentage of correct punches
- Paper used during a given period versus actual output in finished pages

Data Processing

- Keypunch cards thrown out for error
- Computer downtime due to error
- Rerun time
- Promptness in output delivery
- Effectiveness of scheduling
- Depth of programmers' investigations
- Program debugging time
- Keypunch efficiency

Engineering: Design

- Adequacy of systems specifications
- Accuracy of system block diagrams
- Thoroughness of system concepts
- Simulation results compared to original design or prediction
- Success in creating engineering designs that don't require change to make them perform as intended
- Success in developing engineering cost estimates versus actual accruals
- Success in meeting self-imposed schedules
- Success in reducing drafting errors
- Success in maximizing capture rates on request for proposals for which the company was a contender
- Success in meeting engineering test objectives
- Number of error-free designs
- Correct readings of gauges and test devices
- Accurate specifications and standards
- Proper reporting and control of time schedules
- Reduction of engineering design changes
- Changes in tests or in illustrations of reports
- Rework resulting from errors in computer program input
- Advance material list accuracy
- Design compliance to specifications
- Customer acceptance of proposals
- Meeting schedules
- Thoroughness of systems concepts
- Accuracy and thoroughness of reports
- Adequacy of design reviews
- Compliance to specifications
- Adequacy of design reviews

- Accuracy of computations
- Accuracy of drawings
- Reduction in number of engineering change notices to correct errors

Engineering: Manufacturing
- Accuracy of manufacturing processes
- Timely delivery of manufacturing processes to the shop
- Accuracy of time-study data
- Accuracy of time estimates
- Timely response to bid requests
- Asset utilization
- Accuracy and thoroughness of test processes
- Adequacy and promptness of program facilitation
- Application of work simplification criteria
- Minimum tool and fixture authorization
- Labor utilization index
- Methods improvement (in hours or dollars)
- Contract cost
- Lost business due to price
- Process change notices due to error
- Tool rework to correct design
- Methods improvement

Engineering: Plant
- Effectiveness of preventive maintenance program
- Accuracy of estimates (dollars and details)
- Accuracy of layouts
- Cost of building services
- Completeness of plant engineering drawings
- Adequacy of scheduling
- Fixed versus variable portions of overhead
- Maintenance cost versus floor space and manpower
- Lost time due to equipment failures
- Janitorial service
- Success in meeting or beating budgets
- Instrument calibration error
- Fire equipment found defective
- Lost time due to equipment failures
- Purchase requisition errors

- Schedule compliance
- Timely response to bid requests
- Adherence to contract specifications
- Effectiveness of customer liaison
- Effectiveness of cost negotiations
- Status "ship not bill"
- Change orders due to errors
- Drafting errors found by checkers
- Late releases
- Time lost due to equipment failure
- Callbacks on repairs

Finance

- Billing errors (check accounts receivable overdues)
- Accounts payable deductions missed
- Vouchers prepared with no defects
- Clock card or payroll transcription errors
- Keypunch errors
- Computer downtime
- Timeliness of financial reports
- Effectiveness of scheduling program "debugging" time
- Rerun time
- Accuracy of predicted budgets
- Clerical errors on entries
- Inventory objectives met
- Payroll errors
- Discount missed
- Amounts payable records
- Billing error

Forecasting

- Can departments function with maximum effectiveness with budgets set for them?
- Can the company buy needed capital equipment, keep inventories supplied, pay its bills?
- Do projects meet time schedules?
- Assistance to line organizations (e.g., scheduling, planning, and control functions)
- Methods for finance and cost control
- Timeliness of financial reports
- Assets control

- Minimizing capital expenditures
- Realistic budgets
- Clear and concise operating policies
- Timely submission of realistic cost proposals
- Completeness of financial reports
- Effectiveness of disposition of government property
- Effectiveness of cost negotiations

Legal

- Amount of paper used versus finished pages produced
- Misdelivered mail
- Misfiled documents
- Delays in execution of documents
- Teletype errors
- Patent claims omitted
- Response time on request for legal opinion

Management

- Management can be gauged by the output of staff elements, overall defects rates, budgets and schedule controls, and other factors that reflect on managerial effectiveness. In other words, managers' accomplishments are the sum totals of those working under them.
- Success in developing estimates of costs versus actual accruals
- Success in meeting schedules
- Performance record of employees under manager's supervision
- Success in developing realistic estimates on a program evaluation and review technique (PERT) or PERT/cost chart
- Success in minimizing use of overtime operations
- All nonproduction departments can be measured.
- Each department should be measured against itself, using time comparisons, preferably by itself.
- The best primary goals are those that measure cost, delivery, and quality performances of the department. Secondary goals can be derived from these primary goals.
- There should be a base against which quality, cost, or delivery performance can be measured as a percentage improvement. Examples of such a base would be direct labor, sales dollars, material dollars, or budget dollars. A dollar base is more meaningful to management than a physical quantity of output.
- Success in affecting pricing actions to preclude subsequent revisions
- Pages of data compiled with no defects

- Clarity and conciseness of operating procedures
- Evaluations of capital investment
- Errors in applying standards on process sheets
- Accuracy of estimates; actual costs versus estimated costs
- Effectiveness of work measurement programs

Marketing

- Success in reducing defects through suggestion submittal
- Success in capturing new business versus quotations
- Responsiveness to customer inquiries
- Accuracy of marketing forecasts
- Response from news releases and advertisements
- Effectiveness of cost and price negotiations
- Success in response to customer inquiries (i.e., customer identification)
- Customer liaison
- Effectiveness of market intelligence
- Attainment of new order targets
- Operation within budgets
- Effectiveness of proposals
- Exercise of selectivity
- Control of cost of sales
- Meeting proposal submittal dates
- Timely preparation of priced spare-parts lists
- Aggressiveness
- Effectiveness of G-2
- Utilization of field marketing services
- Dissemination of customer information
- Bookings budget met
- Accuracy of predictions, planning, and selections
- Accurate and well-managed contracts
- Exploitation of business potential
- Effectiveness of proposals
- Control of printing costs
- Application of standard proposal material
- Standardization of proposals
- Reduction of reproduction expense
- Contract errors
- Order description error
- Sales order errors

Material

- Savings made
- Late deliveries
- Purchase order (PO) errors
- Material received against no PO
- Status of unplaced requisitions
- Orders open to government agency for approval
- Delays in processing material received
- Damage or loss items received
- Claims for product damages after shipment from plant
- Delays in outbound shipments
- Complaints or improper packing in shipments
- Errors in travel arrangements
- Accuracy of route and rate information on shipments
- Success in meeting schedules; material shortages in production
- Success in estimating inventory requirements
- Clock card errors by employees
- Damaged shipments
- Stock shelf life exceeded
- Items in surplus
- Purchase requisition errors
- Effectiveness of material order follow-up
- Adequacy and effectiveness of planning and scheduling
- Application of residual inventories to current needs
- Inventory turnover
- Manufacturing jobs without schedules
- Timeliness of incorporating ECNs
- Timely replacement of rejected parts
- Adequacy of reject control plan
- Effectives of packing operation
- Application of residual inventories to current needs
- Floor shortages
- Labor utilization index
- Data processing rerun time on material programs
- Bad requisitions
- Value of termination stores and residual inventory
- Manpower fluctuations around mean
- Percent supplier material (in dollars) rejected and returned; total materials (in dollars) purchased

- Number of defective vendors (repetitive); total number of vendors
- Number of single-source vendors; total number of vendors
- Percent of supplier material (in dollars) holding up production; total material (in dollars)
- Number of late lots received (actually holding up production); total lots received
- Percent of purchased material (actual); total material bid or budgeted
- Percent of reductions in bills of material affected through purchasing effort; total material bid or budgeted
- Correct quotations or rates
- Customers call back as promised
- Installation of exact equipment requested by customer
- Appointments kept at the time promised customers
- Prompt handling of complaints
- Accurate meter readings
- Courteous treatment of customers
- Right packages of goods ordered shipped
- Number of telephone numbers correctly dialed
- PMI rejects
- Savings made
- Material handling budget met
- Travel expense against open shop orders
- Orders to government for approval disapproved, resubmitted, and open but not approved

Personnel

- Success in eliminating security violations
- Hiring effectiveness
- Thoroughness and speed in responding to suggestions
- Employee participation in company-sponsored activities
- Administration of insurance programs
- Accident prevention record
- Processing insurance claims
- Provision of adequate food services
- Personnel security clearance errors
- External classified visit authorization errors
- Speedy processing of visitors through lobbies records accuracy
- Adequacy of training programs
- Thoroughness and speed of investigating suggestions grievances
- Employment requisitions filled
- Administration of insurance program
- Acceptance of organization's development recommendations

- Effectiveness of administration of merit increases
- Overhead budget performance

Product Assurance

- Participation in design reviews
- Customer liaison
- Technical society participation
- Accuracy of proposals and contracts
- Application of program policies
- Prevention of filed complaints
- Effectiveness of reporting and recording
- Customer rejects
- Rejected material on the floor
- Adequacy of vendor ratings
- Effectiveness of field quality control
- Rejects
- Screening efficiency
- Inspection documentation
- Quality assurance audits

Product Control

- Success in developing realistic schedules
- Success in developing realistic estimates
- Success in identifying defective specifications
- Process sheets written without errors
- Transportation hours without damage to product
- Parts shortages in production
- Downtime due to shortages

Production

- Success in reducing the scrap, rework, and "use-as-is" categories
- Success in maintaining perfect attendance records
- Success in identifying defective manufacturing specifications
- Success in meeting production schedules
- Success in cost reduction through suggestion submittal
- Success in improving first article acceptance
- Performance against standard
- Success in reducing required material review board action
- Utilities improperly left running at close of shift

- Application of higher learning curves
- Floor parts shortages
- Delays due to rework and material shortage
- Control of overtime (i.e., nonscheduled)
- Prevention of damage to work in process
- Cleanliness of assigned areas
- Conformance to estimates
- Suggestions submitted
- Labor utilization index
- Defects
- Asset utilization
- Scrap
- Utilization of correct materials, drawings, and procedures
- Prevention of damage
- Safety records
- Inches of weld with no defects
- Logbook entries with no defects
- Security violations
- Compliance to schedules
- Accuracy of estimates

Program Management

- Liaison with customer
- Financial
- Quality of proposals (e.g., technical approach, cost, time)
- Soundness of project plans
- Coordination of support activities
- Satisfactory field sell-off
- Backlog
- New business volume versus budgeted

Publications

- Compliance to specifications
- Errors corrected
- Thoroughness of coverage
- Usefulness of material
- Quality of production

Quality Control
- Inspection errors
- Sampling program errors
- Timeliness of inspection reports
- Adequacy of vendor quality ratings
- Returned goods and field rework due to inspection oversight; customer rejects
- Quality assurance audits
- Inspection documentation
- Customer liaison

Research and Development
- Can it be applied?
- Can it be developed?
- Can it be manufactured?
- Can it be marketed?

Security
- Personnel security clearance errors
- Timely and accurate processing
- External classified visit authorization errors
- Accurate processing of visitor identification
- Effectiveness of security program
- Guards, security checks, badges, passes
- Records accuracy
- Fire watch

Services: General
- Promptness in reply to requests
- Quality of service rendered
- Blueprint and drawing control, reproduction, and distribution
- Test equipment maintenance and calibration
- TRW communication
- Reproduction facilities

Purchasing
- Purchase order changed due to error
- Late receipt of materials
- Rejections due to incomplete description

Hotel Front Desk

- Guests taken to unmade rooms
- Reservations not honored

Supervision

Supervisors' performance is measured by the overall effectiveness of their department; in other words, they're judged by the sum total of accomplishments of people working for them. The worth of individual or group achievements should be evaluated against the following criteria:

- Effect of potential error (e.g., abort of mission or cost effect on schedules)
- Contributions of the individual or group to preventing error
- Difficulty of the job and level of skill required
- Work schedules and load impact on error potential
- Ability of individual to correct his or her own errors
- Attitude of the individual toward work, project, or command mission

APPENDIX C

ABC CO. KEY PERFORMANCE INDICATORS

Division or Department	Measurement	Defects by Percentage or Number				
		Aug.	Sept.	Oct.	Nov.	Dec.
International						
	Procedural writing (std.)	57%	54%	77%		
	Telex communications	57%	53%	64%		
	Order entry	13%	11%	34%		
	Invoicing	—	61%	95%		
Business systems and services						
Business systems development	Nonconformance per employee-phase worked in the month	—	—	1.2		
Business systems support	Failures in active production programs	—	—	—		
Operations	Data entry errors in:					
	■ Accounts payable input	—	—	128		
	■ General ledger input	—	—	12		
	Data center—late reports:					
	■ Finance	1.2%	4.8%	2.7%		
	■ Customer service	1.6%	7.4%	5.0%		
	■ Manufacturing	3.0%	4.8%	5.3%		
	System software errors	—	—	1		
Office methods and planning	Number of tasks for which the actual time varied from the estimate by more than the allowed percentage	—	—	5		
Office services	Word processing percentage of pages retyped	2.5%	3.2%	3.5%		
	Printing services percentage of impressions printed	1.0%	2.0%	2.5%		
	Mail and office supply error hours per hour worked	—	—	—		

Division or Department	Measurement	Defects by Percentage or Number				
		Aug.	Sept.	Oct.	Nov.	Dec.
Design engineering						
Project management	Percentage not on schedue	—	21%	14%		
	Percentage over budget	—	6%	5%		
	Percentage not meeting objectives	—	9%	5%		
Corrective ECOs	Marten	62	76	44		
	Cougar	46	17	8		
Corrective	Sweepers and scrubbers	23	41	44		
ECO processing	Within engineering	11%	31%	7%		
	Released to manufacturing	1%	0%	0%		
	Test nonconformance	—	—	—		
	Engineering work request and/ or test request on plan, correct prints, and/or information	—	—	—		
Finance						
	Profit-sharing cerificate errors	1.3%	1.4%	2%		
	Credit turnaround (deviation from standard processing time)	40%	8%	21%		
Billing	Machine billing turnaround (shipment through invoicing)	32%	21%	18%		
	Billing department errors as a percentage of total volume	4.6%	2.8%	3.1%		
	Shipments requiring more than one attempt to invoice	27%	36%	38%		
Accounts payable (A/P)	Processing of untimely vendor invoices	13%	11%	16%		
	Total processing errors	3.1%	3.1%	3%		
	Percentage of above caused by A/P	42%	46%	52%		
	Average number of days from receipt to processing	7.5	7.5	9		
Accounts receivable	Early customer contact	54%	24%	45%		
Sales financing	Mailing contracts in two days or less	—	57%	39%		
Corporate accounting	Financial statements (includes errors in data entry, handwriting, date entries, and improper accounts)	5.6%	0.3%	—		

Division or Department	Measurement	Defects by Percentage or Number				
		Aug.	Sept.	Oct.	Nov.	Dec.
Personnel	Employee change notices	8.8%	4.3%	—		
	Address changes	—	14.3%	—		
Manufacturing						
Quality control	Nonconforming lots:					
	■ Purchased	6.7%	7.4%	6.8%		
	■ Manufactured	9.5%	5.9%	11.7%		
	Parts rejected in plant I:					
	■ Purchased parts	150	252	161		
	■ Manufactured parts	163	198	262		
	Parts pulled from stock for inspection:					
	■ Number of manufactured parts	25	32	24		
	■ Number of purchased parts	26	18	35		
	■ Number OK					
	Used parts returned under warranty:					
	■ Number of scrap for credit	—	16	5		
	■ Number of scrap no credit	—	27	19		
	■ Number returned to vendor	—	2	16		
	■ **Total number**	—	58	81		
	New parts returned:					
	■ Number of UPS returns	—	—	5		
	■ Number damaged in shipment	—	—	1		
	■ Number of duplicate shipments	—	16	15		
	■ Number shipped in error	—	32	43		
	■ Number ordered in error	—	38	40		
	■ Number of customer overstock	—	12	5		
	■ Number of credit requests	—	48	93		
	■ **Total number of returned shipments**	—	148	202		

Division or Department	Measurement	Defects by Percentage or Number				
		Aug.	Sept.	Oct.	Nov.	Dec.
	Installation reports returned with something wrong:					
	■ Percentage of something wrong	15.9%	14.8%	16.5%		
	■ Vendor correction action	—	—	—		
	■ Number of problems	—	—	—		
	■ Number of problems solved	—	—	—		
Tool and die	Number of defects:					
	■ Tool records	54	74	98		
	■ Tool design	45	15	12		
	■ Jigs and fixtures	32	12	10		
	■ Template and die	27	24	17		
	■ Tool crib	200	200	200		
Manufacturing	Number of process defects	34	36	52		
Engineering	Number of method layout defects	11	11	10		
	Number of labor standard defects	46	23	14		
	Number of nonconforming programming defects	1	4	1		
	Number of bills of material defects	3	0	5		
Sheet metal	Rework labor (in dollars)	—	—	—		
	Inventory spoilage (in dollars)	7,400	400	6,400		
	Rework transfers (in dollars)	—	—	—		
Machine shop	Rework labor (in dollars)	—	—	—		
	Inventory spoilage (in dollars)	4,800	2,400	7,100		
	Rework transfers (in dollars)	—	—	—		
Brush	Rework labor (in dollars)	—	—	—		
	Inventory spoilage (in dollars)	500	300	700		
	Rework transfers (in dollars)	—	—	—		
Shipping and receiving	Rework labor (in dollars)	—	—	—		

Division or Department	Measurement	Defects by Percentage or Number				
		Aug.	Sept.	Oct.	Nov.	Dec.
Plant II						
	Gross profit red. (in dollars)	—	—	—		
	Inventory spoilage (in dollars)	200	10	300		
	Rework transfers (in dollars)	—	—	—		
	Inventory accuracy	—	—	—		
Paint	Rework labor (in dollars)	—	—	—		
	Inventory spoilage (in dollars)	—	—	—		
	NSR labor (in dollars)	2,358	1,582	1,219		
	Rerun labor (in dollars)	—	—	—		
Welding	Rework labor (in dollars)	—	—	—		
	Inventory spoilage (in dollars)	3,449	6,592	5,160		
	NSR labor (in dollars)	—	—	—		
Assembly (03)	Rework labor (in dollars)	—	—	—		
	Inventory spoilage (in dollars)	5,550	5,800	5,100		
	Rework transfers (in dollars)	—	—	—		
	Number of defects per machine	—	—	—		
	240 north and south	6.3	6.4	5.3		
Assembly (07)	Rework labor (in dollars)	—	—	—		
	Inventory spoilage (in dollars)	11,000	700	3,400		
	Rework transfers (in dollars)	—	—	—		
Shipping and receiving	Rework labor (in dollars)	—	—	—		
Crating	Gross profit red. (in dollars)	—	—	—		
	Inventory spoilage (in dollars)	1,000	1,100	100		
	Rework transfers (in dollars)	—	—	—		
	Number of receiving department miscounts	—	2	4		
	Number of bills of lading errors	—	—	—		
	Not caught in shipping	50	5	0		
	Number of shipping errors	—	1	2		
Stockroom	Rework labor (in dollars)	—	—	—		
	Gross profit red. (in dollars)	—	—	—		
	Inventory spoilage (in dollars)	1,700	2,200	2,200		
	Rework transfers (in dollars)	—	—	—		
	Inventory accuracy	94.7%	94.7%	94.9%		

Division or Department	Measurement	Defects by Percentage or Number				
		Aug.	Sept.	Oct.	Nov.	Dec.
Materials control	Gross profit red. (in dollars)	—	—	—		
	Inventory spoilage (in dollars)	4,100	6,300	5,000		
	Rework transfers (in dollars)	—	—	—		
Marketing and/or sales						
Machine order processing	Percentage of machine orders reprocessed due to errors	79%	65%	64%		
Warranty	Warranty costs	51,000	—	—		
Field services	Percentage of time to bill repair orders	—	—	67%		
Technical publications	Number of manual illustrator errors	0	0	1		
	Number of manual parts list originator errors	4	3	3		
	Number of manual typing and/ or proofreading errors	3	2	1		
	Number of instruction bulletins delayed	6	3	6		
	Average number of days instruction bulletins delayed	5.5	1.5	1.5		
Service center		—	—	—		
Marketing	Timeliness of bids:	—	—	—		
	■ Number of bids completed in Mpls.	34	23	28		
	■ Number of bids returned in time from Mpls.	34	23	28		
	■ Number of bids returned late	0	0	0		
	■ Percentage handled in a timely manner	100%	100%	100%		
	■ Accuracy of bids	100%	100%	100%		
	Customer satisfaction letters:	—	—	—		
	■ Number of replies received	39	23	4		
	■ Number of replies answered in two weeks	35	20	3		
	■ Percentage handled in "timely" manner	90%	87%	75%		

Division or Department	Measurement	Defects by Percentage or Number				
		Aug.	Sept.	Oct.	Nov.	Dec.
	FTM failure reports:					
	■ Number of reports received	10	14	10		
	■ Number replied to within seven days	8	14	6		
	■ Percentage handled in a "timely" manner	80%	100%	60%		
	Special:					
	■ Number of requests received	—	—	50		
	■ Number replied to in forty-eight hours	—	—	50		
	■ Percentage handled in a "timely" manner	—	—	100		
Advertising traffic	Number of on-hand notices	41	28	32		
	Unapplied freight costs	8,760	5,600	6,900		
Supply order processing	Same-day orders processed:					
	■ Sent to shop and shipped	—	—	—		
	■ Percentage of orders processed	69%	73%	72%		
	■ Percentage sent to shop	53%	53%	56%		
	■ Percentage of same-day orders shipped	31%	29%	33%		
	Number of shipping order errors:					
	■ Total number of shipping order errors	927	957	889		
	■ Total number of same-day shipment orders	521	631	583		
Communications	Errors on warehouse shipping memos:					
	■ Number processed	356	488	522		
	■ Number of errors	11	41	36		
	■ Percentage correct	97%	92%	94%		
	Same-day rush orders:					
	■ Number processed	229	207	273		
	■ Number shipped same day	143	110	175		

Division or Department	Measurement	Defects by Percentage or Number				
		Aug.	Sept.	Oct.	Nov.	Dec.
	■ Percentage shipped same day	62%	53%	64%		
Field warehousing	Ship complete results:					
	■ Current results: percentage of orders	72%	73%	71%		
	■ Current results: percentage of lines	80%	80%	80%		

INDEX